THE POLITICS OF CONSTITUTIONAL REVIEW IN GERMANY

Constitutional courts have emerged as central institutions in many advanced democracies. This book investigates the sources and limits of judicial authority, focusing on the central role of public support for judicial independence. The empirical sections of the book illustrate the theoretical argument in an in-depth study of the German Federal Constitutional Court, including statistical analysis of judicial decisions, case studies, and interviews with judges and legislators.

The book's major finding is that the interests of governing majorities, prevailing public opinion, and the transparency of the political environment exert a powerful influence on judicial decisions. Judges are influenced not only by jurisprudential considerations and their policy preferences, but also by strategic concerns. By highlighting this dimension of constitutional review, the book challenges the contention that high court justices are largely unconstrained actors, as well as the notion that constitutional courts lack democratic legitimacy.

Georg Vanberg was educated at the College of William and Mary and at the University of Rochester. He has taught at Florida State University, the University of Wisconsin-Milwaukee, and the University of North Carolina at Chapel Hill. His research focuses on comparative constitutional and judicial politics as well as on coalition theory. His work has appeared in such journals as the *American Journal of Political Science*, the *British Journal of Political Science*, and *Comparative Politics*.

POLITICAL ECONOMY OF INSTITUTIONS AND DECISIONS

Series Editors

Randall Calvert, Washington University, St. Louis
Thrainn Eggertsson, Max Planck Institute, Germany, and University of Iceland

Founding Editors

James E. Alt, Harvard University
Douglass C. North, Washington University, St. Louis

Other Books in the Series

Alberto Alesina and Howard Rosenthal, *Partisan Politics, Divided Government, and the Economy*

Lee J. Alston, Thrainn Eggertsson and Douglass C. North, eds., *Empirical Studies in Institutional Change*

Lee J. Alston and Joseph P. Ferrie, *Southern Paternalism and the Rise of the American Welfare State: Economics, Politics, and Institutions, 1865–1965*

James E. Alt and Kenneth Shepsle, eds., *Perspectives on Positive Political Economy*

Josephine T. Andrews, *When Majorities Fail: The Russian Parliament, 1990–1993*

Jeffrey S. Banks and Eric A. Hanushek, eds., *Modern Political Economy: Old Topics, New Directions*

Yoram Barzel, *Economic Analysis of Property Rights*, 2nd edition

Yoram Barzel, *A Theory of the State: Economic Rights, Legal Rights, and the Scope of the State*

Robert Bates, *Beyond the Miracle of the Market: The Political Economy of Agrarian Development in Kenya*

Charles M. Cameron, *Veto Bargaining: Presidents and the Politics of Negative Power*

Kelly H. Chang, *Appointing Central Bankers: The Politics of Monetary Policy in the United States and the European Monetary Union*

Peter Cowhey and Mathew McCubbins, eds., *Structure and Policy in Japan and the United States: An Institutionalist Approach*

Gary W. Cox, *The Efficient Secret: The Cabinet and the Development of Political Parties in Victorian England*

Gary W. Cox, *Making Votes Count: Strategic Coordination in the World's Electoral Systems*

Continued on page following index

THE POLITICS OF CONSTITUTIONAL REVIEW IN GERMANY

GEORG VANBERG
University of North Carolina at Chapel Hill

CAMBRIDGE UNIVERSITY PRESS
Cambridge, New York, Melbourne, Madrid, Cape Town, Singapore, São Paulo, Delhi

Cambridge University Press
The Edinburgh Building, Cambridge CB2 8RU, UK

Published in the United States of America by Cambridge University Press, New York

www.cambridge.org
Information on this title: www.cambridge.org/9780521111683

© Georg Vanberg 2005

This publication is in copyright. Subject to statutory exception
and to the provisions of relevant collective licensing agreements,
no reproduction of any part may take place without the written
permission of Cambridge University Press.

First published 2005
This digitally printed version 2009

A catalogue record for this publication is available from the British Library

Library of Congress Cataloguing in Publication data
Vanberg, Georg, 1971–
The politics of constitutional review in Germany / Georg Vanberg.
p. cm. – (Political economy of institutions and decisions)
Includes bibliographical references and index.
ISBN 0-521-83647-6
1. Judicial review – Germany – Public opinion. 2. Judicial review – Political
aspects – Germany. I. Title. II. Series.
KK5475.V36   2005
347.43012–dc22   2004045894

ISBN 978-0-521-83647-0 hardback
ISBN 978-0-521-11168-3 paperback

*To my parents,
Monika and Viktor*

Contents

Acknowledgments		*page* xi
1	The Politics of Constitutional Review	1
	EXAMPLES	2
	CONSTITUTIONAL REVIEW IN COMPARATIVE PERSPECTIVE	9
	APPROACH OF THE BOOK	12
	PLAN OF THE BOOK	17
2	Implementation, Public Support, and Transparency	19
	PUBLIC SUPPORT AND JUDICIAL AUTHORITY	20
	MODELING CONSTITUTIONAL REVIEW	24
	PREDICTIONS OF THE MODEL	28
	INTERPRETATION AND COMPARATIVE STATICS	39
	TRANSPARENCY	45
	PUBLIC SUPPORT	49
	INFORMATION, POLITICAL COMPETITION, AND SEPARATION OF POWERS	53
	CONCLUSION	56
	APPENDIX: PROOF FOR THE SIX PURE-STRATEGY PBE OF THE GAME	58
3	The Federal Constitutional Court in Comparative Perspective	61
	ESTABLISHING A COURT	62
	WEATHERING THE FIRST STORM	67
	ORGANIZATION AND STRUCTURE	77
	THE APPOINTMENT PROCESS	81
	JURISDICTION AND CASELOAD	87

	DECISION-MAKING PROCEDURES	91
	DECISIONS	92
	CONCLUSION	93
4	Transparency and Judicial Deference	95
	FOCUSING ON TRANSPARENCY	97
	HYPOTHESES	100
	THE DATA	102
	ANALYSIS AND RESULTS	106
	CONTROLLING FOR THE LEGAL ENVIRONMENT	108
	SUBSTANTIVE IMPACT	111
	CONCLUSION	113
5	From the Inside Looking out: Judicial and Legislative Perceptions	116
	PUBLIC SUPPORT AND JUDICIAL AUTHORITY	119
	PUBLIC SUPPORT AS CONSTRAINT ON JUDICIAL BEHAVIOR	124
	EVASION AND THE COSTS OF COMPLIANCE	130
	CONCLUSION	137
	APPENDIX A: AFFILIATIONS OF INTERVIEWEES	138
	APPENDIX B: BUNDESTAG QUESTIONNAIRE	139
	APPENDIX C: COURT QUESTIONNAIRE	140
6	Pushing the Limits: Party Finance Legislation and the Bundesverfassungsgericht	143
	PARTY FINANCE IN GERMANY	146
	THE COURT'S INITIAL APPROACH TO PARTY FINANCE	147
	LEGISLATIVE RESPONSE TO PARTY FINANCE II AND THE 1986 DECISIONS	152
	THE REVISION OF 1988 AND THE 1992 PARTY FINANCE DECISION	162
	CONCLUSION	166
7	Prudent Jurists	168
	BEYOND GERMANY	172
	BROADER NORMATIVE IMPLICATIONS	175

Bibliography 179
Index 189

Acknowledgments

A book is never really the product of a single mind. In the course of thinking through issues, developing arguments, and gathering data, I have benefited from the critical discussion, suggestions, assistance, and encouragement provided by countless people. I can thank only a few of them by name. This book began its life during my graduate training in the Department of Political Science at the University of Rochester, which provided a rich intellectual atmosphere. My two advisors, Bing Powell and Randy Calvert, gave generously of their time and analytic abilities during the early phases of this project and have had a profound impact on my thinking. I am grateful for all they have done. I also want to thank other colleagues from whose comments and insights I have profited along the way, especially Gregory Caldeira, Cliff Carrubba, Lee Epstein, Gail McElroy, Jeff Staton, and Keith Whittington. Barry Friedman, Lanny Martin, Kevin McGuire, Jim Rogers, and two anonymous readers generously provided invaluable suggestions on various chapters as the manuscript was nearing completion.

I also want to thank several individuals who were critical in the data collection effort and in making possible the interviews with judges and legislators reported in Chapter 5, especially Dr. Gotthard Wöhrmann, Director of the Federal Constitutional Court, Professor Ernst Wolfgang Böckenförde, and Professor Hans Hugo Klein (both formerly judges of the Bundesverfassungsgericht). I am also grateful to all the judges and legislators who agreed to be interviewed for this project. Their names are listed in Appendix A of Chapter 5.

For encouragement and support in what sometimes seemed to me (and surely to them!) an interminable process, I thank our friends and especially my wife, Julia. Last, but not least, I want to express my deep gratitude and appreciation to two people without whom this book and my occupational choice would never have come to be. In acknowledgment of that debt, I dedicate this book to them.

I

The Politics of Constitutional Review

Constitutional review – defined as the power of judicial bodies to set aside ordinary legislative or administrative acts if judges conclude that they conflict with the constitution – has emerged as an almost universal feature of Western-style democracy. The commitment to this institution has become so pervasive that it is now virtually unthinkable to draft a democratic constitution without providing for its inclusion. Whether in postfascist Spain, postapartheid South Africa, or postcommunist Eastern Europe, recent transitions to democracy have been transitions to *constitutional* democracy, including judicial oversight of the political process. As Mauro Cappelletti has observed, in much of the Western world, constitutional review has come to be understood as "the necessary 'crowning' of the rule of law" (1989:205).

The experiences of totalitarianism provided a natural impetus for this development. In writing his monumental survey of American democracy in the 1830s, Alexis de Tocqueville praised the role of the judiciary in the new political system, arguing that "the power granted to American courts to pronounce on the constitutionality of laws is yet one of the most powerful barriers ever erected against the tyranny of political assemblies" (1835/1988:103f.). Similarly, constitution writers following World War II, and again in the wake of the peaceful revolutions of 1989 in Eastern Europe, turned to courts armed with the power of constitutional review in the hope of creating effective limitations on the power of legislative majorities.[1]

---

[1] See, for example, Konrad Adenauer's remarks during the West German Constitutional Convention: "Dictatorship is not necessarily dictatorship by a single person. There is also dictatorship by a parliamentary majority. And we want protection against such dictatorship in the form of a constitutional court" (Verhandlungen des Parlamentarischen Rates, 2nd session, p. 25).

And yet, Tocqueville's seemingly uncontroversial observation raises a critical question: *How can courts, and the judges who serve on them, constrain governing majorities in practice?* For governing majorities, constitutional courts often pose an unwelcome constraint on power and a potential threat to a majority's legislative program. Moreover, it is widely accepted that courts constitute, in Alexander Hamilton's well-known phrase, the "least dangerous" branch of government. In contrast to legislatures, which control the "purse," and executives, which control the "sword," courts enjoy few formal powers to enforce their rulings. Given their apparent weakness, how can courts manage (and have managed) to predominate in interactions with the more powerful branches? Under what circumstances will they fail to do so? And what are the broader implications for the nature of constitutionally constrained government? This book provides one answer to these puzzles and considers the implications of this answer for our broader understanding of constitutional review. Before outlining the argument in greater detail, we will consider several examples that highlight the difficult position courts occupy.

EXAMPLES

Example 1: The Crucifix Decision in Germany

In August 1995, the German Federal Constitutional Court (FCC) issued a decision on the constitutionality of a Bavarian school ordinance that required the display of a crucifix in public elementary school classrooms.[2] The requirement had been challenged by adherents of the nature philosophy of Rudolf Steiner, who argued that forcing their children "to learn beneath the cross" constituted a violation of the children's constitutional right to religious freedom, guaranteed under Article 4, Section 1 of the Basic Law: "Freedom of creed, of conscience, and freedom to profess a religious or non-religious faith are inviolable." In characteristically dry German legal language, the first two sentences of the court's ruling read:

1. The display of a cross or crucifix in classrooms of a public school, which has no denominational affiliation, constitutes a violation of Article 4, Section 1 of the Basic Law.

[2] Decisions of the FCC are published in serial format and are referenced by the volume and page number on which the decision appears. The *Crucifix* decision is BVerfGE 93, 1, indicating that it can be found in volume 93, page 1, of the court's decisions. All references to decisions by the FCC follow this convention.

2. Article 13, Section 1, Sentence 3 of the School Ordinance for Elementary Schools in Bavaria is incompatible with Article 4, Section 1 of the Basic Law and void.

Within days, a storm of public protest against the decision erupted. Church leaders condemned the ruling as an attack on Germany's Christian heritage. Politicians, mostly affiliated with the ruling Christian Democrats, joined the chorus. Even the chancellor, Helmut Kohl, weighed in, calling the decision "incomprehensible." In a hastily arranged press release, the court made an attempt to defuse the situation by claiming that the decision's first sentence had been "misformulated." The clarification seemed to imply that the ruling only precluded the state-*mandated* display of a cross. But the concession did little to assuage the protests. The Bavarian premier, Edmund Stoiber, vowed that crucifixes would remain in elementary schools. A genuine constitutional crisis appeared at hand. One of the court's judges (a member of the majority) became so concerned over calls for defiance that he wrote an editorial entitled "Why a Judicial Ruling Deserves Respect," published in one of the major national newspapers (*Frankfurter Allgemeine Zeitung*, August 18, 1995).

Naturally, opposition to the verdict was not unanimous. Some commentators and politicians, while often critical of the ruling, argued against open defiance of the court. But the conflict lingered. As the school year began, crucifixes remained in Bavarian schoolrooms. A mass demonstration organized by the Catholic Church in opposition to the decision brought more than 30,000 protesters to Munich's Odeonplatz. By the end of the year, a campaign in Bavaria had collected more than 700,000 signatures against the verdict. In late December, the Bavarian parliament finally passed a revision of the school ordinance to implement the court's decision. The new ordinance reads:

Article 7, Section 3: In light of Bavaria's historical and cultural traditions, a cross is displayed in every classroom. This act symbolizes the desire to realize the highest educational goals of the constitution on the basis of Christian and occidental values while respecting religious freedom. If parents challenge the installation of the cross for genuine and acceptable reasons of faith or secular belief, the school principal shall attempt a compromise solution. If it is not possible to find a solution, the principal shall notify the school authorities and then devise an individual solution that respects the religious freedom of the person who has objected and which balances the religious and secular beliefs of all persons in a class appropriately. In doing so, the will of the majority must be considered as much as possible.

Obviously, the extent to which this new regulation is consistent with the court's decision is open to question. Crosses are still required in schoolrooms. Even if a student or a parent objects, the new regulation does not require the removal of the cross. The nature of the prescribed "compromise solution" is left open. In a year-end article on the crisis, the *Neue Zürcher Zeitung*, one of the most influential European newspapers, concluded that "except for a few extremely rare cases, nothing has changed in everyday school life in Bavaria" (December 16, 1995). As a judge of the FCC quipped during a lecture at the University of Freiburg: "There are more crucifixes hanging in Bavarian schoolrooms now than before the decision."

Example 2: German Party Finance

As in many European countries, established political parties in Germany are provided public subsidies for their political activities. The precise form of these subsidies, and the terms on which they are granted, have been subject to a continuous tug of war between parliament and the constitutional court ever since public party finance was first established in 1959.[3] The party finance law in effect during the late 1980s and early 1990s included a so-called base amount as part of the funding scheme. This base amount provided a fixed amount of money to each party that had received at least 2 percent of the vote in a given federal election. In a 1992 decision, the FCC declared this provision unconstitutional. The practical consequence of the base amount, the court concluded, was to divorce (at least in part) a party's public financial support from its ability to gather votes, donations, and membership dues from citizens (by paying a "premium" on the first votes a party secured). Such a provision, the court argued, violates the constitutionally guaranteed independence of political parties from the state (BVerfGE 85,264:294).

In 1994, the federal parliament (Bundestag) passed a revision of the party finance law in response to the FCC's decision. Under the new law, a party receives 1 deutsche mark (DM 1) for every vote it captures in a federal, state, or European Union election. For the first 5 million votes captured, however, parties receive an additional DM 0.30 above the regular amount.[4] Naturally, this "bonus payment" constitutes, in practice,

---

[3] West Germany was the first industrialized Western democracy to introduce such public financing for political parties, although other countries quickly followed suit.

[4] In the latest revision of the party finance law, this bonus payment was modified to Euro 0.70 with a Euro 0.15 bonus payment for the first 4 million votes captured.

little more than the base amount that was declared unconstitutional by the court, as several prominent constitutional lawyers have pointed out (Rudzio 1994; von Arnim 1996:107). In fact, the constitutionality of this provision was so questionable in light of the 1992 decision that fifteen Social Democratic members of the Bundestag publicly stated their constitutional objections and refused to vote for the new law (BTD 12:16448f.). Federal President Richard von Weizsäcker also voiced his constitutional concerns and signed the new law only after considerable delay – an unprecedented step by a German president, who ordinarily has only ceremonial functions.

Example 3: The Legislative Veto in the United States

A final example comes from the United States. In *INS v. Chadha* (462 U.S. 919), a landmark separation-of-powers decision issued in 1983, the U.S. Supreme Court invalidated congressional use of the "one-house legislative veto." This device allows Congress to delegate authority to executive agencies, but Congress retains the right to veto decisions that executive agencies subsequently take by a resolution of one house of Congress, that is, without having to pass a new law. In declaring this procedure unconstitutional, the Court held that the separation-of-powers principle inherent in the U.S. Constitution requires that whenever Congress acts to change the legal environment, it must do so by passing a statute, including (1) passage of the same bill in both houses and (2) the opportunity for the president to sign or veto the bill. Congress cannot reserve the right to change executive agency decisions without following these procedures.

The congressional reaction to the *Chadha* decision is particularly interesting. On the one hand, Congress removed legislative vetoes from a number of statutes, generally replacing them with a requirement for joint resolutions of approval. On the other hand, Congress simply continued to employ the legislative veto *even after* the decision was handed down. As Louis Fisher has documented, in the ten-year period between 1983 and 1992 alone, Congress passed more than 200 new statutes containing a legislative veto, usually subjecting the actions of executive agencies to approval by particular congressional committees (Fisher 1993:288). These vetoes appear to be in clear conflict with the Court's holding in the *Chadha* decision. As Fisher has concluded, "the meaning of constitutional law in this area is evidently determined more by pragmatic agreements hammered out between the elected branches than by doctrines announced by the Supreme Court" (1993:273).

These examples are suggestive because they underscore the crucial distinction between *announcing* and *implementing* a legal decision. Courts do not act in a vacuum. While they often enjoy broad powers of review, few possess direct means to oversee the implementation of their rulings. Instead, implementation usually requires the cooperation of other actors – on many occasions, even the cooperation of the very institutions whose acts the court has just struck down. As Canon and Johnson put it in their influential treatment of judicial implementation, "in virtually all instances, courts that formulate policies must rely on other courts or on nonjudicial actors to translate those policies into action" (1999:1).[5]

This is true in several senses. Implementation of a ruling may require another institution to refrain from engaging in certain behavior (as in *Chadha*). A decision may require a person or an institution to take a certain action (e.g., the order to President Richard Nixon to turn over White House tapes upheld in *United States v. Nixon*, 418 U.S. 683). More commonly, a decision that attacks the constitutionality of a statute or administrative action, like the German *Crucifix* and *Party Finance* decisions, may require a legislative majority or an agency to revise an existing statute or regulation in light of the court's ruling. Even where no action is formally required to implement a decision, a ruling may evoke a legislative response as governing majorities attempt to adjust policy in light of the judicial action (e.g., if a court strikes down a particular income tax provision, a government usually does not stop collecting income tax; instead, a new tax statute is passed). In other words, judicial decisions ordinarily require or induce a response by other policy makers. As our examples show, this fact calls attention to the relationship between judicial decision and response. To what extent does a legislative or executive reaction correspond to the court's ruling?

Putting the same point slightly differently, a judicial ruling is typically *not* the last act in the adjudication of many constitutional disputes. To be sure, the traditional account of the role and purpose of constitutional review does not deny the formal need for implementation. Rather, it is often assumed implicitly that the response to a decision is a straightforward technical matter that does not afford legislators or bureaucrats much

---

[5] More than 200 years ago, Alexander Hamilton made essentially the same observation in *Federalist 78*: "The judiciary, on the contrary, has no influence over either the sword or the purse; no direction either of the strength or the wealth of the society, and can take no active resolution whatever. It may truly be said to have neither Force nor Will but merely judgment; and must ultimately depend upon the aid of the executive arm even for the efficacy of its judgments" (1961:465).

discretion.[6] Putting it loosely, nonjudicial governmental actors are assumed to translate judicial rulings faithfully into law. Our examples suggest that the reality is more complex. The need for courts to rely on other institutions to implement decisions provides legislators and bureaucrats with opportunities to attempt to evade judicial decisions they oppose.

The possibility is not simply academic. Evasion of constitutional decisions in Germany, for example, is sufficiently frequent that an article published in one of the nation's preeminent newspapers, the *Süddeutsche Zeitung*, recently concluded that legislative majorities in Germany routinely evade or circumvent FCC decisions that are politically costly or have significant budgetary implications.[7] In post–World War II Italy, the first president of the Italian Constitutional Court resigned in protest after the government repeatedly failed to enforce judicial decisions (Volcansek 1991:120). Nor has resistance to implementation disappeared since the court's early years. For example, Mary Volcansek, a prominent scholar of the Italian court, concluded in a survey of decisions on media pluralism issued in the 1980s and 1990s that the court's

> influence in directing the legislative process was minimal. Twice the Court enumerated what would be necessary in constitutionally accepted laws, and both times Parliament passed laws that did not conform. The Mammi Law served only to replicate by law the situation that the Court had earlier deemed unacceptable. (2000:139)

The Russian Constitutional Court, similarly, has had to contend with "persistent noncompliance with and frequent delays in the implementation of its decisions by federal and regional authorities" (Trochev 2002:96; see also Schwartz 2000). In the Russian case, the Constitutional Court's difficulties in securing compliance led to a particularly interesting episode. Since the demise of the Soviet Union, there has been a persistent struggle between Moscow and several regions intent on asserting their autonomy. In this struggle, the Constitutional Court soon proved to be a valuable ally of the central government, quashing regional claims of sovereignty in several cases. Regional governments, however, were little bothered by these decisions and routinely ignored them, in one case even refusing to publish the court's rulings (Trochev 2002:96). In response, President

---

[6] I focus on legislative and administrative responses, not on responses by lower courts. However, judicial responses raise similar issues and can be analyzed within the framework provided here.

[7] See "Was nicht paßt, wird ignoriert" ("If it does not sit well, it is ignored"), *Süddeutsche Zeitung*, January 10, 1998, page 2.

Vladimir Putin in late 2001 proposed and pushed through the Duma a new statute establishing strict deadlines for compliance with Constitutional Court decisions. However, Putin may have been less motivated by a genuine concern for compliance with judicial decisions than by an interest in using the court to bring recalcitrant regional governments to heel. The law provides sanctions only for *regional* governments that fail to comply in a timely manner. Federal institutions are exempted from penalties for noncompliance (Trochev 2002: 101).

All of these episodes powerfully underscore a central point: Because judicial decisions often require or induce a response from other governmental actors, constitutional courts face a potential *implementation problem*. While judges may possess the formal power to declare legislative and administrative actions unconstitutional, the substantive effect of such a declaration in specific cases will often turn on the manner in which other political actors implement the decision. The actual, as opposed to formal, influence judges can exercise over the use of political power will therefore be determined, in part, by the strategic interactions between constitutional courts and parliaments.[8] All of this raises questions that go to the heart of our understanding of constitutional democracy:

- What factors determine how legislative majorities respond to judicial rulings?
- Does the potential for evasion shape judicial deliberations and perhaps even decisions?
- Under what circumstances can courts successfully constrain legislative majorities, and when will they not do so?
- What are the deeper implications for the possibility of democratic yet constitutionally constrained government?

An answer to these questions requires a theory of judicial–legislative relations. Over the past decade, a growing literature has tried to construct such a theory from a strategic, game-theoretic perspective, mostly with application to the U.S. Supreme Court (e.g., Epstein and Knight 1998; Ferejohn and Shipan 1990; Ferejohn and Weingast 1992) but also in comparative politics (Epstein, Knight, and Shvetsova 2001; Helmke 2002; Vanberg 1998a, 2000, 2001). Building on these efforts, I investigate the strategic interactions between courts and legislatures and the

---

[8] Although I will focus on legislative–judicial relations in the remainder of the analysis, a similar argument applies to administrative–judicial relations.

role of public support in shaping these interactions. I then test the theoretical argument in a detailed study of the relations between the German Bundesverfassungsgericht and Bundestag. Before I sketch the outlines of the theory and the plan for this book, a brief detour to consider the historical origins of constitutional review is useful.

CONSTITUTIONAL REVIEW IN COMPARATIVE PERSPECTIVE

Perhaps surprisingly, the pervasive popularity of constitutional review is of relatively recent vintage. While the ideal of constitutionally constrained government has a long tradition in Western political thought (see Gordon 1999), the notion that judges can (and should) act as guardians of the constitutional order emerged as a significant practical political force only after the founding of the United States. Although the U.S. Constitution does not mention constitutional review explicitly, it was widely understood and expected during the founding era that judges would exercise such power. Thus, Alexander Hamilton famously commented in *Federalist 78*:

> By a limited constitution, I understand one which contains certain specified exceptions to the legislative authority.... Limitations of this kind can be preserved in practice no other way than through the medium of courts of justice, whose duty it must be to declare all acts contrary to the manifest tenor of the Constitution void. (Hamilton 1961:466)[9]

By the early nineteenth century, judicial review of state laws had become common in the American political system, and the U.S. Supreme Court's historic decision in *Marbury v. Madison* (5 U.S. 137) set a precedent for the invalidation of a federal statute on constitutional grounds.

In continental Europe, on the other hand, constitution writers as well as legal and constitutional scholars initially resisted the idea of judicial oversight precisely because it places limits on the authority of representative assemblies. An explicit adoption of constitutional review, it was feared, might lead to the establishment of a "government of judges,"

---

[9] Similarly, in arguing against ratification of the U.S. Constitution, "Brutus" warned against the power that judges would be able to exercise under the new constitution: "If, therefore, the legislature pass any laws, inconsistent with the sense the judges put upon the constitution, they will declare it void; and therefore in this respect their power is superior to that of the legislature" (Ketcham 1986:307).

who would lack the popular legitimacy enjoyed by an elected assembly.[10] Nonetheless, against the backdrop of the American experience, the idea gained increasing intellectual support over the course of the nineteenth century.[11] Thus, the draft constitution for a unified German state produced by the national assembly convened in Frankfurt's Paulskirche during the unsuccessful 1848 revolution already included a provision creating a Reichsgericht with wide-ranging powers of constitutional review. With the adoption of a republican constitution in Portugal in 1911, constitutional review was introduced into European political practice. Under the constitution, ordinary courts were authorized to review the constitutionality of legislation as part of their proceedings, much as American courts had been doing for more than a century (Magalhaes 2003:31).

It was with the Austrian Constitution of 1920, drafted by the well-known legal scholar Hans Kelsen, that constitutional review finally gained a secure foothold on the European continent. Significantly, Kelsen developed an alternative institutional structure that differs in important respects from the decentralized form of review exercised by American courts. While the American model provides for a decentralized system in which any court can exercise constitutional review,[12] the European model concentrates the power of review in a constitutional court that acts outside of the ordinary judicial hierarchy and has exclusive jurisdiction over constitutional questions. Moreover, unlike American courts, which are constrained to decide only "cases and controversies" that arise out of disputes between litigants with provable injuries, European constitutional courts usually have broad jurisdiction and open rules of access that allow (and often require) them to decide abstract constitutional questions in the absence of a concrete dispute.

In the face of the rise of totalitarianism in the 1930s, the initial experiment with constitutional review in Europe turned out to be short-lived. But in the aftermath of the horrific suffering and destruction wrought by Nazi Germany, Kelsen's model quickly gained acceptance in other European countries. Constitution writers across Europe tried to secure the limitation of legislative powers that Tocqueville had identified as one

---

[10] For example, in France, an explicit prohibition of constitutional review was adopted in August 1790, which is still valid for the ordinary French judiciary: "Courts cannot interfere with the exercising of legislative powers or suspend the application of the laws" (see Stone Sweet 2000:33).

[11] For an excellent review, see Stone (1992, chapter 9) and Cappelletti (1989, chapters 3–5).

[12] Subject, of course, to the opportunity for appeal and the principle of *stare decisis*.

beneficial consequence of constitutional review more than a century earlier. Capelletti summarizes the development well:

After the sad experiences of the first half of this century, there arose in Europe an awareness of the need to put a check upon the legislature itself, for it had become evident that even legislation could be the source of great abuses. Hence, Europeans, and non-Europeans as well, embarked on the path taken by the Americans so long before. Higher law was to be expressed in constitutions that were difficult to amend. The judiciary, or a part of it, was to be the instrument for assuring conformity to this higher law. The Old World moved from legal to constitutional justice. (1989:148)

Following World War II, the Austrian Constitutional Court was reestablished, and the new, democratic constitutions for Italy (1948) and West Germany (1949) included provisions for a constitutional court. With Charles de Gaulle's constitution for the Fifth Republic (1958), constitutional review, although in a more constrained form, was introduced in France.[13] When authoritarian regimes were replaced by democratic constitutions in Portugal (1976) and Spain (1978), constitutional courts received a prominent place in the new institutional structure. More recently, almost all former Soviet bloc countries, including Russia, have established constitutional courts on the Kelsen model (Schwartz 2000). Nor is the spread of constitutional review restricted to nation-states. Even in supranational organizations, judicial oversight of legislation is becoming more common. Thus, the European Court of Justice (ECJ), armed with the authority to check the conformity of member state legislation to higher-order European Union law, has emerged as a key institution of the European Union (Alter 2001; Dehousse 1998).

Not only has the institution of judicial review, whether in the decentralized American version or the centralized European model, become commonplace; comparative judicial scholars have argued that over the past decade, courts around the world have begun to use their powers more aggressively and play an increasingly active and important role in the policy-making process. Thus, scholars have identified a "global expansion of judicial power" (Tate and Vallinder 1995), a "rights revolution," (Epp 1998), and a "judicialization of politics" (Stone 1992). Stone Sweet expresses the emerging consensus this way:

The work of governments and parliaments is today structured by an ever-expanding web of constitutional constraints. In a word, European policy-making

---

[13] It was only in 1974 that legislative minorities in France gained the right to bring cases to the Constitutional Council.

has been judicialized. Constitutional judges routinely intervene in legislative processes, establishing limits on law-making behavior, reconfiguring policy-making environments, even drafting the precise terms of legislation. (2000:1)

Viewed against the backdrop of this emphasis on growing judicial influence, the examples provided here serve to highlight the importance of the puzzle posed by judicial review. Are courts in fact becoming ever more dominant institutions? Are they, at least on occasion, helpless to secure compliance, as the examples suggest? Or are both observations consistent with a general understanding of how courts and legislative majorities interact? In other words, is there an explanation of judicial influence that accounts for the circumstances under which courts will impose effective constraints on legislative majorities and for those circumstances under which courts themselves will be constrained by the need to secure cooperation for the implementation of their decisions?

APPROACH OF THE BOOK

The approach I take in this book diverges from most traditional treatments of legislative–judicial relations by moving the implementation problem and its implications to the center. I adopt a strategic outlook that stresses the *mutual* interdependencies among legislative majorities and constitutional courts. This is not to say that strategic considerations have not played a role in other treatments of legislative–judicial relations. Many comparative judicial scholars have focused on the fact that legislators must anticipate the possibility of constitutional censure of their enactments. Such strategic anticipations are central to the "judicialization of politics" identified by Stone Sweet (1992, 2000), Landfried (1984), Tate and Vallinder (1995), and others. But complementary strategic considerations on the judicial side have received much less attention. Especially among European (legal) scholars, courts are still often assumed to be "above politics," and their decisions tend to be treated as purely legal texts that can be understood in isolation from their political context. But if courts face a potential implementation problem, it is plausible that just as legislators may anticipate constitutional review, judges are likely to be aware of the fact that implementation requires cooperation by other institutions. Anticipations of reactions to their decisions may therefore shape their jurisprudence. As a result, to accurately understand how constitutional courts shape policy making, we need to understand the mutual strategic interplay between courts and legislatures instead of treating courts as unconstrained actors above the political fray.

In treating constitutional courts as strategic political actors, I extend a rich literature that has developed over the past decade. This research has focused mostly on the U.S. Supreme Court.[14] More recently, scholars have begun to extend the strategic approach to courts in other countries, including applications to executive–judicial relations in Russia (Epstein et al. 2001), strategic behavior by Argentinean judges during periods of regime change (Helmke 2002), strategic use of media relations by the Mexican Supreme Court (Staton 2003), and the ability of the ECJ to build its institutional power through strategic use of its power of judicial review (Carrubba 2003). It is my hope that this book, like these efforts, will contribute to demonstrating the value of thinking about judicial institutions as strategic political actors.

I should note at the outset that my approach is largely *positive*: I am concerned with explaining how judicial–legislative relations work in practice (and with evaluating the adequacy of that explanation empirically), not with the normative question of how this interaction *ought* to work in an ideal world. At the same time, I believe that such a positive enterprise is central in helping us think through our normative commitments. As John Ferejohn has argued, "it seems impossible to engage in meaningful normative discourse – to criticize practices or give advice – without some conception of how political institutions either do or could be made to work" (1995:192). In this sense, I hope that the theory outlined here can contribute to fundamental discussions about the value of constitutional government and the appropriate role for judicial institutions in a democratic society. In the concluding chapter, I consider some of the normative implications of the analysis for the possibility of a judicially enforced, constitutional order.

The argument I put forward is disarmingly simple. Because the implementation of judicial decisions often requires legislative action, a crucial component in determining the de facto power of constitutional courts concerns the incentives facing other policymakers in reacting to a court decision. Do legislators have reason to respect a ruling, even when doing

---

[14] Game-theoretic treatments of the U.S. Supreme Court have grown tremendously over the last few years, and it would be impossible to list all citations that deserve mention. A few of the more prominent ones are Ferejohn and Weingast (1992), Epstein and Knight (1996), Shipan (2000), and Rogers (2001). This research agenda has, of course, much older roots going back to Walter Murphy's (1964) seminal contribution.

so is contrary to their immediate interest in the continuation of a policy that has been struck down? A number of alternative enforcement mechanisms have been proposed in response to this question.[15] I focus on one particular central mechanism: the role of public support. I argue that the principal inducement for governing majorities to comply with high court decisions is the threat of a loss of public support for elected officials who refuse to be bound by them. That is, governing majorities will be motivated to respect court decisions primarily when they are concerned about the electoral consequences of not doing so.

Such an account carries implications for judicial behavior. To anticipate: Policy environments differ in the extent to which they hold out the possibility of a public backlash for evasion of constitutional decisions. For example, the complexity of an issue area determines, in part, how easily citizens, with the help of opinion leaders, can monitor legislative responses. Furthermore, judges are likely to be aware of the implementation problem, and their anticipation of the potential for evasion may shape their jurisprudence. For example, if public support represents a principal judicial resource, judges may be concerned about maintaining such support. Similarly, if they are concerned about avoiding evasion, they may be led to temper their decisions so as not to exceed the tolerance threshold of governing majorities. In short, the judges who serve on constitutional courts are likely to be *prudent* jurists: They are influenced not only by jurisprudential considerations and their policy preferences, but also by strategic concerns, including the larger political environment in which they act, public views of an issue, and the interests of governing majorities. As a result, constitutional courts may be more constrained in their ability to curb the exercise of legislative power than is presumed by the conventional view. The remaining chapters flesh out this argument theoretically and empirically.

At this point, it is important to make clear what I am *not* arguing. Much of the discussion in the book focuses on the limits to judicial power imposed by the need to generate compliance. However, a focus on the limits to judicial power does not imply that I regard courts as powerless or irrelevant institutions. On the contrary, under the right circumstances, courts can be tremendously influential institutions, able to successfully

---

[15] The most prominent alternatives, apart from the one discussed here, focus on the interest that political parties may have in preserving an independent judiciary in an uncertain electoral environment in order to constrain other parties (see Carrubba 2003; Ramseyer 1994; Whittington 2003). I return to a discussion of this mechanism in Chapter 2.

curb the exercise of political power by more democratic, directly elected parliaments. Rather than viewing courts either as all-powerful or as paper tigers, the goal is to develop a realistic assessment of their capabilities. In other words, the point is to develop an understanding of the circumstances under which courts will be in a strong position vis-à-vis legislative majorities and of the circumstances under which they will be constrained. The implementation problem, and the mechanisms that allow judges to solve this problem, are key to such an understanding.

It is also useful to say a few words about the intended scope of the theory, that is, about the range of cases on which the argument has bearing. The short answer is that the argument applies wherever courts with the power of constitutional review confront a potential implementation problem and where the need for elected officials to maintain sufficient public support is a primary consideration in their calculus about how to respond to judicial decisions. In this book, the focus of the analysis is on constitutional courts in Europe and, in particular, the FCC. But the argument also applies to high courts in decentralized systems of judicial review, as in the United States. Throughout the book, references to the U.S. Supreme Court will try to indicate the relevance of the argument beyond Europe. Naturally, in applying the argument to courts in different institutional and political contexts, it is important to be sensitive to the manner in which such context shapes the precise nature of legislative–judicial interactions. For example, the implementation problem may be more acute for European constitutional courts than for the U.S. Supreme Court. These courts must routinely rule on legislative enactments and typically confront an efficient parliamentary majority that can respond to rulings quickly. The U.S. Supreme Court, on the other hand, deals less frequently with legislative enactments (since it also serves as a court of last appeal) and also faces legislative institutions that are highly fragmented and sometimes even controlled by opposing parties, which makes a response to judicial decisions much more difficult to achieve.

In confronting these issues, I employ a "triangular" approach that combines game-theoretic analysis with statistical and qualitative evidence. Furthermore, the empirical analysis focuses on legislative–judicial relations in one particular country. Let me briefly explain why I believe this research strategy is appropriate for the problem at hand.

As indicated earlier, in constructing a theory about judicial–legislative interactions, I am concerned with a strategic problem, that is, with a situation in which the optimal course of action for each actor depends not just on her preferences, but also on her anticipations of how she expects others to react to her decisions. Game theory is an especially useful analytical tool in such a context. Game-theoretic analysis allows researchers to model a strategic interaction formally. It requires a statement of assumptions from which conclusions are derived deductively. Imposing this sort of rigor has at least three desirable consequences. First, formalization provides "a clear and precise language for communicating insights" (Kreps 1990:6). All the relevant actors in a situation, their possible courses of action, and their motivations must be specified explicitly. As a result, the path from assumptions to conclusions can be retraced readily. Second, by proceeding deductively, formalizing an argument "allows us to subject particular insights and intuitions to the test of logical consistency" (Kreps 1990:7). Finally, formalization may lead to new insights by forcing us to think through the implications of our assumptions. That does not mean that formalization is necessary to gain those insights, but it is one suitable method for doing so (see also Huber 1996:14ff.; Kreps 1990:6).

The empirical test of the theory rests on a combination of statistical and qualitative evidence. Relatively little needs to be said about the importance of statistical corroboration of a theory. Statistical testing has become the standard tool of the social sciences. The ability to analyze a large number of cases systematically is crucial in assuring researchers that empirical results are not idiosyncratic properties of particular cases, but that they are indeed general features of a certain class of phenomena. The purpose of the statistical test presented here is precisely to furnish this assurance.

In addition to statistical analysis, I turn to qualitative evidence, including interviews with jurists and legislators and case studies. A little more needs to be said about why I consider this kind of evidence to be at least as important as statistical evidence in evaluating the theory presented. Equilibrium analysis in formal modeling rests on two pillars: the structure of the game that is assumed (including the relevant players and their possible strategies) and the equilibrium beliefs that are imputed to players about the strategies of others. Both of these components of a formal model are fundamentally subjective in the sense that they reside in the minds of the real-world actors being modeled. Moreover, both usually involve beliefs about *counterfactual* situations that never occur along the path of play. That is, equilibrium behavior is, in part, explained by player A's beliefs about what player B would do if A ever deviated from the equilibrium path of play.

A crucial concern in assessing the power of a formal model must therefore consist in determining whether the beliefs and perceptions of real-world actors about the interactions they are engaged in and about the strategies of other players correspond closely to the beliefs imputed to players in the model. Ariel Rubinstein has called attention to this connection, arguing that it is difficult to "see how we can avoid the interpretation of a game as an abstract summary of the players' actual perceptions of the complicated situations they are in" (1991:917). This need to demonstrate that the expectations that sustain equilibrium behavior match up well with the subjective beliefs of real-world actors creates a fundamental place for qualitative evidence in testing game-theoretic models. Historical case studies based on archival evidence or interviews with judges and legislators that can reveal the actors' motivations and expectations provide a unique opportunity to paint an accurate picture of the subjective perceptions of the various players. In short, the centrality of perceptions in strategic analysis supplies an important reason to engage in "analytic narratives" that has not been highlighted sufficiently (Bates et al. 1998; Vanberg 2000).

Finally, some explanation for the empirical focus on the German FCC and parliament is appropriate. Next to the U.S. Supreme Court, the German Bundesverfassungsgericht is widely considered to be one of the most powerful and influential constitutional courts in the world. It almost certainly ranks as the most important high court in Europe. It has served as the model for many of the new constitutional courts in Eastern Europe as well as for the South African constitutional court. In other words, among high courts, the FCC appears among the least likely to be constrained by the need to generate compliance. Empirical results indicating that even this court is constrained by strategic concerns would therefore be especially powerful evidence for the theory. Finally, while cross-national studies can be desirable, the focus on one country allows a detailed, in-depth analysis that would be difficult to achieve in a cross-national context. Given the centrality of qualitative evidence in evaluating a strategic theory, this provides another powerful reason for the empirical focus. All of these reasons suggest that the relations between the German FCC and legislature provide a useful forum for testing the theory.

PLAN OF THE BOOK

The book is organized as follows. In Chapter 2, I present the theoretical argument. To stress the generality of the theory and to make it easier to "transport" the account to other contexts, the theory is strictly separated from the particulars of the German case. Chapter 3 provides an overview of the establishment of the FCC and its institutional structure in comparison to that of other constitutional courts. Chapter 4 begins the systematic empirical evaluation of the theory. I begin with a statistical analysis of decision making by the FCC to demonstrate that aggregate judicial behavior is consistent with central implications of the argument. In Chapter 5, I analyze data gathered in in-depth interviews with judges of the FCC and key members of the Bundestag. This chapter demonstrates that the way these central actors think about what they are doing comports well with the argument. In Chapter 7, I present a case study of the interactions between the FCC and the Bundestag over public financing of political parties that illustrates central aspects of the theory. The concluding chapter considers the broader implications of the findings.

2

Implementation, Public Support, and Transparency

In much of the Western world, the institution of constitutional review has become a central component of constitutional democracy. In the previous chapter, I argued that how and under what circumstances courts are able to exercise influence over the policymaking process poses a puzzle. While many courts have successfully established a claim to the power of constitutional review, most have few means at their disposal to force compliance with their decisions. President Andrew Jackson's apocryphal reaction to the U.S. Supreme Court's decision (written by Chief Justice John Marshall) in *Worcester v. Georgia* (31 U.S. 515), invalidating attempts by the State of Georgia to assert jurisdiction over the Cherokee Indians provides a poignant illustration: "John Marshall has made his decision, now let him enforce it" (see Smith 1996:518). This lack of formal enforcement powers is potentially significant because implementation of a judicial decision often requires or induces a response by other policymakers. As the examples presented in the previous chapter suggest, governing majorities may be tempted to exploit the opportunity to evade, or at least limit, the impact of unwelcome judicial decisions. How then do courts constrain other political institutions?

Scholars have investigated various bases of judicial authority, including the value that political parties that alternate between government and opposition may place on judicial independence (Landes and Posner 1975; Ramseyer 1994), the fact that courts can help parties to solve Prisoner's Dilemma–type problems (Carrubba 2003), and the informational gain that legislative majorities may achieve from judicial review (Rogers 2001). Toward the end of this chapter, I will consider some of these enforcement mechanisms. The main focus of the chapter, however, is on a different mechanism that may give force to judicial decisions in light of the implementation problem: public support for an independent judiciary. Importantly, this particular enforcement mechanism has significant implications for judicial behavior and for the ability of constitutional courts to effectively constrain governing majorities. Before I launch into this argument, several general remarks are useful. By occupying its own chapter, the theory is separated physically from the rest of the book, which focuses on the interactions between the German FCC and the Bundestag. This separation is not accidental. The account is intended as a *general* statement of relations between courts with the power of constitutional review and legislative majorities. In other words, the theoretical framework is applicable across countries, across legal systems, and across time; it is not peculiar to the German case. Separating the argument from the specifics of any particular country symbolizes this generality. Hopefully, it will also make it easier to "transport" the account to different contexts and to assess its applicability.

One drawback of presenting the theoretical treatment in a separate chapter is that the chapter demands a certain amount of patience on the part of the reader before we engage the substantive application in later chapters. As much as possible, I have tried to confine the technical aspects of the argument to an appendix and to provide as many substantive illustrations as possible. I hope the reader will bear with me and agree in the end that the investment was worth it.

PUBLIC SUPPORT AND JUDICIAL AUTHORITY

The linchpin to the argument is the observation that the interactions between courts and other policymakers do not occur in a vacuum. Politicians in advanced democracies require sufficient public backing to remain in power and to be effective. This simple relationship between public support and political power can provide a powerful enforcement mechanism for judicial decisions. If citizens value judicial independence and regard respect for judicial rulings as important, a decision by elected officials to resist a judicial ruling may result in a loss of public support (i.e., citizens may withdraw their support at the voting booth, in an opinion poll, etc.). The fear of such a public backlash can be a forceful inducement to implement judicial decisions faithfully. Moreover, the number of such citizens need not be very large. Politicians and party leaders are concerned about shifts in support *at the margin*. Thus, to be effective in deterring evasion, the mechanism does not require that all, or even many, citizens are motivated by concerns for judicial authority. Only a sufficiently numerous group of citizens to sway the calculations of politicians is necessary.[1] *Why* citizens might support courts in such a way is, naturally, a central question to which I return later.

A number of scholars have pointed to the central role of public support for an independent, effective judiciary as an important resource for judicial authority (e.g., Caldeira 1986; Murphy and Tanenhaus 1990:992), and this insight has provided a prominent justification for empirical investigations of public support for courts. In considering support of high courts from a cross-national perspective, Gibson, Caldeira, and Baird, for example, argue that "with limited institutional resources, courts are therefore uncommonly dependent upon the goodwill of their constituents for both support and compliance" (1998:343).

However, to serve as an effective enforcement mechanism, public support alone is insufficient. It requires two central conditions that tap separate dimensions of the enforcement problem:

Condition 1: There must exist sufficient public support for the court (or for a specific decision) to make an attempt at evasion unattractive.

Condition 2: It must be sufficiently likely that citizens will become aware of an evasion attempt so that any support the court enjoys can be brought to bear against legislative majorities that choose not to comply with a decision.

If either condition fails, public support cannot act as an effective enforcement mechanism. While both conditions are necessary, the second raises an especially vital issue. In many advanced industrial democracies, courts do enjoy considerable support among their publics, especially compared to other institutions (Gibson et al., 1998). But the threat of losing public support for failure to faithfully implement a judicial decision will deter noncompliance only if policy makers who attempt to evade a decision are sufficiently likely to be caught. In other words, *monitoring* of responses to judicial rulings and *activation* of the court's support in cases of noncompliance are crucial. Yet neither is a trivial task. Legislative majorities usually do not challenge judicial decisions openly and publicly (unless they are convinced that the court has little support, as in the *Crucifix*

---

[1] In a similar vein, Barry Weingast (1997) has argued that constitutional maintenance requires broad, coordinated agreement by citizens that certain rules of the game must be respected, thereby threatening a loss of support for politicians who violate them. Institutional structures such as constitutions can play a central role as devices that coordinate citizens' expectations about what these limits are and when resistance is appropriate.

case). Rather, they attempt to avoid compliance implicitly. For example, congressional policymakers did not openly attack the *Chadha* decision; instead, they simply continued to employ the legislative veto. Similarly, the German Bundestag did not explicitly challenge the constitutional court's 1975 order to pass a prohibition against "consulting" contracts between legislators and special interest groups; it just did not act on it (BVerfGE 40, 296). Sometimes a legislative majority may even claim to implement a judicial decision but may craft the new policy in such a way as to evade aspects of the decision it opposes; recall the *Crucifix* and *Party Finance* decisions discussed in Chapter 1.

Because legislative majorities will usually not pursue noncompliance in an open, explicit fashion, the second condition takes center stage. The effectiveness of public support in lending authority to courts will depend on the likelihood that citizens will become aware (and convinced) that an attempt at evasion has taken place. To illustrate, suppose a judicial decision is announced that requires a legislative majority to revise the tax code in accordance with certain constitutional mandates,[2] and the legislature responds by passing a revised tax statute. A key question then becomes how easy it is for those voters who may be influenced (at the margin) by a concern for compliance with judicial rulings to check the correspondence between the ruling and the subsequent legislative revision. Does the new tax code comport with the court's demands? And if not, will citizens become aware and convinced that the legislature has failed to adhere faithfully to the decision?

Obviously, a number of factors will influence how effective such monitoring can and will be. One factor concerns the institutional structure of the political system. Systems that provide greater transparency in the policymaking process and allow greater opportunities for scrutiny by opposition parties make it more difficult for legislative majorities to hide attempts at evasion. Also, the configuration of public awareness of (and interest in) an issue matters. On issues that have low saliency, evasion is a much safer alternative than on issues that voters are intensely aware of. Such public awareness, of course, is directly influenced by opinion leadership. Situations in which the media, interest groups, or opposition groups face strong incentives to call attention to legislative responses make evasion more difficult. Moreover, the effectiveness of opinion leadership (and monitoring more generally) will depend on characteristics of the issue at

---

[2] The FCC made a number of such decisions during the 1990s, such as, BVerfGE 87, 153.

stake, most importantly its complexity. Some issues present straightforward, open-and-shut cases in which compliance is easy to establish (Did Nixon turn over the tapes?). Others are much more complex and subtle, and as a result, compliance is more difficult to verify and claims of noncompliance are more difficult and controversial to establish. (Is the new German tax code structured so as to provide the "existence minimum" to all taxpayers?) I will consider these factors in greater detail later in this chapter. For current purposes, I will simply say that the more *transparent* a political environment is, the more likely it is that citizens will become aware of legislative attempts to evade a judicial decision. In other words, transparency is a term that summarizes how easy it is for citizens to discover the relationship between a judicial decision and a legislative response. The more transparent the environment, the more likely an attempt at evasion of a decision will be caught.

In the next section, I develop a simple game-theoretic model that investigates how public support and transparency affect the interactions between legislative majorities and courts. Naturally, like any model, the one presented here is "stylized" and does not capture the full complexity of the politics of constitutional review. Along the way, I will point out how the model simplifies the real-world interaction and how this simplification may affect the model's results. Nevertheless, in abstracting away from these additional considerations and crystallizing the causal mechanism, the model provides valuable insights into the dynamics of constitutional review when courts must rely on public support to lend force to their decisions.

In addition to sometimes generating unexpected insights, a central advantage of a formal approach is that a model serves as a crucial "consistency check" in constructing a theory. Looking at the experiences of constitutional courts around the world, we can observe instances in which courts appear to be powerful, unconstrained institutions, able to impose their will on legislative majorities. We also observe courts that appear to kowtow to the other branches, apparently too timid to exercise their formal powers. And we observe courts and legislative majorities locked in struggles as each side attempts to defend a particular conception of good policy or good law. Sometimes we may observe all three types of interactions by the same court. Scholars often treat these different types of interactions as sui generis, that is, as interactions that require particularized explanations. The model developed in this chapter shows that this broad array of phenomena is consistent with one general framework that rests on a fairly simple set of assumptions. In addition, the model predicts the conditions under which each of the different types of interactions should be expected.

MODELING CONSTITUTIONAL REVIEW

Consider a simple policy-making game played by a "Constitutional Court" and a "Legislature" (For our purposes, it is easiest to think of a legislative majority, but of course, we could substitute any agent whose decisions are subject to review by the court and who may play a role in implementing the court's decision.) The game consists of a simple one-shot interaction. First, the legislature decides whether to "legislate" (L) or to forego doing so ($\sim L$). If the legislature chooses not to legislate, the game ends. If it legislates, the court has an opportunity to review the statute. It can choose to uphold the statute (U) or to veto it (V).[3] Finally, if the court decides to veto the statute, the legislature has an opportunity to respond to the decision. It can choose to evade the decision (E), thus sidestepping aspects of the court's decision, or it can choose to implement the ruling faithfully ($\sim E$). Thus, the interaction captures the central feature of legislative–judicial interactions that we are concerned with: the potential for legislative reactions to judicial decisions.

Naturally, we still need to incorporate the two conditions that are central to the enforcement mechanism we want to investigate – public support and transparency. One convenient way to do so is to think of these as characteristics of the political environment in which the interaction between court and legislature takes place. Simplifying to ease the exposition, I will treat each as dichotomous. In an environment that is transparent (T), the legislature's response to a judicial decision can be monitored effectively, and citizens will become aware of an attempt at noncompliance. If the legislature chooses to evade a decision, its attempt to do so is revealed and becomes public knowledge. In a nontransparent environment ($\sim T$), the legislature's evasive maneuver remains undetected. Similarly, in an environment in which the court enjoys sufficient support (PS), a legislature's attempt to evade a decision, provided that the attempt becomes public, results in a backlash that is politically so costly that the legislature abandons its evasion attempt and abides by the court's decision. If the court does

---

[3] Notice that this modeling choice assumes that the court has no docket control. This is an appropriate choice in the European context, since constitutional courts, including the FCC, generally do not have a discretionary docket.

not enjoy sufficient support ($\sim PS$), evading its decision is not politically costly.[4]

The combination of these two dimensions produces four environments in which the interaction between court and legislature can take place:

1. *Transparent environment with public support*: This environment puts the court in a strong position. Evasion attempts by the legislature will become public, and the court enjoys sufficient public support to make a backlash for evasion so costly that the legislature prefers to comply.
2. *Transparent environment with no public support*: This environment places the legislature in a strong position. Although any evasion attempt will become public knowledge, the court enjoys so little public support that an evasive legislature will not fear a backlash that is so costly that it would prefer to comply.
3. *Nontransparent environment with public support*: This environment favors the legislature. Even though the court enjoys public support, attempts at evasion are not detected and therefore do not trigger a backlash.
4. *Nontransparent environment with no public support*: Again, the legislature is in a strong position. Evasion is not detected. Even if it were, the court has insufficient public support to induce compliance.

If legislature and court knew in which type of environment their interaction takes place, we would have straightforward expectations about their behavior. In environments 2, 3, and 4, we would expect the legislature successfully to ignore any judicial decisions with which it disagrees. In environment 1, on the other hand, the legislature would comply and we would therefore expect the court to veto any statute that it does not agree with.

But of course, judges and legislative majorities usually cannot know which kind of environment they will find themselves in. In real-world

---

[4] This modeling choice simplifies a much more complex reality. Nevertheless, it captures the fundamental point that political actors must worry about potential backlash for noncompliance under some circumstances and that, under others, defying a court may not be sufficiently costly to deter noncompliance and can even be politically advantageous. In a slight variation on this story in the spirit of Barry Weingast's (1997) framework, one can interpret the presence of public support as signifying the existence of a citizens' consensus that evading a court decision is an action that triggers citizens' reactions.

interactions, majorities at the legislative stage cannot anticipate perfectly whether a constitutional court will enjoy public support should it later rule on a statute currently being considered. Similarly, when deciding how to react to a judicial decision, a legislative majority cannot anticipate perfectly whether the public will become aware of an evasion attempt. Finally, in deliberating, judges cannot know precisely what the constellation of public support following different rulings will be or whether evasion attempts can be successfully concealed. In the language of game theory, the players have incomplete information about the environment in which they act.

I capture this uncertainty through the use of two probabilities that capture the subjective beliefs that the actors have about their environment. We will denote the actors' subjective belief that the court enjoys sufficient public support by $q \in (0,1)$. Their subjective belief that the environment is transparent is represented by $r \in (0,1)$. A high q (i.e., q close to 1), for example, implies that both players think it highly likely that the court will enjoy sufficient support to make noncompliance unattractive. A low r (i.e., r close to 0), on the other hand, means that both believe that the environment is highly likely to be nontransparent, that is, that it is unlikely that the public will become aware of an evasion attempt.

The last components of the game we need to specify are the preferences of the players. What motivates judges and legislators in the model? The court's payoffs are a function of two components. First, the court has a preference over the policy under review, captured by a policy payoff $A > 0$. The court reaps this benefit whenever the ultimate outcome of the interaction with respect to the issue under review (whether the statute is implemented or not) comports with its preference for or against the bill. A *convergent* (C) court shares the policy preferences of the legislature. In other words, the convergent court reaps the benefit A if the policy is implemented. A *nonconvergent* court (~C), on the other hand, is opposed to the legislature's policy preferences and gains A whenever the policy is not implemented. Obviously, convergence and nonconvergence of preferences can be interpreted as simple policy preferences (the "attitudinal model"; see Segal and Spaeth 1993). Alternatively, one could interpret these preferences as capturing a judicial concern with legal criteria that determine constitutionality or unconstitutionality (the "legal" model). In other words, the model is open to a legal interpretation as well as the standard interpretation that judges are policy-motivated.

Given the potential for evasion, it would be unreasonable to assume that judges are motivated solely by the particulars of the current case. A successful evasion of a ruling is costly for the court as an institution because it undermines the court's authority by challenging its role in the policymaking process and demonstrates its relative weakness. As a result, judges are likely to have an *institutional* concern as well: They would prefer to avoid successful evasion of a decision. We incorporate this aspect by assuming that the court pays a cost of $I > 0$ if the legislature successfully evades the court. (Note that we make no assumption about how *strong* this institutional concern is relative to the value that the judges place on the issue under review.)

For the legislature, trying to anticipate judicial preferences when deciding whether to legislate or not is, of course, an important issue. If the court is convergent and shares the preferences of the majority, the possibility of judicial review poses little threat. On the other hand, if the court is non-convergent, constitutional review might result in a judicial veto. But just as the legislature cannot know whether the environment is transparent or whether the court will enjoy sufficient support, it also cannot know with certainty which type of court it is likely to confront. The legislature's subjective belief that the court shares its preferences, that is, is convergent, is given by $p \in (0,1)$. That is, a high value of p implies that the legislature is fairly certain that a majority on the court shares its preferences for the bill (or, in the alternative interpretation, has no constitutional objections.)

The utility function for the legislature, like judicial preferences, captures policy preferences and institutional concerns. First, we assume that the legislative majority has a policy goal in mind that it is pursuing with the bill it is considering. As a result, the legislature earns a policy payoff of $\alpha > 0$ if it can successfully implement the new policy it has proposed (either because the policy is upheld by the court or because the court is successfully evaded). We capture the potential impact of public support for the court by assuming that the legislature suffers a "public backlash" cost of $\beta > 0$ if it is caught in an evasion attempt when the court enjoys public support (i.e., this must be paid only if the environment is transparent, the court enjoys support, and the legislature has chosen to evade). Finally, we need to capture the fact that legislating is costly for a legislative majority. Agreement must be secured on a particular bill. Moreover, time on the legislative calendar is scarce, and therefore spending time on one bill precludes consideration of other bills. We capture these legislative transaction and opportunity costs by assuming that the majority must pay a cost of ε to legislate, where $\alpha > \varepsilon > 0$.

A strategy for the court is a set of instructions that explains how each type of court will react to a legislative enactment.[5] For example, the strategy $s_C = \{U|C; V|\sim C\}$ is a strategy under which the convergent court will uphold the legislature's decision and the nonconvergent court will veto it. Alternatively, under the strategy $s_C = \{U|C; U|\sim C\}$, both types of court uphold the decision. Since a convergent court shares the policy preferences of the legislature, it is clear that this court will always uphold the legislature's action. A strategy for the legislature specifies whether the legislature will legislate and how it will react to a judicial veto. For example, the strategy $s_L = \{L, \sim E\}$ is a strategy in which the legislature legislates and does not evade a judicial veto.

PREDICTIONS OF THE MODEL

The predictions of the model revolve around a central intuitive insight and its implications. If public support is a central enforcement mechanism, the court requires *both* public support and transparency to be in a strong position. Higher public support and greater likelihood of transparency constitute the court's resources in its interactions with the legislature. It is therefore not surprising that the *joint probability that the court enjoys sufficient support and that the environment is transparent* will play a crucial role in determining the predictions of the model. The greater this probability, the more the environment favors the court, while a reduced likelihood of either strengthens the legislature. This joint probability is given by rq (the probability that the environment is transparent multiplied by the probability that the court enjoys sufficient support). The equilibrium predictions of the model depend on whether this joint probability falls below or above certain thresholds. To reduce the visual clutter of stating the equilibrium conditions, it will be helpful to define several of these thresholds and to consider the intuition behind them before stating and interpreting the results.

Definition: Define the "legislative compliance threshold" as

$$T_L^{Comp} \equiv \frac{\alpha}{\alpha + \beta}.$$

To see the intuition behind this threshold, suppose a legislative majority is confronted with a judicial veto and must decide how to respond.

---

[5] I limit attention to pure strategies. Doing so has no substantive implications for the results.

Predictions of the Model

Evasion holds out the possibility of implementing a policy that the majority favors. But it also risks a costly public backlash. Whether legislative majorities choose to evade or comply therefore depends on their expectations about the likelihood of each scenario. When rq rises above the legislative compliance threshold, the likelihood that evasion will not be successful is so high that the legislature chooses to comply with an unwelcome decision. If, on the other hand, rq falls below the threshold, the legislature is sufficiently confident that it will be able to evade a decision successfully that it chooses not to comply. As we would expect, this threshold depends on legislative preferences. The more important the issue under review is to the legislative majority, the higher the threshold becomes. In other words, legislative majorities are more willing to risk an evasion attempt on issues that are central to their interests. The threshold declines as the cost of a public backlash increases. The more costly a backlash for evasion, the more willing the legislature becomes to defer to judicial decisions.

Definition: Define the "judicial veto threshold" as

$$T_J \equiv \frac{I}{I + A}.$$

Suppose a nonconvergent court expects that a legislative majority will try to evade its decision if the court chooses to annul the statute (i.e., the legislative compliance threshold is not met). At the same time, suppose the court is confident that the environment is highly favorable in the sense that the attempt at evasion is likely to be caught and the court will enjoy sufficient public support to induce the legislature to comply after all. In such a case, the court might decide to go ahead and annul a law despite the expectation of noncompliance. The judicial veto threshold marks this cutpoint. If rq rises above this threshold, the nonconvergent court will annul a statute even if it expects noncompliance. Note that this threshold depends on judicial preferences. The larger the institutional cost to successful evasion, the higher the threshold. In other words, as the institutional cost of being evaded rises for the court, the court must feel more confident that the environment is favorable before provoking a confrontation with the legislature. Similarly, the more the court cares about the issue under review, the lower the threshold becomes, that is, the more willing the court will be to take a chance on invalidating a statute even if it expects noncompliance.

Definition: Define the "legislative passage threshold" as

$$T_L^{Leg} \equiv \frac{\alpha - \varepsilon}{(\alpha + \beta)(1 - p)}.$$

To understand the intuition behind this threshold, suppose rq falls between the judicial veto threshold and the legislative compliance threshold. In this case, if the legislature chooses to pass a law at the initial stage, a showdown between court and legislature ensues as the court invalidates the law and the legislature chooses to evade the ruling. Since legislating is costly (remember the cost ε), the legislative majority at the initial legislative stage must decide whether inviting such a confrontation, which might end with a public backlash against the legislature, is worthwhile. The majority will choose to legislate only if it is sufficiently likely to prevail in the confrontation with the court. The legislative passage threshold marks this cutoff. If rq falls below this threshold, the legislature is sufficiently likely to prevail that it chooses to pass a bill even when it expects a confrontation with the court. If, on the other hand, rq rises above this threshold, the environment is so likely to be favorable to the court that inviting a confrontation with the court is not worth it, given the opportunity costs of legislating, and the legislature chooses not to pass a bill. Not surprisingly, this threshold depends on legislative preferences and the probability that the court will share the legislature's preferences. If the issue under consideration is more important to the legislative majority and the court is more likely to share the majority's preferences, the threshold increases and the legislature is more willing to risk a confrontation with the court. As the cost of a public backlash or the opportunity costs of legislating increase, the reverse is true.

There are five types of equilibrium interactions that the model predicts. In discussing these equilibria, it is useful to group them into four distinct types:

Legislative Self-Censoring Equilibria: In these equilibria, the legislature censors its own behavior in anticipation of judicial review and chooses not to legislate. There are two such equilibria:
Equilibrium A: For $rq < T_L^{Comp}$, $rq > T_J$ and $rq > T_L^{Leg}$, the following strategy profile constitutes a Perfect Bayesian Equilibrium (PBE)
Legislature: $s_L = \{\sim L, E\}$
Court: $s_C = \{U|C; V|\sim C\}$
Equilibrium B: For $rq \geq T_L^{Comp}$ and $p < \frac{\varepsilon}{\alpha}$, the following strategy profile constitutes a PBE:

Predictions of the Model

Legislature: $s_L = \{\sim L, \sim E\}$
Court: $s_C = \{U|C; V|\sim C\}$

Consider equilibrium B first. Because the joint probability that the environment is transparent and the court enjoys public support lies above the legislative compliance threshold, the legislature will choose to respect a judicial veto. Expecting compliance, the nonconvergent court will veto any bill that is passed. Moreover, the probability that the court will in fact be hostile to the legislature's purposes is high ($p < \frac{\varepsilon}{\alpha}$). In other words, in this scenario, the legislature believes that it is likely to face a hostile court that can successfully veto the law. Confronted with this scenario, the legislature concludes that the opportunity cost of passing a bill that is likely to be annulled outweighs the benefit that can be gained by passage. Therefore, it chooses not to legislate. The first equilibrium is similar. The legislative compliance threshold is not met, and the legislature will try to evade an unfavorable decision. However, the joint probability that the environment is transparent and the court enjoys public support is above the judicial veto threshold. That is, the court is sufficiently confident that it will prevail in a confrontation with the legislature to veto the law despite the expectation of noncompliance. Once again, the legislature believes that the court is so likely to be hostile to the legislative initiative (p is low) that the opportunity cost of legislating outweighs the expected benefit of passing the bill and engaging in a showdown with the nonconvergent court.

Substantively, in these equilibria, the legislature censors its own behavior preemptively in anticipation of judicial review by a court that is highly likely to be hostile. In other words, these equilibria demonstrate that one effect of constitutional review is that legislative majorities may decide not to pursue preferred policy initiatives because of the looming threat of a judicial veto.[6] This phenomenon has received attention by scholars of comparative judicial politics under the label "autolimitation." Stone (1992) has identified important instances in which legislative majorities in the French National Assembly have limited their legislative proposals in order to guard against a negative decision by the Constitutional Council. Other studies conclude that such autolimitation may be a more

---

[6] Of course, another intriguing possibility, not explored in this model, is that legislative majorities may decide to pass legislation in an effort to take a position precisely because they believe that they are insulated against actual implementation through a likely judicial veto.

general phenomenon in Europe (Landfried 1984; Stone Sweet 1998, 2000; Vanberg 1998a, 1998b).

These equilibria also have an important methodological implication. It is common to identify judicial power with instances in which courts have successfully struck down a particular piece of legislation. While annulments are clearly important, these equilibria suggest that the substantive impact of constitutional review on public policy may also be expressed in what does *not* happen. Bills that might have enjoyed legislative support in the absence of an anticipated judicial veto may not be passed in the same form or at all when legislators must confront a court with the power of review. This observation highlights the fact that one cannot adequately assess the manner in which the possibility of constitutional review shapes the policy process by considering only instances of judicial intervention. While some work, most notably that of Stone Sweet and Landfried, has begun to investigate the anticipatory influences of judicial review, most empirical work on constitutional courts focuses on analyzing judicial decisions or judicial voting patterns. A fuller appreciation for how the possibility of constitutional review influences policymaking and policy outcomes requires attention to the "passive influence" of judicial review (Brace and Langer 2001) as well.

Judicial Self-Censoring Equilibrium: In this equilibrium, the non-convergent court censors its own behavior in anticipation of the legislature's reaction by upholding the legislature's decision despite its preference for seeing the policy invalidated.
Equilibrium C: For $rq < T_L^{Comp}$ and $rq \leq T_J$, the following strategy profile constitutes a PBE:
Legislature: $s_L = \{L, E\}$
Court: $s_C = \{U|C; U|\sim C\}$

The distinguishing feature of this equilibrium is that the joint probability that the court enjoys sufficient support and the environment is transparent is low – neither the legislative compliance threshold nor the judicial veto threshold is met. The nonconvergent court realizes that it is in a weak position and unlikely to prevail in a confrontation with the legislature. Moreover, it knows that the legislature will choose to evade if the court chooses to annul the law. Consequently, the court decides to circumvent a confrontation that has the potential to damage its institutional standing. It does so by strategically upholding the statute (although it would prefer to annul). Put differently, an environment that leaves the court in a weak position creates conditions for "legislative supremacy."

Predictions of the Model

Despite its formal powers, the court cannot effectively act as a counterweight to the legislature. This equilibrium is significant because the anticipatory reactions it embodies demonstrate that observed compliance with judicial rulings does not *necessarily* imply that courts are powerful actors able to constrain legislative majorities at will. Perhaps judges are simply astute at avoiding confrontations they cannot reasonably hope to win.

The argument that anticipations of noncompliance can push courts to be more deferential toward legislative majorities than they otherwise might be has been important in several empirical studies. Consider Volcansek's analysis of the Italian Constitutional Court's jurisprudence on decree laws. Under Article 77 of the Italian Constitution, Italian governments may issue decree laws in cases of "necessity and urgency." The article also specifies that decree laws are temporary and lose effect retroactively unless they are confirmed within sixty days of issue by both houses of parliament. Italian governments routinely circumvented this limitation on the decree power by reissuing decrees that parliament had refused to ratify, even though there was no constitutional basis for doing so. By the 1980s, hundreds of decree laws were regularly reissued, on several occasions "not once or even twice, but up to six times" (Volcansek 2000:42). Despite the fact that numerous challenges to the practice had reached the court, the "Constitutional Court stood on the sidelines as the practice was transformed into a clear abuse of power" (2000:46). In case after case, the court declined to censor the government's conduct. Only in 1996, after the momentous upheaval that transformed the Italian political landscape in the early 1990s, did the court issue a decision declaring all reissued decree laws unconstitutional. In explaining the court's deference to the government over a span of more than three decades, Volcansek moves anticipations of noncompliance to the center: "Parliament's inability to stem the tide of decree laws would argue that, from a strategic perspective, a judicial action might also be ineffective.... The Court could have rightly calculated until 1996 that its best strategy was to avoid making what might well have been no more than a useless gesture" (2000:48). Similarly, Epstein et al. argue that the Russian Constitutional Court, reestablished in 1993 following President Boris Yeltsin's suspension of the court after the invalidation of several presidential decrees, has been careful to avoid cases and decisions that would provoke noncompliance by other institutions of governance (2001:152ff.).

Expectations of noncompliance have also played a central role in interpretations of seminal U.S. Supreme Court decisions, especially during the Court's early years. Consider Robert Lowry Clinton's (1994) analysis of the Court's historic decision in *Marbury v. Madison* (5 U.S. 137), often hailed as the case in which the Court "successfully asserted its authority to invalidate acts of Congress in one of the cleverest coups of American history" (Pritchett 1977:126). The case revolved around the refusal of the newly elected Republican administration of President Thomas Jefferson to recognize judicial appointments made during the last few days of the outgoing Federalist administration of President John Adams. The Supreme Court, despite the fact that most justices had strong Federalist ties, famously declined to order the administration to deliver the commissions that would allow the appointees to take up their judgeships by arguing that the Constitution prevents Congress from granting the Court the power to issue such orders. Clinton explains the decision in part by assuming that the justices expected that the Jefferson administration would ignore the Court's decision if it issued a writ of mandamus to force delivery of William Marbury's commission as a justice of the peace. Mark Graber (1998:232) is even more explicit in his evaluation of *Marbury* and another Marshall Court decision that involved the return of a captured vessel to its original French owners: "When read in conjunction with *Marbury* and other early Marshall Court decisions, however, *Schooner Peggy* evinces a court desperately avoiding clashes with a potentially hostile administration."

Similarly, in his biography of Chief Justice John Marshall, Jean Edward Smith alludes to anticipations of noncompliance in explaining the Court's seminal decision in *Cohens v. Virginia* (19 U.S. 264). The case revolved around a Virginia law prohibiting the sale of out-of-state lottery tickets. The Supreme Court's opinion upheld the Court's authority to hear appeals from state courts but declined to overturn convictions under the Virginia statute. Smith concludes that the decision may have been motivated, at least in part, by an expectation of noncompliance: "If Virginia defied the Court and persisted in arresting those selling out-of-state ducats, there would be little the justices could do. Marshall was too astute to press an issue that the Court could not win" (Smith 1996:459). The judicial self-censoring equilibrium captures the underlying logic of these examples.

Separation-of-Powers Equilibrium: In this equilibrium, the legislature legislates. The nonconvergent court vetoes the law, and the legislature respects that decision.
Equilibrium D: For $rq \geq T_L^{Comp}$ and $p \geq \frac{\varepsilon}{\alpha}$, the following strategy profile constitutes a PBE:

Legislature: $s_L = \{L, \sim E\}$
Court: $s_C = \{U|C; V|\sim C\}$

This equilibrium captures what at first appears to be the normal interaction between legislative majorities and constitutional courts in successful constitutional democracies. Along the path of play, the legislature legislates. The law is upheld by a convergent court and vetoed by a nonconvergent court. Confronted with a judicial veto, the legislature chooses to comply. The sense in which this constitutes a Separation-of-Powers Equilibrium is immediate: The legislature exercises its power to initiate policy change, but the nonconvergent court can effectively prevent the legislature's decision from being implemented. Successful initiation of a new policy thus requires the consent of *both* players – the legislature acting as an agenda setter and the court as a veto player. The conditions that are necessary to sustain this equilibrium are intuitive. First, the joint probability that the court enjoys public support and the environment is transparent must be sufficiently high to induce the legislature to respect a judicial veto. Second, given that the nonconvergent court can successfully prevent implementation of the policy, the probability that the court will share the preferences of the legislature must be high enough to forestall self-censoring behavior by the legislature. In other words, successful separation-of-powers arrangements are not purely defined by formal institutional arrangements (which are equivalent across all of our equilibria). They also depend on the presence of external conditions (such as public support and transparency) that support mutual respect and balance among the branches and prevent any one branch from becoming overbearing (as in the Self-Censoring Equilibria). If these conditions are met, however, the court is largely unconstrained in pursuing its sincere preferences when reviewing legislation. As a result, we might expect that the attitudinal model, which posits that justices largely vote on the basis of their personal policy preferences (Segal and Spaeth 1993), would predict judicial behavior under this equilibrium well. One important implication of this argument is that there is no necessary conflict between the strategic and attitudinal models. The attitudinal model may simply reflect a special case of a more general model, such as the one presented here, in which judges may or may not be able to vote their sincere preferences, depending on the political environment in which they find themselves (for a similar argument with special reference to the U.S. Supreme Court, see Segal 1997).

Contentious Equilibrium: In this equilibrium, the legislature passes a law and chooses to evade any judicial veto. The nonconvergent court chooses to veto the law nevertheless.

Equilibrium E: For $rq < T_L^{Comp}$, $rq > T_J$, and $rq \leq T_L^{Leg}$, the following strategy profile constitutes a PBE:
Legislature: $s_L = \{L, E\}$
Court: $s_C = \{U|C; V|\sim C\}$

This final equilibrium captures an intermediate case. Because the joint probability that the court enjoys public support and the environment is transparent does not meet the legislative compliance threshold, the legislature feels secure in evading a judicial veto. At the same time, this probability is sufficiently high that the nonconvergent court hopes to win in a confrontation with the legislature and chooses to annul the statute despite the expectation of evasion. Unlike Equilibrium A, however, the court is likely to share the legislature's preferences, convincing the legislative majority to pass the statute. Of the five equilibria, this is the *only* one in which evasion of a judicial veto actually occurs. In the next section, we will return to a substantive discussion of the conditions that make such a tug of war between judges and governing majorities particularly likely.

For now, it is important to note that, empirically, this equilibrium is particularly interesting and significant. It demonstrates that struggles or confrontations in which a court invalidates a measure, only to encounter resistance and noncompliance (recall the examples in Chapter 1), are not necessarily the result of accidents or miscalculations on the part of politicians or judges. Instead, they are consistent with fully rational behavior when public support constitutes a central enforcement mechanism for judicial decisions. In the next section, we will flesh out the empirical circumstances in which such confrontations are particularly likely. In Chapter 6, we will consider an in-depth case study of party finance legislation and jurisprudence in Germany that illustrates this type of equilibrium well.

The model's equilibria can be ranked according to the degree of judicial power in each. For this ranking, we need only consider the perspective of the nonconvergent court (since there is no conflict between the legislature and the convergent court). An intuitive way to think about judicial power in this context is to say that the court is more powerful the more likely it is to prevent successful implementation of the legislature's policy. Given this definition, the court is most powerful in the Legislative

Predictions of the Model

Self-Censoring Equilibria (the legislature does not even attempt to legislate) and the Separation-of-Powers Equilibrium (the legislature complies with the court's ruling). It is less powerful in the Contentious Equilibrium (the legislature will successfully evade if the court has insufficient support or if the environment is not transparent) and least powerful in the Judicial Self-Censoring Equilibria (the court simply upholds the legislature's policy). Naturally, the analogous power ranking for the legislature is given in the reverse order.

One of the central lessons of this simple, parsimonious model is that a wide array of empirically relevant and observable forms of interaction between legislatures and courts are fully consistent with the assumption that public support provides a central enforcement mechanism for judicial decisions. In other words, the model furnishes a unified, general explanation of legislative–judicial interactions. The predictions of the model are illustrated graphically in Figures 2.1 and 2.2.[7] Each figure maps the probability that the court enjoys public support (q) along the vertical axis, while the horizontal axis displays the probability that the environment is transparent (r).

Consider Figure 2.1 first. This figure graphs the model's predictions when the court is sufficiently likely to share the legislature's preferences so that legislative majorities do not engage in self-censoring $(p \geq \frac{\varepsilon}{\alpha})$. In the northeastern section of the probability space, the court is in a strong position, since the environment is likely to be transparent and the court is likely to enjoy public support. Here we find the Separation-of-Powers Equilibrium in which the nonconvergent court can successfully veto the statute. As we move out of this area into the region in which the joint probability rq is in an intermediate range, the Contentious Equilibrium is predicted. Finally, as we move to the southern and western edges of the figure, where the probability of transparency and the probability of public support are low, the court is in a weak position and begins to censor its own behavior. Figure 2.2 is directly analogous to Figure 2.1. It shows the equilibrium predictions when the court is highly likely to be hostile to the legislative initiative $(p < \frac{\varepsilon}{\alpha})$. As a result, environments that place the court in a strong position (the northeast corner) now induce the legislature to engage in the Self-Censoring Equilibrium (instead of giving rise to the Separation-of-Powers Equilibrium).

---

[7] The regions displayed in the figure are illustrative only. While the general shape and location of the equilibrium regions is accurate, the precise cutoffs depend on the values of the payoff parameters and the probability p.

Implementation, Public Support, and Transparency

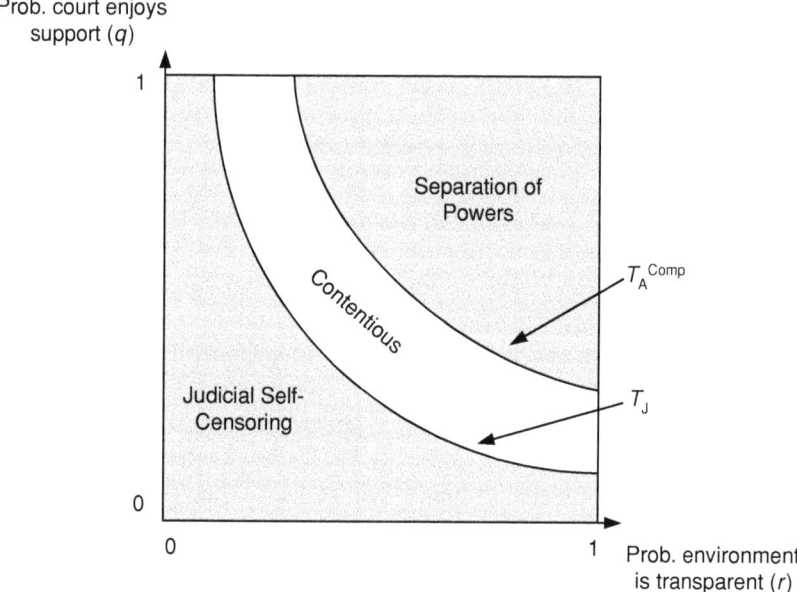

Figure 2.1. Equilibrium Predictions When Court Is Likely to Be Convergent ($p > \frac{\varepsilon}{\alpha}$).

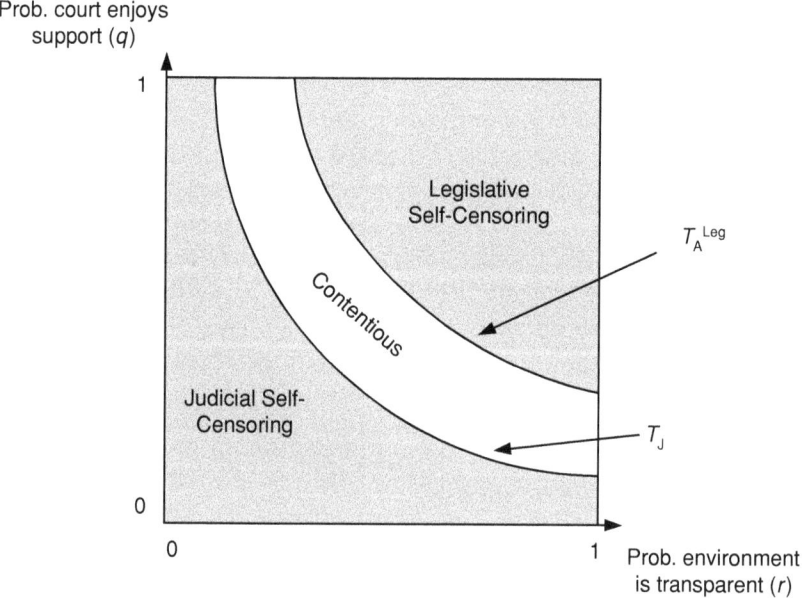

Figure 2.2. Equilibrium Predictions When Court Is Likely to Be Hostile ($p < \frac{\varepsilon}{\alpha}$).

INTERPRETATION AND COMPARATIVE STATICS

The discussion and interpretation of these results is organized around a series of observations:

Observation 1: If public support is central to the enforcement of judicial rulings, courts become more deferential and less powerful as the political environment becomes less transparent and as they are less likely to enjoy public support.

Environments in which transparency is high (making it likely that citizens would become aware of an evasion attempt) and in which the court is likely to enjoy sufficient public support favor effective judicial control. On the other hand, environments in which the court is not likely to enjoy public support or that are nontransparent hold out little promise for effective judicial oversight. Instead, the legislature is largely able to pursue its preferred policies without judicial interference. Figures 2.1 and 2.2 illustrate this finding graphically. The court is in a powerful position in the northeastern section of the probability space, where the joint probability that the environment is transparent and the court enjoys support is high (resulting in the Separation-of-Powers Equilibrium or the Legislative Self-Censoring Equilibrium). In this region, the nonconvergent court is able to prevent implementation of the legislature's proposal. As either probability begins to decline, the court finds itself in a weaker position and the legislature may begin to evade its rulings (the Contentious Equilibrium). In the southern and western parts of the figure, the court is so disadvantaged that it censors its own behavior in anticipation of successful evasion (the Judicial Self-Censoring Equilibrium). As a result, the legislature is unconstrained by judicial oversight.

Corollary: The power of constitutional courts in constraining legislative majorities varies cross-nationally. Even for the same court at the same time, influence varies across different issue areas.

Courts in some countries enjoy much higher levels of support than courts in others (see Gibson et al. 1998). Some courts are highly visible institutions in their political systems, and their decisions are disseminated through the mass media and generally receive some public attention (e.g., the U.S. Supreme Court or the German FCC). Other high courts linger in relative obscurity.[8] Because of such differences in support and transparency, courts that are institutionally equivalent may diverge greatly in the extent to which they can pose powerful counterweights to legislative majorities. Moreover, even for the same court, the issues at hand will vary in the degree to which the court is likely to enjoy support and in the transparency surrounding an issue (see later sections of this chapter). Courts will be less able to police complex policy areas than simple ones in which evasion can be spotted easily. Similarly, the court's leverage will be reduced on issues that generate little media attention and public interest or on which there is substantial public opposition to the court's position. Judicial power varies not only across courts and across time, but also for the same court at the same time across different issue areas.

The next observations draw on Table 2.1, which demonstrates how changes in the model's parameters affect or change its predictions. Specifically, for each type of equilibrium and each exogenous parameter, the corresponding cell in Table 2.1 shows how an increase in the given parameter may affect the equilibrium prediction of the game. For example, an increase in q (the probability that the court enjoys public support) or r (the probability that the environment is transparent) may induce a shift from the Judicial Self-Censoring Equilibrium to any of the three other equilibrium types (which implies greater judicial power).[9]

Observation 2: If public support is central to the enforcement of judicial rulings, courts become more powerful and less deferential as their public support increases.

A natural way to interpret the payoff parameter β is as a measure of the severity of the public backlash that a governing majority must endure if it is caught in an evasion attempt. As Table 2.1 indicates, increases in the magnitude of this sanction can only induce movements to equilibria that make the court more powerful. The intuition underlying these results is straightforward: Because a more severe sanction raises the expected costs of evasion, the legislature will comply with judicial decisions even in circumstances that are less favorable for the court. This increased willingness to abide by judicial decisions induces the court to exercise its powers more aggressively. In other words, if an exogenously imposed sanction such as public support acts as the major enforcement mechanism

---

[8] See Staton (2003) for a fascinating study of attempts by the Mexican Supreme Court to generate media attention for its decisions. I return to this later.
[9] For the parameters r and q, the same information can be seen in Figures 2.1 and 2.2.

Table 2.1 Comparative Statics Predictions

	Increase in q (Favors Court)	Increase in r (Favors Court)	Increase in p (Favors Legislature)	Increase in α (Favors Legislature)	Increase in β (Favors Court)	Increase in A (Favors Court)	Increase in I (Favors Legislature)
Legislature self-censoring (S.C.)	No change	No change	Contentious Separation	Contentious Separation Judicial S.C.	No change	No change	Judicial S.C.
Separation of powers	No change	No change	No change	Contentious Judicial S.C.	No change	No change	No change
Contentious	Separation Legislature S.C.	Separation Legislature S.C.	No change	No change	Separation Legislature S.C.	No change	Judicial S.C.
Judicial self-censoring	Contentious Separation Legislature S.C.	Contentious Separation Legislature S.C.	No change	No change	Separation Legislature S.C.	Contentious Legislature S.C.	No change

Note: The table shows the movement from the equilibrium types listed on the left that can be induced by an increase in the exogenous parameters.

for judicial rulings, the magnitude of the sanction constitutes a crucial resource for a court. As one would expect, the court's power increases as this resource grows and diminishes where it is absent. This observation calls attention to the dynamics of public support for courts. How is such support generated? Can support be influenced by judges? I return to these issues later.

> **Observation 3:** If public support is central to the enforcement of judicial rulings, courts become more deferential and less powerful as the political importance of the issue under review increases for legislative majorities.

Not all issues are of equal importance to governing majorities. The preference parameter α signals the importance placed on the issue under review by the legislature. As Table 2.1 reveals, an increase in α can only provoke movement toward equilibria in which the court is less powerful. (For example, an increase in α may lead to a shift from the Separation-of-Powers Equilibrium to the Contentious Equilibrium or even to the Judicial Self-Censoring Equilibrium.) The more important the issue is to the governing majority, the more committed the majority will be to preserving its policy, if necessary by evasion. Faced with a more committed opponent, the court may decide to back down because it is not sufficiently likely to prevail in a confrontation. In other words, courts will be less likely to be influential on an issue as the preferences of other actors become more intense. This result is consistent with Gerald Rosenberg's argument, drawing on careful studies of several major policy areas in the United States, that courts are constrained in preventing or initiating policy change in opposition to strong preferences by other political players (Rosenberg 1991). Ironically, judicial oversight is thus least likely to be effective in cases in which the *external* constraint on governing majorities may be particularly important because their preferences are so intense.

> **Observation 4:** If public support is central to the enforcement of judicial rulings, courts become more deferential and less powerful as judges
>
> - place greater value on avoiding evasion
> - place less importance on the issue under review

Both of these results are intuitive. The more judges are concerned to avoid a successful evasion, the more timid they will be in exercising their powers. As Table 2.1 shows, an increase in the parameter I can only induce a shift to judicial self-censoring. Similarly, the less judges are motivated by the issue under review (as indicated by A), the less aggressive they will be in reviewing the legislature's action.

Taken together with Observation 3, these results have a direct bearing on the Contentious Equilibrium. As Figures 2.1 and 2.2 indicate, the Contentious Equilibrium is predicted in the region *between* the legislative compliance threshold (T_L^{Comp}) (or, for Figure 2.2, the legislative passage threshold, T_L^{Leg}) and the judicial veto threshold (T_J), that is, in the region in which the legislature (given its preferences) feels sufficiently secure to evade a judicial veto and the court feels sufficiently confident (given its preferences) to annul the law despite the expectation of evasion. As the importance of the issue under review increases for the court (A increases), the T_J curve shifts downward toward the southwest region. As importance increases for the legislature (α increases), the T_L^{Comp} and T_L^{Leg} curves shift upward toward the northeast. Together, these two effects lead to an expansion of the region in which the Contentious Equilibrium is expected. This has a direct empirical implication: Actual confrontations between legislative majorities and judges (in which judges veto a law and legislative majorities ignore the decision) are most likely in cases in which judges and legislators place substantial importance on the issue under review.

The model also generates several interesting counterintuitive empirical implications:

Observation 5: Empirically, confrontations between legislative majorities and courts, as well as evasion of judicial decisions, *may* become more frequent as courts are more likely to enjoy public support and as the political environment is more likely to be transparent.

Observation 6: Empirically, confrontations between legislative majorities and courts, as well as judicial vetoes and evasion of judicial decisions, *may* become more frequent as courts are more likely to share the policy preferences of legislative majorities.

At first, these two observations appear counterintuitive. As conditions that strengthen the position of the court increase (public support and transparency), we might expect confrontations between majorities and courts to decline. Similarly, as a court is more likely to be sympathetic to the goals of a legislative majority, we might expect conflict between the institutions to diminish. The key to making sense of these observations lies in the fact that the formal model allows us to capture the full "equilibrium response" of the players. That is, it allows us to capture how *both* players adjust their behavior to changes in their environment. As conditions for the court improve, legislative majorities are more willing, ceteris paribus, to accept judicial rulings. But things do not remain equal: Courts respond to their new environment by becoming *more aggressive* in using their power of review. As a result, there may be a shift from a Judicial Self-Censoring Equilibrium to a Contentious Equilibrium, which results in more confrontations. Similarly, when the court is more likely to share the preferences of the legislature, it is more likely to uphold a given enactment. But because the legislature is more optimistic about its chances at the review stage, it responds to this change by passing legislation that it would not have passed if the court were less likely to be convergent. That is, we may observe a shift from a Legislative Self-Censoring Equilibrium to a Contentious or a Separation-of-Powers Equilibrium.

These observations nicely illustrate the power of formal approaches: By focusing on equilibrium behavior, that is, on the complete adjustment of all players to their environment, models can generate unexpected insights. In this case, we have uncovered interesting and unexpected relationships that provide testable empirical hypotheses. For example, if courts usually enjoy little support when first established and then build support over time (as Gibson et al. 1998 have argued), we might expect few confrontations between court and legislature initially, as the court largely defers to the legislature. As the court begins to build support, there may be a period of more intense confrontations. And if the court continues to grow in public esteem, these confrontations may subside again as the legislature is forced to defer to the court more and more often.

All six observations call attention to the fact that if public support is important in lending force to judicial decisions, legal and constitutional considerations are not the only variables determining how a constitutional court makes use of its powers and how legislative majorities respond to judicial decisions. The *political* environment matters as well. In addition to the preferences of judges and governing majorities, transparency and public support for the court are central. A high joint probability that the environment is transparent and the court enjoys support favors the court, while an absence of either strengthens the position of the legislature. Clearly, it is worthwhile to unpack the substantive meaning of transparency and public support further, and to investigate the implications of each for judicial and legislative behavior.

TRANSPARENCY

So far, transparency has functioned as a blanket concept. It is intended to capture the likelihood that citizens become aware of and convinced that a legislative majority has attempted to evade a judicial decision. Transparency in this broad sense is influenced by many factors. In this section, I discuss several influences that are particularly central: the impact of opinion leadership and media coverage, the presence of organized interests that have an incentive to call attention to evasion attempts, and the complexity of the issue at hand.

Most citizens acquire what knowledge they possess about politics from sources that are readily available, primarily the mass media, including television and newspapers (Page, Shapiro, and Dempsey 1987; Zaller 1992). The issues covered and the views expressed in these media are heavily shaped by opinion leaders, that is, by a fairly small number of people (in proportion to the population as a whole) who, for various reasons, can exercise more influence on what is reported, and how it is reported, than most citizens. Opinion leaders include, obviously, news editors, editorial writers, and reporters. They also include sources that these individuals rely on, especially political insiders, experts, and interest groups. Several studies have shown that opinion leaders have predictable and considerable effects on the development of public awareness and opinion on particular issues through a two-step process in which information filters down to the mass public via elite opinion (McCloskey and Zaller 1984; Page et al., 1987; Zaller 1992). In the current context, this implies that opinion leaders, through their influence on media coverage surrounding a judicial decision and the legislative response, play a central role in raising public awareness of a decision and of potential evasion attempts. More intense media coverage of a decision and the legislative response increases transparency and makes it more difficult to evade a decision without detection.

The role of opinion leadership in raising transparency (and in shaping public opinion; see the later discussion) suggests that judges and politicians will be particularly attentive to opinion leaders in gauging potential public attention (and public opinion) on a particular issue. For example, in its first confrontations with the newly established FCC in 1952, the Adenauer administration decided to back down in attempts to pressure the court despite the absence of systematic public opinion polls on the issue. It did so largely because of concerns generated by negative newspaper editorials, which suggested that the cabinet's actions might result in a considerable backlash (Vanberg 2000). Moreover, the importance of opinion leadership suggests that politicians and judges will not react to *current* public interest and opinion in a case, but rather to what public attention and opinion, once mobilized, may be. As Zaller has put it, when political actors "pursue a certain policy because of perceived public pressure to do so, it is often the anticipation of that pressure, rather than actual pressure, that is critical" (Zaller 1992:270; see also Arnold 1990; Key 1961).

Another crucial factor that impacts transparency is whether organized interests that have incentives to call attention to an evasion attempt are present. On any given issue, certain individuals or organized groups may have a particular interest in raising public awareness of legislative evasion to deter such action (because they have a genuine interest in seeing the decision implemented) or simply to embarrass or hurt the majority politically (because they hope to profit by damaging the majority's political standing independently of the issue at stake).[10] The legislative opposition constitutes an obvious candidate. If (some) citizens are willing to sanction governing majorities for failing to implement judicial decisions faithfully, such punishment will usually directly benefit current opposition parties. As a result, opposition groups, regardless of the issue at stake, generally face incentives to monitor compliance with judicial decisions and to call attention to attempts at evasion. However, the ability of the opposition to increase transparency is conditioned by its institutional environment and by the characteristics of the issue at stake. Legislative processes that are open to the public (at the floor and committee stages), that allow opposition groups to initiate public hearings, or to shape the agenda of committee hearings or floor debate, enhance the ability of the opposition to call attention to legislative evasion.

Like opposition parties, organized groups that have a stake in a particular decision can have a direct impact on transparency by raising awareness of an issue or calling attention to attempts at noncompliance. Such groups can provide financial resources and expertise that are valuable in monitoring legislative compliance and can facilitate renewed court challenges if necessary. Through their membership and their media connections, organized groups can also create publicity and call attention to evasive

---

[10] I borrow this insight from Arnold's treatment of the U.S. Congress. He uses the term "instigator" to refer to individuals who have an incentive to call attention to the stakes citizens have in various policy areas and thereby to raise the importance of those issues in citizens' electoral calculations (1990:30).

maneuvers. For example, in a detailed study of the judicial enforcement of constitutional rights provisions in the United States, Canada, India, and Britain, Charles Epp has shown that whether a "rights revolution" occurs is directly connected to the presence of organized interest groups that can sustain systematic litigation and provide "the judiciary with active partners in the fight against the opponents of implementation" (1998:22). In short, the presence of large, well-organized interest groups that favor implementation of a specific judicial decision increases transparency surrounding that decision, thereby making it more difficult for legislative majorities to resist or evade a ruling.

Transparency depends not only on the institutional environment and the actions of outside actors, but also on the characteristics of the issue at hand. The inherent complexity of the policy area is one such factor. It is more difficult to establish whether a judicial decision has been faithfully implemented in policy areas that are technically more complex and demanding. For example, a legislative reaction to a decision declaring the death penalty unconstitutional is transparent because it is fairly straightforward to determine (at least in a liberal democracy) whether executions still take place. By contrast, a technical decision involving several tax code provisions is much harder to monitor. Does the tax code as revised satisfy the court's demands? In general, policy areas that involve regulation of substantive outcomes (as opposed to procedural rules) and cases that involve multiple policy areas rather than a single issue tend to be more complex.

Moreover, complexity has a secondary (interactive) effect on the ability of outside groups to increase transparency. As the complexity of an issue increases, claims that evasion has taken place are more difficult to verify and therefore become more contentious. In other words, opposition parties and other outside groups may have a more difficult time convincing a sufficient number of citizens that a particular legislative response does, in fact, evade a particular court decision. To summarize, increasing issue complexity tends to reduce transparency, thereby making legislative evasion easier.

In the interests of tractability, the model I have presented treats transparency as an exogenous variable. But of course, within constraints, legislators and judges have some influence over how difficult or easy it is to police compliance with a decision; in other words, they have some influence over transparency. When contemplating an evasive maneuver, legislators will generally favor lower transparency, and they have several options in trying to hide evasion.[11] For example, they may try to reduce the publicity of parliamentary debate on a particular bill (e.g., scheduling a highly restricted debate during a late night session) or they may try to close committee hearings. Instead of presenting a single bill that consolidates the legislative revision, they may break up the response into a number of statutes, making it more difficult to grasp the entire response. Similarly, complex statutory language may be used to hide evasion. For example, in 1995 the main parliamentary parties in Germany, the Christian Democrats (CDU/CSU) and the Social Democrats (SPD), initiated a statutory change to raise legislators' salaries – a situation in which reducing transparency is desirable. After studying the proposed bill, a commentator (who is widely acknowledged as a preeminent authority on party finance and legislative compensation in Germany) concluded:

> The sponsors of the statute to increase legislative compensation were so wary of the light of day that they drafted a largely undecipherable law. The bill did not list specific monetary amounts, but expressed salaries as percentages that referred to statutes and regulations governing civil service salaries and benefits that are difficult to track down. It took this author two weeks and uncountable inquires at the parliamentary administration to gain a reliable picture of the content of the bill. (von Arnim 1996: 343f.)

Clearly, legislators can use similar strategies to try to reduce transparency when they decide to evade a particular judicial decision. Naturally, whether they can do so depends to some extent on the nature of the issue at stake.

Unlike legislators, judges generally have an interest in increasing transparency since greater transparency will make it more difficult to evade a decision. There are several methods they can use. The precise wording of an opinion is one. The more clearly an opinion enunciates the constitutional principles that sustain the decision, as well as the implications of the decision for policy, the easier it is to verify whether a legislative response complies with the ruling. Naturally, achieving such precision is, in part, a function of the issue at stake. Some issues allow courts to issue highly focused rulings ("President Nixon, turn over the tapes"), while others demand more diffuse rulings that are more difficult to state in precise

---

[11] Under some circumstances, there may be such strong public opposition to a particular decision that noncompliance can be politically advantageous; in this case, there is no need to hide evasion, and it may even be advantageous to highlight noncompliance. The *Crucifix* decision in Germany and the reaction of elected officials in the American South to *Brown v. Board of Education* (347 U.S. 483) are examples.

language.[12] Systematic studies of implementation of U.S. Supreme Court opinions seem to suggest that greater precision in judicial decisions does indeed promote implementation (Baum 1976, 1981; Spriggs 1997). One implication of this analysis is that judges' desire to increase pressure for compliance by making decisions more explicit may be one reason for the (sometimes lamented) judicial tendency to write specific policy prescriptions into opinions. Specificity of judicial language may be a response to the problem of transparency. In addition to specificity in rulings, judges may also try to increase the pressure on legislative majorities to comply by raising public awareness of a decision. For example, in a careful study of the Mexican Supreme Court, Jeffrey Staton (2003) has investigated the strategic use of the court's press office to raise public awareness of decisions that may be opposed by legislative majorities.[13]

PUBLIC SUPPORT

If public support is central in creating judicial authority, transparency is obviously a necessary condition for the mechanism's effectiveness: Citizens must become aware of an evasion attempt.[14] But unless a sufficiently large number of citizens are also willing to express their dissatisfaction by withdrawing support from politicians and parties that do not respect judicial decisions, transparency alone is insufficient. The centrality of public support naturally raises two questions: What determines public support for a constitutional court? And do the foundations of public support have implications for judicial behavior?

A long tradition in political science research separates institutional support into two components: specific and diffuse support (Easton 1975). "Specific support" refers to satisfaction with the particular policy outputs of an institution; in the current context, it refers to satisfaction with particular judicial decisions. "Diffuse support" refers to more general support for an institution qua institution, divorced from immediate reference to specific policy outputs. Clearly, this distinction makes analytic sense: I may well regard a constitutional court as a valuable

---

[12] I would like to thank Barry Friedman for bringing this important distinction to my attention.
[13] Under certain circumstances, it may be in the interests of judges to reduce transparency in order to hide evasion. I return to this point later.
[14] Again, it is important to stress that this number must not be large in absolute terms. Elections are won and lost at the margin. There must simply be a sufficiently numerous group of citizens to sway legislators' calculations.

institution in the political system and oppose threats to the court's independence even if, on occasion, I intensely disagree with particular judicial rulings.

In one sense, the distinction between these two types of support does not matter for the efficacy of the enforcement mechanism that we are considering here. If the expectation of a public backlash for noncompliance is a primary factor in politicians' calculus about how to respond to a decision, it does not matter if citizens withdraw their support because they approve of the court's specific decision (specific support) or because they support the court as an institution (diffuse support). What matters is that in the aggregate, a sufficient number of citizens are expected to support the court to make evasion unattractive. In another sense, however, the distinction is of central importance.

Considerable research by political psychologists suggests a dynamic relationship between specific and diffuse support. Over time, the support that an individual exhibits for a court is, at least in part, a function of how that person evaluates the substantive outcomes of the court's decisions. Some caveats are in order before we consider these studies more closely. Empirically, it may be difficult to separate specific and diffuse support reliably. Operationalizing these concepts in survey questions that meaningfully tap the two attitudes when presented to respondents is extraordinarily difficult, and perhaps impossible (Loewenberg 1971, but see Canache 1999). Most scholars readily admit the difficulty (e.g., Gibson et al. 1998:356). Second, nonexperimental studies typically utilize cross-sectional data taken at a specific point in time, not longitudinal data that track individual attitudes over time. Thus, the data provide a snapshot of attitudes, not the dynamics of attitudinal change.

Within these limitations, several studies conclude that specific support influences diffuse support for a court. In several experiments using college students, Mondak (1991, 1992) demonstrated that respondents' diffuse support for the U.S. Supreme Court increased after they had been exposed to hypothetical court decisions consistent with their ideological predispositions. In a nonexperimental design, Grosskopf and Mondak (1998) showed that evaluation of specific decisions by the U.S. Supreme Court affected diffuse support for the Court. Similarly, Gibson et al. found in their survey data collected in 1993–6 that in "Greece, West Germany, the Netherlands, [and] the former East Germany, diffuse support closely mirrors specific support" (1998:351). In short, considerable evidence suggests that substantive evaluations of particular court decisions do affect the level of public support for a court, especially for opinion leaders (see also

Caldeira and Gibson 1992; Franklin and Kosaki 1995; Marshall 1989). Importantly, as we will see in Chapter 5, German judges and legislators also believe that this is the case.

This link between specific and diffuse support has significant implications for judicial behavior. Because public support constitutes an important judicial resource, a concern about maintaining support for the court may influence judicial deliberations. Specifically, judges may recognize that their current decisions have implications for future support. This recognition, coupled with a desire to retain or build the court's support, may induce judges to be sensitive to public opinion. This does not imply that a constitutional court will act as a "preference barometer" and decide cases on the basis of opinion polls. Nor does it imply that judges cannot, on occasion, get away with an unpopular decision. But judges are likely to be aware that the support they enjoy is a valuable resource that can be "spent" quickly if too many unpopular decisions convince too many citizens that the court exercises an undesirable influence on the direction of policy (see also Durr, Martin, and Wolbrecht 2000; Mondak and Smithey 1997).

As a cursory example, consider President Franklin D. Roosevelt's 1937 Court-packing plan. Throughout the 1930s, Roosevelt had to contend with a Supreme Court that consistently struck down central programs of the New Deal. These programs constituted the core of the president's legislative program and enjoyed widespread public support. After winning reelection in an unprecedented landslide in 1936, Roosevelt decided to confront the Court head on by proposing a plan that would allow him to "pack" the Court with up to six additional justices. In a series of spectacular decisions following the announcement of the plan, the Supreme Court reversed its position and began to uphold New Deal programs.[15] Whether the Supreme Court (or, more accurately, Justice Owen Roberts) performed this "switch in time that saved nine" as a conscious response to the court-packing plan is debatable (Leuchtenburg 1995). What seems less controversial is that public opposition to the plan, which eventually forced Roosevelt to give up on it, would have dissipated quickly had the Supreme Court continued to oppose New Deal legislation. In a highly interesting and original paper using Gallup poll data, Caldeira has shown, in fact, that opposition to the court-packing plan was significantly linked

---

[15] The most important cases, handed down over a two-week period in the spring of 1937, are *West Coast Hotel v. Parrish* (300 U.S. 379) and *National Labor Relations Board v. Jones & Laughlin Steel Corporation* (301 U.S. 1).

to the timing of the decisions in which the court performed its about-face (Caldeira 1987).

Naturally, satisfaction with particular decisions over time may not be the only determinant of (diffuse) support for courts.[16] Courts are usually understood to be different from other political institutions in the sense that they are supposed to act as impartial, apolitical referees that are required to advance legal (and sometimes constitutional) arguments in defense of their decisions. Whether judges are in fact motivated in this way is, of course, a question of intense disagreement among defenders of the "legal" and "attitudinal" models. But as long as the public perception that courts are supposed to be different is sufficiently widespread, public support for courts is likely to be a function of courts' ability to convey the image of an impartial, apolitical legal body, as several scholars have argued (see Capelleti 1989:176; Gibson 1989, 1991; Schwartz 2000; Shapiro 1981:16f.; Tyler and Raskinski 1991). As a result, even judges who are purely policy-motivated probably also wish to project the appearance that they reach their decisions in impartial, principled, and consistent ways. To summarize, the fact that public support is central to judicial authority, coupled with the foundations of public support for courts, leads to the expectation that judges will be concerned to maintain the appearance of impartiality and consistency while, at the same time, being sensitive to prevailing public opinion.

Naturally, these dimensions of public support – sensitivity to public opinion and the appearance of impartiality – interact in complex ways. Significantly, there can be tension between them. Most obviously, the impartial, consistent application of established constitutional principles may require a highly unpopular decision in a specific case. For example, in the early 1990s, the FCC was confronted with a series of highly controversial cases known as the *Soldier* cases (BVerfGE 93,266). These cases may have presented the court with the dilemma of reconciling sensitivity to public opinion with a concern for consistency. The cases were the result of appeals filed by pacifists who had been convicted and fined for publicly displaying banners featuring the Kurt Tucholsky slogan "Soldaten sind Mörder" ("Soldiers are murderers"). In two separate decisions the FCC overturned the convictions, arguing that the trial court had not sufficiently weighed the defendants' right to free expression. These decisions clearly appeared consistent with established freedom-of-expression

---

[16] However, as pointed out earlier, the empirical evidence is strong that for politically aware individuals, specific and diffuse support are extremely closely linked.

jurisprudence. To many citizens, however, the court had (seemingly) endorsed insults leveled at military personnel. The decisions immediately sparked public controversy. A wave of public protest and court-bashing (led predominantly by CDU/CSU politicians) dominated the public sphere for months. In short, in weighing concerns for impartiality, consistency, and sensitivity to public opinion, judges may be caught in a delicate balancing game. My interviews with judges of the FCC (see Chapter 5) suggest that they may not have realized that the *Soldier* cases involved this trade-off. To them, the cases seemed to present a fairly straightforward freedom-of-expression issue. As one judge put it: "the feeling was: We've already said this a thousand times. No one realized that this particular sentence would cause a special reaction."

INFORMATION, POLITICAL COMPETITION, AND SEPARATION OF POWERS

As I have argued, public support for the constitutional order and an independent court provides one crucial exogenous enforcement mechanism for judicial decisions. Of course, there are other mechanisms that have been investigated and that deserve brief mention here. The most prominent candidate mechanism takes off from the reciprocal relationships among competing parties (Carrubba 2003; Landes and Posner 1975; Ramseyer 1994; Stephenson 2003; Whittington 2003). In democratic political systems, policy makers do not have complete and permanent control of the policy-making process. Instead, they must share power with other policy makers. Most obviously, such sharing occurs over time as parties win and lose elections. In such an environment, policy makers may seek to establish and maintain an independent judiciary that can protect their interests while they are out of government by constraining their political opponents. While in power, each party may be willing to respect the court's decisions because it realizes that its opponent's *future* compliance is contingent on the party's own respect for the court at present. As Ramseyer has put it in the most complete articulation of this theory, "political leaders agree to increase their control over the judiciary *into the future*, by decreasing their control over the judiciary *in the present*" (1994:741).[17]

In other words, maintaining an effective and independent judiciary poses a Prisoner's Dilemma problem: While policy makers most prefer

---

[17] Landes and Posner (1975), who focus on the role of an independent judiciary in enforcing interest group bargains, make a similar argument.

the discretion to ignore court decisions unilaterally while their opponents are bound by them, all are likely to prefer a regime in which *all* policymakers (including they themselves) comply with judicial decisions to a regime in which *none* do. Since there is no fixed endpoint to this interaction (i.e., political competition is essentially open-ended), the standard result for an infinitely repeated Prisoner's Dilemma problem applies. Under the right circumstances, judicial independence may be sustained as a cooperative equilibrium in which parties comply with judicial rulings, where their willingness to do so is contingent on everyone's expectation that others will exhibit similar respect for the court. Importantly, to sustain such cooperation, competing politicians must expect that the "game" will continue for an indefinite time, there must be sufficient electoral uncertainty, and politicians must value the *future* expected results from a system of effective judicial review sufficiently compared to the *present* loss in complying with an undesirable decision.

While Ramseyer (1994) (as well as Landes and Posner 1975) focus on intertemporal cooperation, a similar argument applies when policymakers must share power across different parts of the political system – for example, in a separation-of-powers system or across levels of government in a federal arrangement. In such circumstances, politicians in different positions may value judicial constraints on *other* policymakers and agree to be bound by judicial decisions provided that others similarly comply.

A second line of argument in explaining why politicians may have an interest in preserving a system of judicial review has focused on the central informational aspects of judicial review (Rogers 2001). At the policymaking stage, legislators must base their support for particular proposals on their projected impact. Unfortunately, for many policies, the actual impact may depend on empirical circumstances that cannot be perfectly anticipated and foreseen. As a result, it is possible that a policy, once implemented, has unintended and undesirable consequences that, had they been anticipated at the legislative stage, would have prevented passage of the bill. It is at this point, Rogers argues, that courts can be extremely useful from the perspective of legislative majorities. Courts often (but not always; see later) review policies in light of a concrete dispute, that is, after its implementation. This means that judges, in general, will have access to better information about the actual impact of policies than legislators had at the legislative stage. Judges may therefore be able to screen out bad legislation. Given the high political costs that a legislative majority may face in rescinding a statute and the scarcity of legislative time, eliminating undesirable legislation through a judicial veto may be more efficient, from the perspective of legislators, than for legislators to police themselves. In other words is, when striking down legislation that has produced undesirable and unintended consequences, judges may be performing a service that legislative majorities value. This informational benefit provides one reason why legislative majorities may support a system of judicial review.

Reciprocity among political competitors and the informational gain that judicial review may generate can provide powerful incentives for establishing and maintaining a system of judicial review. Both mechanisms are compatible with the role of public support and may work in conjunction with it. However, both face potential challenges as enforcement mechanisms for *specific* judicial decisions as opposed to mechanisms that help explain a commitment to the *institution* of judicial review. As Ramseyer has pointed out, cooperation is only *one* among many potential equilibria in the "judicial independence game." In many equilibria, judicial independence is not maintained (Ramseyer 1994:747). Moreover, while an independent judiciary may be in the institutional interests of policymakers, such support for the judiciary as an institution does not *necessarily* translate into a willingness to comply with a *specific* decision. Unless the maintenance of the system can be made contingent on unwavering compliance in all instances, the enforcement problem remains. That is, as Carrubba has recently demonstrated (2003), even when political competition provides incentives to establish and maintain a court, policymakers may prefer a regime of "selective compliance" in which they are exempted from compliance in instances in which bowing to judicial demands would be particularly costly.[18]

The informational theory, while an important contribution to our understanding of judicial review, faces another challenge when the object is to explain compliance with decisions that majorities would prefer to evade. When courts provide "informational review," legislative majorities

---

[18] Carrubba's argument (2003) is most closely related to the theory advanced here. He considers an infinitely repeated Prisoner's Dilemma game with private information that is played between two "governments." The governments have an incentive to establish a court as a monitoring device to help them play this game, but this institutional interest in the court is only sufficient to maintain a regime of "selective compliance" in which governments can defect when they face high costs for cooperation. Carrubba then extends the model to demonstrate that public support for courts can generate full compliance. The major difference between the two approaches is that Carrubba focuses attention on the process by which public support is built up, but does not consider the impact of transparency.

actually *want* to comply with the decision: As soon as the court makes it clear that the negative consequences of the law outweigh the benefits the legislature expected when it passed the legislation, the majority no longer wants to see the law implemented. Putting it differently, informational review can be performed by a completely dependent judiciary, which is routinely manipulated by the other branches to bring its preferences in line with those of governing majorities. The court then acts as a perfect agent to weed out bad laws – but there is never any genuine conflict between court and legislature.[19]

CONCLUSION

At bottom, democratic politics is sustained by the accountability generated by the potential for shifts in public support among parties and politicians. This is true not only with respect to particular public policies, but also the constitutional order itself. I have argued that this generic democratic mechanism can furnish a crucial inducement for legislative majorities to comply with the decisions of independent constitutional courts even when they would prefer not to see a policy annulled. To be effective, however, this mechanism requires not only that a sufficient number of citizens are willing to support a court in a confrontation with a legislative majority, but also that these citizens will become aware and convinced that a governing coalition has chosen to evade a judicial ruling. And the ease with which such monitoring can take place depends fundamentally on the political environment surrounding a decision, including the complexity of the issue at stake, the constellation of public interests, the presence of organized interest groups, and the behavior of opinion leaders. Judicial decision making as well as legislative responses to judicial rulings will be shaped by this environment. Moreover, because public support is vital to the influence judges can exercise, judicial decision making will be shaped by a concern for maintaining public support.

These conclusions carry normative significance for our understanding of the role of courts in a constitutional, democratic system. A constitutional court will create a powerful constraint on governing majorities

---

[19] In Rogers's model, such conflict is possible because there is an exogenously assumed probability that the court does not share the legislature's preferences. In the context of a one-shot model, this modeling choice is sensible. But of course, over time, we would expect legislative majorities to reduce this probability as much as possible, that is, to ensure that the court shares its policy preferences perfectly.

Conclusion

when the court (or the court's specific ruling) enjoys popular support and it is likely that such support can be activated or brought to bear if an attempt at evasion is made. Under such circumstances, courts can exercise considerable influence over policy. On the other hand, in cases characterized by a lack of transparency or in which the court's specific ruling meets widespread popular opposition, a constitutional court is not likely to provide much of a brake on the legislative process. Moreover, given the dynamics of public support, constitutional courts will find it difficult to take a sustained stand against prevailing public opinion. Courts are constrained in their ability to function as an independent, countermajoritarian check on the exercise of political power. Over a series of cases, they are limited by the need to sustain public support. In particular cases, they are limited by the effectiveness of public support as an enforcement mechanism, which is determined by transparency and the constellation of public opinion. In the concluding chapter, I will return to a more extensive discussion of these normative implications.

But first, it is time to turn to an empirical evaluation of the theory. The model, and the broader argument surrounding the model, have a number of empirical implications, some of which we have already encountered in the observations. While we will not test all of these implications, the next chapters will focus on providing evidence for several of the more prominent ones:

Hypothesis 1: Ceteris paribus, a constitutional court will be more aggressive in using its powers of review as transparency increases (Chapter 4).
Hypothesis 2: Judges are motivated by a concern to maintain public support and are sensitive to prevailing public opinion (Chapter 5).
Hypothesis 3: Judges are sensitive to the interests of governing majorities (Chapters 5 and 6).
Hypothesis 4: The potential for a public backlash is an important consideration for legislators in deciding how to respond to a judicial ruling (Chapter 5).
Hypothesis 5: When evading a decision, legislators will try to hide evasion by reducing transparency. When anticipating evasion, judges will try to increase transparency in their decisions (Chapter 6).

Before we turn to these chapters, the next chapter provides an overview of the establishment of the FCC and of the court's structure and powers against the backdrop of other constitutional courts.

APPENDIX: PROOF FOR THE SIX PURE-STRATEGY PBE OF THE GAME

Tie-Breaking Assumptions

- If indifferent between evading and not evading, the legislature will choose to comply.
- If indifferent between upholding and vetoing the bill, the court will choose to uphold.
- If indifferent between legislating and not doing so, the legislature will choose to legislate.

Result 1: In any PBE, a convergent court will always choose to uphold the statute as constitutional. Thus, in equilibrium, the judicial strategy must have the form $s_C = \{U|C; *|\sim C\}$.

Proof of the Equilibria

I. Consider the Last Stage of the Game, in Which the Legislature Must React to the Court's Decision. Given that the legislature is not certain about transparency or the court's support, the expected utilities from evading and not evading are given by

$$EU_A(\sim E) = -\varepsilon$$
$$EU_A(E) = rq(-\beta - \varepsilon) + (1 - rq)(\alpha - \varepsilon)$$

The legislature will choose to evade the decision iff

$$rq(-\beta - \varepsilon) + (1 - rq)(\alpha - \varepsilon) > -\varepsilon$$
$$\Leftrightarrow \qquad\qquad\qquad\qquad\qquad\qquad\qquad (1)$$
$$rq < \frac{\alpha}{\alpha + \beta}$$

Denote this threshold as the "legislative evasion threshold." If this condition holds, the legislature evades. Otherwise, it complies with the decision.

II. Consider the Convergent Court at the Review Stage. Result 1 applies. The convergent court will always uphold the legislation.

III. Consider the Nonconvergent Court at the Review Stage:

CASE 1. $rq < \dfrac{\alpha}{\alpha + \beta}$ (i.e., the legislature will evade)

$$EU_C(U) = 0$$
$$EU_C(V) = qrA - (1 - rq)I$$

Appendix

Therefore, the court will choose to veto iff

$$qrA - I + qrI > 0$$
$$\Leftrightarrow \qquad (2)$$
$$rq > \frac{I}{I+A}$$

Denote this threshold as the "judicial veto threshold." If this condition holds, the court vetoes under case 1. Otherwise, it upholds.

CASE 2. $rq \geq \frac{\alpha}{\alpha+\beta}$ (i.e., the legislature will comply)

$$EU_C(U) = 0$$
$$EU_C(V) = A$$

Therefore, the court will veto.

IV. Consider the Legislature at the Initial Legislative Stage

CASE 1. $rq < \frac{\alpha}{\alpha+\beta}$ and $rq > \frac{I}{I+A}$ (i.e., the court vetoes and the legislature evades)

$$EU_A(\sim L) = 0$$
$$EU_A(L) = p(\alpha - \varepsilon) + (1-p)[rq(-\beta - \varepsilon) + (1-rq)(\alpha - \varepsilon)]$$

These imply that the legislature will choose to legislate iff

$$rq \leq \frac{\alpha - \varepsilon}{(\alpha + \beta)(1-p)} \qquad (3)$$

Denote this threshold as the "legislative passage threshold." If this condition holds, the legislature passes the bill under case 1. Otherwise, it chooses not to legislate.

CASE 2. $rq < \frac{\alpha}{\alpha+\beta}$ and $rq \leq \frac{I}{I+A}$ (i.e., the court upholds and the legislature evades)

$$EU_A(\sim L) = 0$$
$$EU_A(L) = \alpha - \varepsilon$$

The legislature will always choose to legislate.

CASE 3. $rq \geq \frac{\alpha}{\alpha+\beta}$ (i.e., the legislature complies)

$$EU_A(\sim L) = 0$$
$$EU_A(L) = p(\alpha - \varepsilon) - (1-p)\varepsilon = p\alpha - \varepsilon$$

Legislature will choose to legislate iff

$$p \geq \frac{\varepsilon}{\alpha} \qquad (4)$$

If this condition is met, the legislature passes the bill under case 3. Otherwise, it does not legislate.
QED.

3

The Federal Constitutional Court in Comparative Perspective

In the remainder of the book, I explore and test the empirical implications of the theory laid out in the previous chapter by applying the framework to the FCC. In the roughly fifty years since its creation, this court has emerged as "the most active and powerful constitutional court in Europe" (Kommers 1994:470), and it has served as a model for many of the new constitutional courts of Eastern Europe (Schwartz 2000). Aside from the intrinsic importance of this court as one of the most significant legal actors in the world today, the FCC therefore provides an appropriate testing ground for the argument. Before we dive into the details of the politics of constitutional review in Germany, it is useful to briefly survey the Bundesverfassungsgericht and its history. How was this court established? How is it organized, and what are its powers? And how does it compare to other European constitutional courts? This chapter provides answers to these (and other) questions. Readers who are already familiar with the structure, jurisdiction, and powers of the FCC can skip without much loss to the next chapter.

I begin with a short account of the history and establishment of the court. One of the implications of the argument in the previous two chapters is that establishing a court, maintaining its institutional integrity, and generating compliance with its decisions constitute separate (though interrelated) problems. The book's central argument is not concerned with the first two issues but focuses on the last: the politics of constitutional review once a court has been created. The central claim is that public support provides one important enforcement mechanism for judicial decisions, and that the nature of this enforcement mechanism has important

---

Parts of this chapter first appeared in *Comparative Politics*. Portions of it are reprinted with the permission of *Comparative Politics*.

ramifications for the effectiveness with which constitutional courts can exercise their powers. However, as we will see, the central role that public support can play in establishing the authority of a court is not limited to generating pressure for compliance with specific rulings. As the early struggles of the Bundesverfassungsgericht in asserting its independence demonstrate, public support can also play a key role in the establishment of a court.[1] After recounting the events surrounding the creation of the FCC, the second part of the chapter provides an overview of the institutional structure of the FCC that places the court in the context of other European courts.

ESTABLISHING A COURT

On September 1, 1948, less than four years after the unconditional surrender of Nazi Germany to the Allies, a convention charged with drafting a constitution for a West German state convened in Bonn. The delegations to the Parliamentary Council had been elected by the state (*Land*) legislatures, and reflected a rough balance between the CDU/CSU and the SPD. The remaining seats in the Parliamentary Council were distributed among the Liberals (FDP/DVP), the conservative German Party (DP), the Catholic Zentrum, and the Communists (KPD). Despite having to resolve several controversial issues, and facing occasional tension between the delegates and the Allied High Command, the convention completed its work quickly. Following ratification by the *Länder* parliaments, the Basic Law was promulgated on May 23, 1949, and elections to the first Bundestag were held in August. The elections produced a clear victory for a center–right coalition, and the CDU/CSU, along with the FDP/DVP and the DP, formed a coalition under the leadership of Chancellor Konrad Adenauer.

One of the least contentious issues in the Parliamentary Council was the decision to create a constitutional court, established by Section IX of the Basic Law. As most constitutions do, the Basic Law leaves crucial details, including the institutional structure of the court, its precise jurisdiction, the number of judges, and their terms of service, to be specified by ordinary legislation. After a lengthy process of negotiations between the governing coalition and the opposition, the Federal Constitutional Court Act (FCCA) was passed on February 1, 1951, to fill in these gaps.

---

[1] More detailed treatments of the establishment of the FCC can be found in Vanberg (2000).

Perhaps the most distinctive organizational feature of the court as established in the FCCA is the fact that it is a *Zwillingsgericht* (twin court). Unlike most constitutional courts, the FCC is divided into two "senates," each of which functions as a separate court with separate jurisdiction. In April 1951, the southwestern city of Karlsruhe was chosen as the seat of the court. Only the appointment of judges remained to bring the establishment of the court to successful completion.

At this stage, serious difficulties emerged. Under the process that had just been enacted, half of the judges were to be appointed by the upper house, the Bundesrat, with a two-thirds majority. The other half were to be appointed by a judicial selection committee of the lower house, the Bundestag, with a three-fourths majority. As a result, any appointments would require agreement between the SPD and the CDU/CSU. Behind the "veil of ignorance" during the Parliamentary Council, there had been virtually unanimous agreement on the desirability of a judicial check on legislative and executive power. But with the veil lifted and the immanent establishment of the constitutional court as a potentially forceful check on the Adenauer administration, the partisan affiliations of the various candidates took on central significance. The appointment of the court's president became particularly contentious. By July 1951 no agreement had been reached, and the issue was postponed until after the parliamentary recess. For months the final establishment of the court had proven elusive, and the prospects for breaking the deadlock seemed dim.

Meanwhile, a pressing political problem emerged that pitted the Adenauer government against one of the German states. The confrontation revolved around the issue of territorial reorganization of the southwestern German states.[2] When creating the occupation zones for southern Germany in 1945, the Allies had split the two existing states of Baden and Württemberg between the American and French zones. The northern half of each state was assigned to the American occupation forces, which unified the territory into a new state called Württemberg-Baden. French forces occupied the southern regions and separated the territory into two states, Baden and Württemberg-Hohenzollern. Thus, three new states had been created that did not correspond to the historic and cultural boundaries in the region. The division was felt to be unsatisfactory by citizens, political elites, and even the occupying forces. As early as 1948, the

---

[2] Most of the factual information presented in the next few pages can be found in the FCC's decision on the Southwest case (BVerfGE 1:14).

three military governors of the Western zones had urged the governments of the three states to enter negotiations on redrawing boundaries. Negotiations began but eventually failed. The main obstacle to a settlement was disagreement over the precise form that territorial reorganization should take. Political leaders in Württemberg-Baden and Württemberg-Hohenzollern favored the creation of a large, unified Southwest state. The minister president of Baden, Leo Wohlleb (CDU), on the other hand, was wedded to the restoration of historic Baden.

Significantly, under the Basic Law, territorial reorganization, if pursued through a federal law, requires ratification in a referendum. As a result, decisions on the number and boundaries of voting districts that might be used for reorganizing the Southwest immediately took on central significance. Who would vote on any plan that was put forth, and how would those votes be aggregated? Wohlleb insisted on a two-district model, corresponding to the two historic *Länder* of Württemberg and Baden, with a majority in each required for unification. The proponents of the Southwest state, on the other hand, favored a division into four districts, with a majority in three of the four being sufficient for unification. A preliminary "informative referendum" was conducted in September 1950, using the four-district model.

The results revealed that large majorities had voted for unification in Württemberg-Hohenzollern, in the Baden section of Württemberg-Baden, and in the Württemberg section of Württemberg-Baden. A comfortable 60 percent majority, however, had voted against the Southwest state in Baden. Totaling the votes for Baden and the Baden section of Württemberg-Baden revealed a slim majority *against* the Southwest state in historic Baden. The implication of these results was clear. If the referendum were held according to Wohlleb's preferred plan, a slim majority in historic Baden would probably vote against unification, thus spoiling plans for a Southwest state. If, on the other hand, the referendum were held under the four-district model, it was expected that only existing Baden would vote against the Southwest state, thus paving the way for unification.

Given these results, there was little prospect of agreement and the battle lines hardened. Rather than continue negotiations between the states, the proponents of the Southwest state decided to make use of Article 118 of the Basic Law, which opened the door for federal action to reorganize the Southwest territory. In April 1951, the Bundestag passed a bill that provided for unification of the Southwest on the basis of the four-district model, scheduling the referendum for September 1951. To save the expense and inconvenience of conducting parliamentary elections in Baden and Württemberg-Hohenzollern shortly before these states were likely to be abolished in the referendum, a second law was passed to extend the legislative periods of both state parliaments until March 1952.

At this point, the fates of the Bundesverfassungsgericht and the Southwest state began to converge. Anticipating the eventual outcome of the referendum, Wohlleb made a last-ditch effort to preserve Baden as a separate state. Using the right of state governments to bring cases to the constitutional court, he challenged the constitutionality of the referendum and the extension of the legislative periods of the state legislatures. Raising genuine constitutional doubts about the laws was not difficult. Could the Bundestag legitimately encroach on *Land* autonomy by extending the legislative period of a state parliament? In addition to the possibility of derailing the referendum through a constitutional prohibition, bringing the case to the FCC had another significant advantage. The deadlock in the appointment of judges meant that no court existed to hear the case, raising the distinct possibility that failure to resolve the constitutional dispute might create a roadblock for the referendum.

Over the course of the summer, this "Southwest problem" took on increased urgency for the Adenauer administration. In early August, Wohlleb announced, in a letter to the government and in various press interviews, that the Baden government would boycott the referendum unless the (still nonexistent) constitutional court ruled on the constitutionality of the two laws before September 16, 1951. The situation for the Adenauer government thus became extremely delicate. The precedent of a land refusing to implement a federal law could have potentially disastrous consequences for the future ability to govern, especially because the confrontation marked one of the first tensions between central and federal governments in the young democracy. In a cabinet meeting in late August, the cabinet unanimously agreed that the best solution would be to establish the constitutional court as soon as possible – presumably because Wohlleb had publicly committed himself to accepting its judgment.[3]

---

[3] It might be asked what other alternatives would have been available to the federal government, and why they were not pursued. The federal government had relatively few resources to ensure a referendum itself, given the nature of German federalism. In this type of federal system, administration of programs is largely left in the hands of *Land* bureaucracies; the federal government has only a very small bureaucracy of its own. To secure compliance through a literal show of force would also have been difficult: The government had no military force to dispose of, and the only force it could command was a relatively small federal police force. Moreover, a

Instead of continuing to insist on their own preferred judicial candidates, Adenauer and the other CDU cabinet ministers agreed to compromise candidates who were acceptable to the SPD and Free Democrats (including the appointment of Hermann Höpker Aschoff as president of the court despite the fact that Adenauer had personally requested Höpker Aschoff's withdrawal from consideration only months earlier). The final election of judges took place on September 4, 1951. More than two years after the ratification of the Basic Law, the Bundesverfassungsgericht had finally been established.[4] Immediately following the selection of judges, the court issued a temporary injunction against the referendum, a step that was greeted enthusiastically by Wohlleb (see the coverage in the two most prominent German newspapers, the *Frankfurter Allgemeine Zeitung* (FAZ hereafter), September 10, 1951, p. 1 and the *Süddeutsche Zeitung* (SZ hereafter), September 11, 1951, p. 1).

The full decision in the Southwest case was handed down in October 1951 and is a landmark in German constitutional history (BVerfGE 1,14). The court declared the law extending the terms of the state legislatures void. It largely sustained the statute that established the procedures for the referendum. However, the importance of the decision lies less in the substantive result than in the principles the court sought to establish. As Donald Kommers has put it in characterizing the decision as Germany's *Marbury v. Madison*, "*Southwest's* foundational character is rooted in the general principles of constitutional interpretation stated therein and in the clarity – and forthrightness – with which the Constitutional Court defines the scope of its authority under the Basic Law" (1997:66). Three of these principles stand out. First, the court held that a decision by the FCC to declare a law void implies that no legislature may debate and enact a similar statute in the future. Second, the court argued that provisions of the Basic Law cannot be interpreted in isolation but must be read in the context of the entire document. Finally, the court enunciated the position that legislation and even constitutional maxims are bound by a higher "preconstitutional" law, giving rise to the possibility of an "unconstitutional constitutional amendment" (for an excellent discussion, see Kommers 1997:62ff.).

---

confrontation in which physical force had to be resorted to would probably have adversely affected the Adenauer government's attempts to persuade the Allies that West Germany should be given sovereignty.

[4] Despite the establishment of the court, another two years passed before the court was able to secure budgetary and administrative independence from the justice ministry. For a detailed treatment, see Vanberg (2000).

WEATHERING THE FIRST STORM

Establishing a court and securing its position as an authoritative institution in the political system are, of course, two different things.[5] Not long after the court's establishment, this important distinction was brought home forcefully as the FCC had to weather the first storm that threatened its authority. In late 1952, a direct and bitter confrontation developed between the court and the Adenauer administration in connection with a series of legal proceedings that had been initiated to test the constitutionality of two treaties. This confrontation, in the course of which the court's authority would be directly challenged, concerned the "Convention on Relations with the Federal Republic of Germany," also known as the General Treaty, and the "Treaty on the European Defense Community," also known as the EDC Treaty. The first treaty formally ended the occupation of West Germany and restored West German sovereignty, while the second treaty established a pan-European system of defense, including German forces.[6] The Adenauer government faced considerable foreign pressure, especially from the Eisenhower administration, to contribute to the defense of Europe and to ratify the treaties as quickly as possible.

Domestically, however, the prospect of ratification caused tremendous political tensions. The confrontation over the treaties between the government and the opposition constituted the single most important political dispute of the first legislative period, and it dominated the public discourse. The intensity of this disagreement arose from the zero-sum view of the political situation held by both participants. Orientation toward and integration into the West provided, in Adenauer's view, the only viable way to return Germany to full sovereignty, to secure its freedom from Soviet aggression, and to pave the way for eventual German "reunification in liberty." For the chancellor, the ratification of the two treaties constituted an essential step in this process, not only as a sign of good will

---

[5] For a similar point in relation to the U.S. Supreme Court, see Friedman (2003).
[6] The treaties, signed on May 26 and May 27, 1952, were the outcome of an extended period of negotiations focusing mainly on the role of a future German state in Europe. The catalyst that had brought these issues to the forefront was the outbreak of the Korean War in June 1950. Although there had been some discussion of German rearmament as early as 1948, the attack on South Korea raised new fear of Communist aggression that strengthened the desire of Allied governments to rearm Germany (see Baring 1969; Herbst 1996). In light of the new world situation, the French government suggested the formation of a European Defense Community. This suggestion (the "Pleven Plan") formed the basis of the EDC Treaty.

toward the Allies, but also because it would foreclose any future agreements among the Allies and the Soviet Union about the status of Germany that might be made without German consent.[7]

While the Adenauer government was deeply committed to the treaties and regarded their ratification as the cornerstone of its foreign policy, the opposition SPD, under the leadership of Kurt Schumacher, was equally committed to preventing their passage. Although the SPD did not in principle reject German rearmament and an orientation toward the West, it decidedly rejected the particular form these goals had taken in the two treaties. SPD leaders argued that the treaties did not treat Germany as an equal and that they demanded excessive concessions on the German side.[8] More importantly, the SPD felt that by moving too quickly in binding West Germany to the Western alliance, the treaties would ultimately make the goal of reunification with East Germany more difficult, if not impossible, to achieve (Bark and Gress 1993; Löwke 1976; Schwarz 1981; Sontheimer 1991).

Given its minority status, however, the ability of the SPD to affect the content or to prevent the passage of the treaties was limited. The Adenauer government generally withheld information on the negotiations and the treaties from the Bundestag, making it difficult for the SPD leadership to attack concrete details or to formulate credible alternatives. Moreover, as the minority party, the SPD's prospects of influencing the substantive content were naturally limited by its lack of voting strength in the Bundestag. The most promising alternative for the SPD was therefore to call on the newly established constitutional court. As Carlo Schmid (SPD), chairman

---

[7] In a passionate speech in the Bundestag on December 3, 1952, Adenauer put this point forcefully: "As things stand now, anyone who says 'No' to the European Defense Community also says 'No' to Europe ... and whoever says 'No' to Europe is the grave-digger of the German people, because he takes from them the only possibility of holding on to a way of life they cherish, a life in liberty, rooted in Christian principles.... These treaties are a matter of our liberty, of our life, and of the future of our children and grandchildren. I call on the German people to be conscious of the magnitude of this decision. It is a fateful question for Germany" (see the legislative record in *Verhandlungen des Deutschen Bundestages* [BTD hereafter] I:11140). See also Adenauer's memoirs (1966:165).

[8] This had been a standard objection by the SPD to Adenauer's foreign policy. The SPD felt that in general, the CDU-led government was too giving in its agreements with the Allies. This difference of opinion about the proper approach to relations with the Allies had already led to one of the deepest rifts between the government and the opposition when Schumacher referred to Adenauer as the "chancellor of the Allies" during the Bundestag debate on the Petersberg Agreement in November 1950 (Schumacher was banned from the Bundestag for twenty days) (Bark and Gress 1993:258ff.; Herbst 1996:65ff.; Sontheimer 1991:32f.)

of the Bundestag foreign affairs committee, put it in April 1952, the only "effective break against the determination to create a fait-accompli in an over-hurried fashion is the Bundesverfassungsgericht" (quoted in Baring 1969:174). The SPD lost little time in pursuing this avenue. On February 1, 1952, before the treaties had even been signed, the FCC received a request for an abstract judicial review proceeding initiated by 144 members of the Bundestag, including all SPD deputies.[9] The request asked the court to determine whether a German defense contribution would be constitutionally permissible under the Basic Law.

Initially, the Adenauer government was not concerned about the constitutional challenge. It expected that the case would simply be dismissed, given that no treaties had been signed and no ratification legislation had been passed (Booms 1989:169). Over the course of the next few months, however, information began to trickle into Bonn that the court's First Senate, which was dealing with the case, would affirm its admissibility and rule against the government on the substantive issue.[10] As concerns that the First Senate might rule against the treaties increased, the Adenauer government began to assess its options in trying to prevent defeat. It was widely believed by the government and the opposition, as well as by the press and other observers, that the court's First Senate was dominated by judges loyal to the SPD, while the Second Senate was believed to be controlled by judges favorable to the CDU.[11] In early June 1952, the cabinet resolved to attempt to exploit this partisan division by moving the proceeding into a more favorable venue. It decided to ask the president of the Federal Republic, Theodor Heuss, to request an advisory opinion on the treaties from the court (Booms 1989:367). The

---

[9] Since the first Bundestag had 402 seats, 134 signatures (one-third) were necessary to initiate such a proceeding. Since the SPD held only 131 seats, it had to secure some outside support from the Zentrum and the BP. The text of the suit is reprinted in a collection of court records on the EDC proceedings published by the Institut für Staatslehre und Politik under the title *Der Kampf um den Wehrbeitrag* (ISP hereafter). See ISP (1952:3–4).

[10] An undated memo by Otto Lenz (one of Adenauer's closest advisors) to the chancellor, probably written in early spring, relays a message from Court President Höpker Aschoff telling Adenauer that a majority of the senate is leaning toward declaring the suit admissible (ACDP I-172-58/1). A trip by Lenz to the court confirmed that a majority was likely to vote against the government. See Lenz's diary (Lenz 1989:268).

[11] According to Udo Wengst (1984:243), of the twelve judges in the First Senate, seven were close to the SPD, four were close to the CDU/CSU, and one judge was neutral. In the Second Senate, three judges were close to the SPD, eight to the CDU/CSU, and again, one was neutral. See also Kommers (1976:122).

strategic importance of this move lay in the fact that an advisory opinion would be delivered by the plenum of the court, that is, by the two senates sitting jointly, thus adding the Second Senate with its CDU majority to the First.[12]

The justices of the court were not oblivious to this strategic maneuvering. In an apparent attempt to escape manipulations that might endanger the authority of the court, the First Senate suggested that the president's advisory opinion be given precedence over the SPD suit. Moreover, the senate suggested that all parties should accept the outcome of the advisory opinion as binding, thus preventing additional suits in conjunction with the treaties from being brought in the future (ISP 1952:227–8). The government, apparently expecting victory in the larger forum, resolved to accept the proposal (Booms 1989:394). The SPD, whose assessment of the advisory proceedings seems to have squared with the government's perceptions, declined the senate's suggestion and insisted on the primacy of its suit. It is difficult to assess what role this refusal by the SPD played in the subsequent deliberations of the First Senate. But in late July, the senate (contrary to the expectations that had given rise to the request for the advisory opinion) dismissed the SPD suit as inadmissible (ISP 1952:436–46).

Having won this victory, the Adenauer government approached the advisory proceedings with general optimism during the summer. Over the course of the fall, however, the government's initial optimism began to fade. In late August, rumors surfaced in the chancellery that only eight of the twenty-two judges would vote in the government's favor (Lenz 1989:412). This impression was solidified in early November when Judge Willi Geiger reported to Lenz that in the First Senate, the split appeared to be 8–4 against the constitutionality of the treaties, while the Second Senate had split approximately 7–4 in the government's favor. As a result, the outcome of the advisory opinion was highly uncertain. Even if the outcome were positive, however, Geiger pointed out that the SPD would move

---

[12] There has been some dispute over whether Adenauer influenced Heuss to request the advisory opinion. In his memoirs, Adenauer himself has claimed that Heuss initiated the proceedings on his accord (1966:169). The publication of the cabinet protocols leaves little doubt that this was not the case. The protocols reveal that the cabinet resolved on June 6 to request that Heuss ask for the opinion, and Heuss's chief of staff, Manfred Klaiber, reported to the cabinet on June 10 that Heuss would request the opinion immediately following the oral arguments held on the 10th (Booms 1989:367, 379). These cabinet protocols also seem to contradict Thomas Dehler's claim, made in an interview with Arnulf Baring, that Adenauer asked Heuss to request the advisory opinion on his own, without cabinet approval (Baring 1969:224).

immediately to bring a proceeding in the First Senate. As a consequence, Geiger advised the government to preempt such a move by initiating a suit in the Second Senate as quickly as possible (Lenz 1989:466).

By early December, the cabinet had decided to follow Geiger's advice by initiating an Organstreit proceeding against the SPD party group, alleging that the SPD's denial of the constitutionality of the treaties violated the majority's constitutional right to legislate (ISP 1958:1–24).[13] That this was a political move designed to shift the proceedings from the plenum to the Second Senate (which is responsible for Organstreit cases) was widely assumed in the press. The judges of the court also felt that this latest move by the government was the final straw in a series of attempt at "forum shopping" by the various sides. They decided that the court had to take a stand to protect its authority. On the morning of December 9, 1952, President Höpker Aschoff opened the proceedings by reading a statement that had been endorsed by the plenum the previous day. The statement strongly condemned the disparaging remarks that had been made "in some political circles" about the court and concluded by declaring that, contrary to the government's intentions, the court would not give precedence to the government's newly initiated suit in the Second Senate. Moreover, the court would treat the advisory opinion as internally binding on both senates:

> The FCC yesterday decided that this advisory opinion, and all future advisory opinions, will be binding on the two senates.... This rule prevents attempts to target a suit to a particular senate's jurisdiction for exogenous and irrelevant reasons. Given this decision, it is ruled out that any pending or future suits on the same substantive issue will be decided in a materially different manner by one of the senates. (ACDP VIII 001–284/4)

This decision implied, of course, that the Adenauer government's attempt to move the proceedings to the Second Senate had failed and that the government would get stuck with an advisory opinion it had wanted to avoid. After requesting a recess, the government spent the rest of December 9 trying to formulate its next move in light of the new situation. In particular, the cabinet considered three responses:

1. Asking President Heuss to rescind his request, thereby ending the advisory opinion proceeding.

---

[13] Even several high-level members of the Adenauer administration were convinced that this was a dubious constitutional argument. See Lenz (1989:480f.).

2. Putting pressure on the court by trying to rally public support for the government's opposition to the plenum decision and raising the possibility of changing the institutional structure of the court.
3. Convincing a sufficient number of government-friendly judges to tender their resignation, thereby crippling the court by reducing its number below its quorum.[14]

The last option was discussed during two cabinet meetings on the 9th, and Adenauer inquired about the feasibility of persuading the requisite number of judges to resign (Booms 1989:730f.; Lenz 1989:492ff.). However, a statement released by the court the following day revealing that twenty of the twenty-two judges supported the decision demonstrated the resolve and unity of the court and must have quashed any hopes of pursuing this avenue. The Adenauer government thus focused on the first two options. A cabinet delegation including the chancellor went to see the president on the evening of December 9. Heuss was convinced quickly and withdrew his request for an advisory opinion the next day.

Instead of letting the matter rest with Heuss's withdrawal, which left the government's suit in the Second Senate as the only pending proceeding, the government decided to also pursue the second option. Justice Minister Thomas Dehler and Adenauer had felt for some time that the court was asserting a role that it was not entitled to, and decided that the current situation presented an opportunity to give the court a "shot across the bow." On the evening of December 10, the government invited journalists to an informal press conference in which Adenauer and Dehler laid out the government's reaction to the court's decision. Adenauer opened with a statement in which he claimed that the FCC's decision "has no basis in either the Basic Law or the Law on the FCC," thus accusing the court, by implication, of having acted unconstitutionally (Küsters 1984:365). He also made it clear that he would not be willing to accept the court's decision: "It is absolutely clear that the court cannot stick to this decision" (377). Dehler became more explicit, going so far as to state that "we will never accept this decision" (377). Both concluded by explicitly raising the possibility of changing the court's institutional structure by revising the FCCA. The same charges were leveled the next day during a Bundestag debate on the crisis, in which Adenauer again asserted that the court's decision was unlawful (BTD I:11650 C). The most concise statement of

---

[14] It was precisely through such a move that the Dollfuss government eliminated the Austrian Constitutional Court in 1932.

the government's position appeared in its publication *Bulletin* on December 12. Once again, the suggestion was made that a revision of the law on the constitutional court would be appropriate.

The Adenauer government had thus taken a clear confrontational stand vis-à-vis the court, and it had announced its intention to resort to institutional changes, if necessary, to prevent implementation of the court's decision and to ensure ratification of the treaties. And yet, within only two weeks, the cabinet would completely negate this position, publish a unanimous declaration of support for the court, and abandon all attempts to change the institutional structure of the FCC. The single most important explanation for this turn of events was the reaction of the mass media and the perceived threat of a public backlash against the government that this media coverage produced in the administration.

This media response to the government's actions, including that of the government-friendly press, was overwhelmingly negative.[15] On the morning of December 10, editorials in support of the court's plenum decision appeared, noting that the court had been drawn into a political fight from which it had to extract itself (FAZ, p. 1; SZ, p. 1). Almost as soon as the crisis intensified, the major newspapers rallied in support of the court. On the morning of the 11th, following Adenauer's press conference of the previous night, the *Süddeutsche Zeitung* published a blistering front-page editorial:

The manner in which the constitutional court has been treated would be unimaginable in any state truly governed by law, and it can only be detrimental for democracy.... What is left when the system of separation of powers breaks down? Only the will of a man who pursues his goals with no regard for the consequences. But of parliamentary democracy one should no longer speak.

Over the next few days, similarly supportive editorials could be read on the front pages of most important newspapers (see FAZ, December 12, p. 1; SZ, December 12, pp. 1, 3; December 13, p. 1). The weekly *Der Spiegel* strongly condemned the government, arguing explicitly that even if the court's decision were questionable (the *Spiegel* supported the plenum decision), the government's conduct would still be unacceptable in a constitutional democracy. "A highest court which errs is still better than one whose authority is undermined by the President and the government" (*Der Spiegel*, December 17, p. 4).

---

[15] A notable exception is the weekly *Die Zeit*, which was critical of the court's plenum decision (see December 11, p. 1; December 18, p. 2).

This considerable support for the court by opinion leaders, and the likely impact of such support on public opinion generally, were not lost on the government. Meeting on December 13, Adenauer's closest advisors agreed that any attempt to manipulate the composition of the court would be politically unacceptable, and that such a move would "constitute a political mistake because it would be viewed as a violation of the democratic rules of the game" (Lenz 1989:500) – a distinct change from the arguments made only days earlier, when the possibility of asking judges to resign in order to cripple the court had been considered. Adenauer as well became convinced that in the face of such strong public sentiment, the government could not afford to move any further against the court.[16]

By December 17, the government was in full retreat. During a radio interview, which the government published in the *Bulletin*, Adenauer declared that "for me, there is only the FCC. I, like everyone else, accept that court as the highest constitutional authority of the Federal Republic. Therefore I cannot conceive of viewing it as a political ally or foe" (*Bulletin* Nr.203/1770). Adenauer attempted to distance himself from any suggestion that the cabinet might have considered threatening the court's institutional structure in order to influence the proceedings: "If we were to consider a revision of the FCCA at all, it would only apply to future cases.... I do not want to prevail at the cost of sacrificing democracy.... I do not think of the Bundesverfassungsgericht or democracy as my enemies. The public should have no concerns in that regard" (*Bulletin* Nr.203/1770). Two days later, the cabinet published a declaration of support for the court, which Adenauer personally delivered to the court's president during a joint meeting with President Heuss:

The cabinet unanimously declares that it never conceived of encroaching on the rights or the dignity of the constitutional court, or even to question them. The cabinet respects the FCC as an integral part of the democratic Rechtsstaat.... (*Bulletin* Nr.205/1785)

Any plans to manipulate the proceedings by convincing judges to resign or otherwise affecting the composition of the court had been given up by this point. As Lenz reported in his diary entry of December 30, Adenauer continued to play with the idea of revising the FCCA to explicitly

---

[16] During a meeting of the CDU leadership on December 15, several speakers referred to the unfavorable press coverage the government had received, and Adenauer explicitly rejected calls by some party leaders for continued attacks on the court (Buchstab 1986:206).

authorize the Second Senate to hear the government's suit against the SPD, thus preventing a possible dismissal of the case. But Adenauer's close advisors continued to argue that any attempts to manipulate the court through institutional changes would be politically unacceptable and had to be resisted. Especially revealing in this context is a top-secret memorandum written by Lenz to Adenauer in late December.[17] Lenz explicitly linked the public reaction to the events of the previous weeks to the conclusion that the court must be "left alone," using FDR's failed court-packing plan to bolster his argument:

It is obvious that any revision [of the FCCA] following a negative decision [by the court] would be regarded... as a kind of coup d'etat. I therefore doubt that it would even be possible to gather a majority for such a revision. I should point out that a similar attempt by Roosevelt failed. To restructure the FCC through a legislative act seems impossible to me at the moment, especially for political reasons.... I must note with special urgency that the events of the last weeks have thoroughly confused the public. The popularity of the government has declined from 38 percent in October to 30 percent in December while the percentage of those with no opinion has increased from 33 percent to 41 percent. This is the largest decline that has occurred all year. Any actions that give the appearance of illegitimate action on the part of the government would lead to further declines. (ACDP I-172–58/2)

In short, the storm of protest that had quickly greeted the government's actions, even in the government-friendly press, had effectively convinced the Adenauer government that the Bundesverfassungsgericht was a constraint that had to be respected. Despite its announcements in the December *Bulletin*, the government did not raise the issue of revising the FCCA in the context of the EDC treaty again and began to use a conciliatory tone toward the court. At the same time, it is clear that this new approach was not indicative of a genuine change of heart, but rather was due to the strategic environment in which the government found itself. This is evident in remarks made by Adenauer to the CDU leadership only a few months later in May 1953:

The Bundesverfassungsgericht... is indeed the dictator of Germany. The Bundesverfassungsgericht decides at its own discretion. There is no power in Germany that can rectify its decisions.... There is nothing we can do about that now; we must take things as they are. But they are painful. (Buchstab 1986:522f.)

---

[17] This memorandum, which I found among Lenz's papers at the Archiv für Christlich-Demokratische Politik in Bonn (ACDP) has, to my knowledge, not been published before.

In March 1953, the Second Senate dismissed the government's suit against the opposition as inadmissible. However, this did not end the court's involvement in the EDC treaty controversy. A new abstract review proceeding would predictably occur after passage of the treaties by the Bundestag and Bundesrat. As a result, the impact of the Bundesverfassungsgericht as a constraint on the Adenauer government's freedom to act was even felt in the cabinet formation following the second Bundestag election in September 1953. The election gave the CDU/CSU an absolute majority. Nevertheless, Adenauer decided to form an oversized coalition that would achieve the two-thirds majority necessary for constitutional amendments in both the Bundesrat and the Bundestag by including the refugee party (GB-BHE). The most important consideration in this decision was the possibility of passing a constitutional amendment to ensure the constitutionality of the treaties.[18]

The theory laid out in the previous chapter focuses on compliance with individual decisions. In contrast, the episode surrounding the EDC concerns the larger question of respect for the institutional integrity and independence of a constitutional court even when no specific decision has yet been rendered. But the episode is fully consistent with the spirit of the argument, and we can clearly see the same enforcement mechanism at work. Given the political salience of the EDC controversy, the conflict between the court and the Adenauer administration played itself out in a highly transparent environment. Opinion leaders and, through them, the general public were well aware of the court's pending decision and the government's actions in trying to affect the outcome. Given this transparent setting, public support could take on a central role in lending authority to the court: Adenauer discovered quickly that manipulation of the constitutional court for political gain would not be acceptable to the broad public (as represented by opinion leaders). It was only in the face of such a potential backlash that the administration decided to back down.

---

[18] See Adenauer's remarks to the CDU leadership following the election (Buchstab 1990:7): "If we include the BHE – provided it is not too expensive – it would have the following advantage: we will have a two-thirds majority in the Bundestag. We may need the two-thirds majority to bring the affair with the Bundesverfassungsgericht to a close." Interestingly, Franz Josef Strauß argued explicitly against inclusion of the BHE on the grounds that the court would not rule against the treaties after the tremendous electoral success of the CDU (Buchstab 1990:22). The necessary amendments were passed in February 1954. The GB–BHE (Gesamtdeutscher Block–Bund der Heimatvertriebenen und Entrechteten) was a nationalist party that aimed its appeal at refugees from the Soviet occupation zone. It existed from 1950 until 1964.

Like the court-packing plan in the United States, the confrontation between the FCC and the Adenauer administration over the EDC treaty has significance as an important precedent. In rather dramatic fashion, the events established that blatant institutional attacks on the court would probably be politically infeasible and that governments would have to respect the formal independence of the constitutional court. Of course, such respect for institutional integrity does not necessarily translate into compliance with specific rulings, an issue to which we will return in the next chapters. But before we do so, it is useful to become more familiar with the institutional structure of the FCC and to situate the court in the broader context of European constitutional courts.

ORGANIZATION AND STRUCTURE

The Bundesverfassungsgericht is a typical example of a European constitutional court. These courts exercise the power of constitutional review in a "European model" that differs in important respects from the "American model" of judicial review. It is therefore useful to sketch the central differences between these two approaches.

The distinctive feature of constitutional review in common law countries such as the United States is that, in principle, *any* court has the power to declare a legislative or administrative act unconstitutional. If, in deciding a case or controversy, an American court confronts a statute that, in the court's judgment, conflicts with the U.S. Constitution or with a state constitution, the judge has the power to declare the law unconstitutional and void. This institutional arrangement reflects the central logic of judicial review claimed by Chief Justice Marshall in *Marbury v. Madison* (1803):

> Those who apply the rule to particular cases, must of necessity expound and interpret that rule. If two laws conflict with each other, the courts must decide on the operation of each. So, if a law be in opposition to the constitution; if both the law and the constitution apply to a particular case, so that the court must either decide that case, conformable to the law, disregarding the constitution; or conformable to the constitution, disregarding the law; the court must determine which of these conflicting rules governs the case: this is of the very essence of judicial duty. If then, the courts are to regard the constitution, and the constitution is superior to any ordinary act of the legislature, the constitution, and not such ordinary act, must govern the case to which they both apply.

Thus, a primary feature of the American model of constitutional review is the *decentralization* that it embodies. No single court monopolizes the power of review.[19] Naturally, a system of decentralized review requires some mechanism that can ensure consistency and coherence. In common law countries, this mechanism consists of the hierarchical organization of the judiciary coupled with the possibility for appeal and the principle of *stare decisis*. The appeals process ensures that litigants who lose but expect a more favorable outcome in the appeals court face incentives to appeal lower court verdicts. *Stare decisis* obliges lower courts to follow the established precedents of higher courts. As a result of the interplay of both components, the American model lodges ultimate judicial authority in the Supreme Court, which stands at the apex of the judicial hierarchy. But it does not grant this court exclusive jurisdiction over constitutional questions.

A second central feature of the American model is the requirement that courts review legislation in the context of a case or controversy. In this sense, the exercise of constitutional review under the American model is incidental to the resolution of a specific dispute that has reached the court. This is not to say that the constitutional issue is not (at least on occasion) at the forefront of the dispute and a primary motivating factor for the litigants or their supporters (thus, a standard tactic for interest groups is to bring test cases to challenge the constitutionality of particular policies). But in order to decide a constitutional question, a court in the American model must first be confronted with a concrete dispute between two parties. American courts cannot decide constitutional questions in the abstract.[20] This requirement to decide cases and controversies has several important consequences. First, courts decide cases in light of the actual consequences of policies once implemented and the information that is generated in an adversarial process between two parties with concrete injuries. Courts thus consider statutes in an environment that is informationally richer than the environment in which legislatures act.[21] A second

---

[19] One consequence of such decentralization is that it adds a layer of uncertainty for legislators trying to anticipate the judicial review process. Legislators face uncertainty not only over how a specific court will rule on a specific issue, but also over which court will review a law in the first place. Such uncertainty can have important consequences for the kinds of bills that legislative majorities adopt in the shadow of judicial review.

[20] In several American states, supreme courts are authorized to deliver "advisory opinions" in which the court does rule on constitutional questions in the abstract. However, these decisions are not binding on policymakers or judges and, in this sense, do not constitute constitutional review (Rogers and Vanberg 2002).

[21] The fact that courts decide cases in light of accumulated experience with a statute has often been hailed as an important benefit of judicial review in the American

consequence of the requirement is that it usually implies considerable delay between the adoption of a statute and the final resolution of a constitutional challenge to its validity, since it requires a law to be implemented, a dispute to arise, and a case to make its way through the legal system.

The central characteristics that set the European model of constitutional review apart from the American version concern both of these features. Under the European model, constitutional review is *centralized* and it can, at least on important occasions, be exercised in the abstract. The European model derives, in large part, from Hans Kelsen's draft of the Austrian constitution of 1920. In trying to import constitutional review into the mainstream of European political practice, Kelsen sought to confront several difficulties that the American model of review might face in the statute-based legal systems of Europe. First, the absence of *stare decisis* in European legal systems might make the development of a consistent jurisprudence difficult, as courts could reach different conclusions on the constitutionality of a statute without a mechanism to resolve the conflict (Cappelletti 1989:140).[22] Second, Kelsen worried that the European system of judicial recruitment, in which judges typically enter a judicial bureaucracy directly from law school and are promoted up the hierarchy according to seniority, would tend to create judges who were "psychologically incapable of the value-oreinted, quasi-political functions involved in judicial review" (Cappelletti 1989:143).[23]

To address both problems, Kelsen proposed that in contrast to American judges, the ordinary European judiciary should not be given the power of constitutional review. Instead, he advocated the creation of a "constitutional court" as a special tribunal outside of the ordinary judicial hierarchy. A "Kelsen court" functions as a separate legal body with exclusive jurisdiction over constitutional questions. Ordinary courts are

---

model (see Note 1956: 1311, Frankfurter 1924, 1930). For a discussion of how this "informational asymmetry" can affect the anticipatory impacts of judicial review on legislative behavior, see Rogers (2001) and Rogers and Vanberg (2002).

[22] Cappelletti (1989:140): "Since the principle of *stare decisis* is foreign to civil law judges, a system that allowed each judge to decide for himself the constitutionality of statutes could result in a law being disregarded as unconstitutional by some judges, while being held constitutional and therefore applied by others. Furthermore, the same court that had one day disregarded a given law might uphold it the next day, having changed its mind about the law's constitutionality."

[23] Cappelletti (1989:143): "Continental judges are usually 'career judges' who enter the judiciary at a very early age and are promoted to the higher courts largely on the basis of seniority. Their professional training develops skills in technical application of statutes rather than in making policy judgments. The exercise of judicial review, however, is quite different from the usual judicial function of applying the law."

prohibited from adjudicating constitutional issues. Of course, this does not imply that Kelsen denied Chief Justice Marshall's contention that courts must, of necessity, confront constitutional questions. Kelsen simply concluded that there is no reason why ordinary courts would have to resolve them. Instead, under the European model, if a court believes that a constitutional question must be adjudicated in deciding a particular case, the court halts its proceedings and refers the question to the constitutional court.

In addition to having a monopoly over the resolution of constitutional questions, constitutional courts, in Kelsen's model, are typically endowed with the power to decide constitutional questions in the absence of a concrete dispute. Under proceedings of abstract judicial review, certain political actors (usually including a parliamentary minority) are entitled to appeal to the court to rule on the constitutionality of a statute immediately following parliamentary passage. Abstract judicial review proceedings, which will be discussed more fully later, thus open up the important possibility of immediate constitutional challenges to decisions taken in the political process. In this sense, these proceedings can plunge a constitutional court directly into a partisan confrontation.

The Bundesverfassungsgericht is a typical example of a Kelsen court. The structure of the court is governed by two documents. The Basic Law provides for the establishment of the constitutional court, defines the court's jurisdiction, and imposes some minimal procedural requirements for the selection of judges. The details of the court's organization are filled in by the FCCA. The most distinctive organizational feature of the court is its division into two separate bodies, the senates. Judges are appointed to a specific senate and serve exclusively in that senate.[24] Each senate has a unique jurisdiction. In a very real sense, the Bundesverfassungsgericht thus consists of *two* constitutional courts – an arrangement that is unusual among constitutional courts.[25] The dual character of the court is even reflected in its physical structure. Each senate occupies a separate floor in the court building in Karlsruhe. The senates come

---

[24] There is one exception to this rule. If a case is urgent and if more than two judges must be excused from deliberations, judges of the other senate can be chosen by lot in order to bring the senate up to its quorum of six.

[25] Most constitutional courts, including the French, Italian, Hungarian, and South African courts, consist of one court. The Russian Constitutional Court is an exception. Like the Bundesverfassungsgericht, the Russian court is split into two senates. However, judges can be reassigned across senates during their tenure, and the composition of the senates must be varied at least every three years.

together as a panel only to resolve jurisdictional conflicts or differences in constitutional interpretation between the senates. Table 3.1 provides an overview of some of the most salient attributes of the FCC in comparison to other European courts. The remaining discussion will be organized around these features.

Each senate is composed of eight judges.[26] As in most European countries, judges on the FCC must meet certain eligibility requirements. Most importantly, a prospective judge must possess advanced legal training. As Table 3.1 shows, this requirement is usual, but not universal, across constitutional courts in Europe. The most notable exception is France, where no eligibility requirements exist and where, in fact, the appointment of a seasoned politician with little legal experience is common. As Stone has documented, the vast majority of the members of the Constitutional Council are former politicians, and professional judges are rarely appointed (Stone 1992:234).[27] For the Bundesverfassungsgericht, the FCCA imposes an additional requirement on the aggregate composition of the court. Of the eight judges in each senate, three must be elected from the benches of the five highest courts of the federal judiciary.

One judge serves as president of the FCC and another as vice-president. They must serve in different senates. The president represents the court in its dealings with other institutions and is responsible for internal administration. Importantly, the president and vice-president do not enjoy special standing in deliberations. Thus, they are not comparable to an American chief justice. The chief justice of the U.S. Supreme Court can exercise considerable influence over deliberations, not least of all because the chief controls opinion assignment (when a member of the majority) and can often set the agenda of deliberations (Epstein and Knight 1998:90f., 125f.). The president and vice-president of the FCC do not possess such status and have no special weight in deliberations.

THE APPOINTMENT PROCESS

The appointment processes for judges to European constitutional courts vary considerably, but two broad types can usefully be distinguished. In

---

[26] When the court was established in 1951, each senate had twelve judges. This number was reduced to ten in 1956 before reaching the current number in 1962.

[27] In the United States there is also no legal requirement that justices of the Supreme Court have legal training. In fact, however, a strong norm of nominating only justices with legal training has developed, and since the mid-nineteenth century, all justices have had formal legal training.

Table 3.1 Structure and Powers of Selected European Constitutional Courts

	France	Germany	Hungary	Italy	Russia
Number of judges	9	16	11	15	19
Appointment	President (3), president of National Assembly (3), president of Senate (3)	Bundestag (8), Bundesrat (8), (2/3 majority)	Parliament (2/3 majority)	President (5), ordinary judiciary (5), parliament (5), (joint session, 3/5 majority)	Federation Council on nomination of president (simple majority)
Length of term	9 years	12 years	9 years	9 years	12 years
Reelection possible	No	No	Two-term limit	No	No
Qualification requirements	None	Must be qualified to be federal judges; 6/16 must be drawn from highest federal courts	Must have legal training. If practicing lawyers, need 20 years' experience	Judges, full professors of law, lawyers with at least 20 years' experience	Lawyers with at least 15 years' experience
Age requirements	None	40-year minimum, 68-year maximum	70-year maximum	None	40-year minimum, 70-year maximum
Abstract review	President, president of National Assembly, president of senate, 60 Senators, 60 deputies	Federal government, *Land* governments, 1/3 of Bundestag	President*	National government and regional governments	1/5 of Duma, 1/5 of Federation Council
Concrete review	No concrete review allowed	Lower courts	Lower courts	Lower courts	Lower courts
Constitutional complaint	Not allowed	Individuals	Individuals	Not allowed	Individuals

*Originally, 50 members of parliament could also initiate abstract review in Hungary. This power was abolished by parliament in 1998.

The Appointment Process

one system, appointments can be made by individual actors, thus reducing the (institutional) need for broad consensus. For example, in France, the president of the Republic, as well as the presidents of the National Assembly and the Senate, each unilaterally appoint three of the nine judges of the Constitutional Council. In the other system, judges are selected by parliaments and appointments usually require supermajorities. For example, Hungarian judges are selected by parliament using a two-thirds majority rule. The most important consequence of these supermajority requirements is not necessarily to depoliticize judicial appointments. Rather, these rules ensure that broad parliamentary consensus is required for appointments. As a result, seats on the constitutional court are usually distributed to reflect the balance of power between parties in the legislature (see also Stone Sweet 2000:48). Some countries incorporate elements of each system. Thus, in Italy, five of the fifteen judges are appointed by the president unilaterally, five are appointed by the ordinary judiciary, and five are appointed by a joint session of parliament using a three-fifths supermajority. In Russia, nominations are made by the president but voted on by the Federation Council using a simple majority rule.

The German system is a variation on the second type. Half of the judges are elected by the lower house of parliament and half by the upper house. The lower house conducts its appointments through the use of a special Judicial Selection Committee (Wahlmännerausschuß), composed of twelve members. Seats on the committee are distributed in proportion to party strength in the Bundestag. Appointments by the upper house, in contrast, are debated and voted on by the full Bundesrat. When a vacancy on the court appears, the federal minister of justice prepares a list of eligible candidates, including persons nominated by the parliamentary parties, state governments, and the federal government. This list is forwarded to the Judicial Selection Committee and the Bundesrat, but neither institution is bound to choose from the list.

To elect a judge, a two-thirds majority is necessary in the Bundesrat and on the Judicial Selection Committee. For practical purposes, this supermajority requirement grants veto power over appointments to each of the two main parties, the CDU/CSD and the SPD. To avoid deadlocks that might arise as a result (as in the first attempt to elect judges in 1951), an informal division of seats on the court has developed. Half of the seats are allocated to the CDU/CSU, the other half to the SPD. If a judge retires, the party with "property rights" over the seat can choose the replacement (subject to an informal norm against choosing extreme candidates). The two minor parties, the liberal Free Democratic Party (FDP) and the

Table 3.2 Composition and Party Balance of the First Senate, 1983–2003

	1/83	7/83	7/83	12/83	6/86	7/87	11/87	7/89	11/89	3/94	9/94	10/95	2/98	1/99	12/99	Since 1/01
Seat 1	Benda (CDU)			Herzog (CDU)							Haas (CDU)					
Seat 2	Faller (CDU)	Henschel (FDP)										Hömig (FDP*)				
Seat 3	Hesse (SPD*)					Grimm (SPD*)									Hoffmann-Reim (SPD*)	
Seat 4	Katzenstein (CDU)						Söllner (CDU)					Steiner (CDU*)				
Seat 5	Simon (SPD)						Dieterich (SPD)									
Seat 6	Niemeyer (SPD)								Seibert (SPD)	Jäger (SPD)				Hohmann-Dennhardt (SPD)		
Seat 7	Heußner (SPD)							Kühling (SPD)								Bryde (Greens*)
Seat 8	Böhmer (CDU*)	Niedermaier (CDU*)			Seidl (CDU*)								Papier (CSU)			
SPD	4 (1)	4 (1)	4 (1)	4 (1)	4 (1)	4 (1)	4 (1)	4 (1)	4 (1)	4 (1)	4 (1)	4 (1)	4 (1)	4 (1)	4 (1)	3 (1)
CDU/CSU	4 (1)	3 (1)	3 (1)	3 (1)	3 (1)	3 (1)	3 (1)	3 (1)	3 (1)	3 (1)	3 (1)	3 (2)	3 (1)	3 (1)	3 (1)	3 (1)
FDP	0	1	1	1	1	1	1	1	1	1	1	1 (1)	1 (1)	1 (1)	1 (1)	1 (1)
Greens	0	0	0	0	0	0	0	0	0	0	0	0	0	0	0	1 (1)

Note: Judges are listed by party membership. For judges who are not party members but who were supported by a particular party, the party affiliation carries a *. The last three rows list the total number of judges by party affiliation. The number of nonparty members included is listed in parentheses.

ecologist Green Party, generally secure a seat from their larger coalition partner when they are in government.

Tables 3.2 and 3.3 show the distribution of seats on the FCC between 1983 and 2003.[28] The equal division of seats between the large parties virtually guarantees that the court will be balanced between the interests and views of the two major parties. The tables clearly reflect this partisan balance. Moreover, the de facto property rights in seats ensure that the ideological balance of the court does not shift radically over time. This stability stands in stark contrast to the situation in France, where the lack of supermajority requirements allows partisan appointments that significantly shift the aggregate composition of the court as control of the presidency, National Assembly, and Senate changes hands (see Stone 1992:50ff.). (Notice, however, that temporary imbalances can occur even in Germany as the seats belonging to small parties are traded to restore balance after a coalition change, e.g., in 1983.)

Unlike the situation in the United States, judges on European constitutional courts typically do not serve for life but are appointed for terms of nine to twelve years. To help insulate judges against electoral concerns, reelection is not permitted in most countries, with some exceptions. In Hungary, judges are eligible for a second term. Judges on the ECJ may also be reappointed. Judges on the FCC serve a twelve-year term and may not be reelected.[29] In addition, as in a number of other European countries, judges are subject to certain age requirements. Most importantly, they must retire when they reach age sixty-eight. The careers of those judges who do not retire from professional life following their years on the court have been varied. Most return to teaching law or take on other leadership duties in key educational institutions. Some return to the bench on one of the high federal courts. Finally, a small number go on to prominent positions in public life, although this option is far from the norm.[30]

---

[28] Other periods show the same patterns. Landfried (1984:21f.) provides a listing from 1951 until 1983.

[29] When the FCCA was passed in 1951, three different classes of judges were created: seats with life tenure and seats with terms of eight or four years. Reelection was permissible. In 1970, this arrangement was changed and a single twelve-year term with no possibility of reelection was introduced.

[30] Roman Herzog, who served as president of the court from 1983 to 1994, went on to the (largely ceremonial) German presidency. Two other members of the court, Jutta Limbach and Paul Kirchhof, were briefly mentioned as potential presidents in the past few years, but neither generated sufficient support. Limbach serves as president of the Goethe Institute, while Kirchhof teaches law.

Table 3.3 Composition and Party Balance of the Second Senate, 1983–2003

	1/83	12/83	10/86	11/87	11/89	7/91	3/94	5/96	12/98	1/2000	1/2001	4/2002	Since 7/2003
Seat 1	Rinck (CDU)		Graßhof (SPD*)										
Seat 2	Rottmann (FDP)	Böckenförde (SPD)						Hassemer (SPD*)					
Seat 3	Wand (CDU)	Klein (CDU)						Jentsch (CDU)					
Seat 4	Niebler (CDU)			Kruis (CSU)					Osterloh (SPD)				
Seat 5	Steinberger (CDU*)			Kirchhof (CDU*)					Bross (CDU*)				
Seat 6	Zeidler (SPD)			Franßen (SPD)		Sommer (SPD)				Di Fabio (CDU*)			
Seat 7	Träger (CDU)				Winter (CDU)		Limbach (SPD)				Mellinghof (CDU)		
Seat 8	Mahrenholz (SPD)											Luebbe-Wolf (SPD*)	Gerhardt (SPD*)
SPD	2	3	4 (1)	4 (1)	4 (1)	4 (1)	4 (1)	4 (2)	4 (1)	4 (1)	4 (1)	4 (2)	4 (3)
CDU/CSU	5 (1)	5 (1)	4 (1)	4 (1)	4 (1)	4 (1)	4 (1)	4 (1)	4 (2)	4 (2)	4 (2)	4 (2)	4 (2)
FDP	1	0	0	0	0	0	0	0	0	0	0	0	0
Greens	0	0	0	0	0	0	0	0	0	0	0	0	0

Note: Judges are listed by party membership. For judges who are not party members but who were supported by a particular party, the party affiliation carries a *. The last three rows list the total number of judges by party affiliation. The number of nonparty members included is listed in parentheses.

JURISDICTION AND CASELOAD

A prominent characteristic of most European constitutional courts is the remarkably broad jurisdiction they enjoy, coupled with open rules of access that enable a wide variety of actors to raise constitutional questions before the court. Typically, three types of proceedings dominate the docket of constitutional courts: referrals of constitutional questions by lower courts ("concrete judicial review"), complaints by individual citizens ("constitutional complaints"), and abstract proceedings initiated by specified political actors ("abstract judicial review").

As Table 3.1 shows, not all European courts allow individuals to challenge the constitutionality of governmental action directly in front of the constitutional court. However, where such constitutional complaints are possible, they typically generate by far the greatest number of cases on the court's docket. This is true in Germany, where the constitutional complaint allows any person (including legal entities) to file a complaint against an alleged violation of his basic rights by state authorities. (The *Crucifix* case discussed in Chapter 1 arose out of a constitutional complaint.) The procedure for filing a complaint is easy and inexpensive. No legal representation, special forms, or fees are required. In fact, "most complaints are handwritten and prepared without the aid of a lawyer" (Kommers 1997:15). The only restriction is that an appellant has exhausted all other legal remedies before appealing to the FCC (and even this requirement can be waived). Given these open rules, it is no surprise that the court has been swamped by constitutional complaints. Table 3.4 shows the caseload of the FCC since its creation in 1951.[31] Since German unification in 1990, the court has received, on average, 4,000 to 5,000 constitutional complaints per year. To help stem this tide, the court can impose (minor) fines for complaints that are obviously frivolous, although it rarely makes use of this provision.

Like most constitutional courts in Europe, the FCC does not have a discretionary docket. This means that unlike the U.S. Supreme Court, which can (largely) choose which cases to review and which to dismiss

---

[31] Discrepancies between the number of cases initiated and the number of cases that have been decided arise for several reasons. The court carries a considerable backlog, sometimes taking several years to issue a ruling. In addition, parties to a dispute may settle their differences and withdraw a case. Finally, the statistics provided by the court only count in lead cases. Often (especially in cases involving constitutional complaints), the court settles several cases in one decision. Since only the lead case is reported, the number of cases that have been decided de facto lies above the total reported in the table.

Table 3.4 *Proceedings before the FCC, 1951–2002*

Proceeding	Initiated	Decided	
Disputes between political institutions	135		72
Abstract judicial review	148		89
Federal-state disputes	39		24
Constitutional complaints	135,968	Senates:	3,879
		Chambers:	109,246
Concrete judicial review	3,210	Senates:	988
		Chambers:	131
Constitutionality of political parties	8		4
Election challenges	144		120
Temporary injunctions	1,378		982
Other	284		95

Source: Gesamtstatistik des Bundesverfassungsgerichts für das Geschäftsjahr 2002 (available at http://www.bverfge.de).

without making a decision on the merits, a European constitutional court is obligated to decide all cases that are properly initiated (Stone Sweet 2000:46). Given the sheer volume of constitutional complaints, it would, of course, be impossible for the senates of the FCC to decide all the cases that are brought to the court. To deal with this practical difficulty, a panel system was created in 1956 and expanded in 1986. When a constitutional complaint reaches the court, it is initially reviewed by a three-judge panel called a "chamber." If all three judges agree that the complaint is inadmissible or has no hope of success, they may dismiss it. If at least one judge considers the complaint to have some prospect of success, it is forwarded to the relevant senate for decision.

In 1986, the chambers were also granted limited power to decide cases. Provided that all judges in a chamber agree that a complaint falls clearly under established precedent and raises no new constitutional issues, the chamber may rule in favor of the complainant without forwarding the case to the full court. However, only a full senate may declare a statute unconstitutional. As Table 3.4 reveals, the vast number of constitutional complaints are handled by the chamber system. Most of these decisions involve highly individualized cases that do not touch on a broader statutory question and have few implications beyond the immediate ruling (many, for example, challenge the constitutionality of a specific ruling by a trial judge in a particular case). It is important to note that this screening procedure does not amount to the full discretionary control of the docket that the U.S. Supreme Court enjoys. The chambers are not free to choose among cases, but instead are bound to accept cases that are properly filed and not clearly without merit. Although proposals to grant the court full docket control have been made, they have not been implemented.

In terms of sheer volume, the second most important proceeding before the FCC involves concrete judicial review. This proceeding, previously mentioned, comes closest to the cases and controversies requirement governing access to the U.S. Supreme Court. If a lower court, in the course of an ordinary proceeding, must apply a statute whose constitutionality is in doubt, the court suspends its proceedings and refers the constitutional question to the FCC. In referring a question, the court must demonstrate that the constitutionality of the statute is relevant for the resolution of the case and is not incidental. (That is, the court must demonstrate that the decision in the case hinges on the constitutional question.) Like constitutional complaints, referrals from lower courts are screened by a chamber. If all three judges on the panel conclude that the lower court has not demonstrated that its decision requires a resolution of the constitutional issue, the chamber may dismiss the case.

For European constitutional courts that allow constitutional complaints and concrete judicial review, these proceedings account for the overwhelming majority of decisions. However, other proceedings involve what are perhaps the most controversial and politically charged rulings. These are proceedings that allow specified political actors to initiate a case in the constitutional court, often immediately after passage of a statute and in the absence of a concrete dispute. For this reason, these proceedings are ordinarily referred to as "abstract judicial review." The specific actors that can initiate abstract review proceedings vary among European countries. Significantly, however, in most countries, parliamentary minorities enjoy the right to challenge legislation immediately after a final vote on the bill. Thus, in France, sixty members of the National Assembly or sixty senators may challenge legislation after passage but before its promulgation. In Russia, one-fifth of the lower house (the Duma) or one-fifth of the upper house (the Federation Council) can initiate proceedings. In Germany, one-third of the lower house can challenge legislation under abstract review. (In Hungary, the right of the parliamentary opposition to initiate abstract review proceedings was eliminated in 1998.)

Politically, cases arising under abstract judicial review tend to be the most significant. Since abstract judicial review occurs immediately after passage, it "extends what would otherwise be a concluded legislative process" (Stone 1992:231). As one might expect, these proceedings, which are usually initiated by opposition parties, are usually highly political and partisan, and often amount to a continuation of the political debate between the government and the opposition by constitutional means (Stone Sweet 1992).[32] The threat of initiating abstract review proceedings is a significant bargaining tool for opposition parties, and the shadow that judicial review casts over the legislative process may be particularly pronounced where referral to the court on final passage is a looming threat (Stone Sweet 1998; Vanberg 1998a, 1998b). For example, central FCC decisions on abortion policy were issued in response to abstract judicial review proceedings brought by CDU/CSU legislators who challenged the liberalization of access to abortion (BVerfGE 39, 1; BVerfGE 88, 203).

In addition to affording parliamentary minorities access to the constitutional court, abstract judicial review is often designed to provide governments with the power to challenge actions by other institutions. Thus, abstract judicial review was introduced in France by Charles de Gaulle's 1958 constitution with the precise aim of providing the president with a tool to guard his constitutional powers through the ability to challenge legislative action (Cappelletti 1989:156).[33] Similarly, in Russia, *only* the president can initiate abstract review, thus providing him with the ability to challenge actions by the Duma and by state governments. In Germany, this feature of abstract judicial review is also incorporated. The federal government as well as state governments have the power to challenge federal and state legislation under the proceeding.

In addition to these three primary proceedings – constitutional complaints, concrete judicial review, and abstract judicial review – the FCC has jurisdiction over a number of other important, though much less prominent, types of cases. It resolves disputes among political institutions and actors about their respective powers (Organstreit). For example, in a recent case, a member of the German parliament challenged the constitutionality of parliamentary procedures for committee assignments after he had been stripped of his committee memberships following his resignation from the Green Party (BVerfGE 80, 188). Institutions that can bring such

---

[32] For example, in France, the Constitutional Council received only nine requests for abstract review in the fifteen-year period from 1958 to 1973, when opposition parties could not initiate review. When opposition parties received the right to initiate challenges in 1974, the number of referrals jumped immediately. In the thirteen-year period from 1974 to 1987, the court received 191 referrals (Stone 1992:233f.).

[33] Parliamentary minorities in France did not receive the right to initiate abstract review until 1974.

a case include the federal president, both houses of parliament, and the federal government, as well as any person or institution vested with independent rights by the rules of procedure of these institutions. Finally, the court adjudicates federal–state disputes, challenges to the constitutionality of political parties, and election challenges.

DECISION-MAKING PROCEDURES

Six judges constitute a quorum in each senate. More than half of the votes cast are required to declare a constitutional violation.[34] The deliberations of the court are closed, and all judges are expected to keep the specific content of deliberations secret. As is true of European constitutional courts generally, all judges who participate in a decision must sign the court's opinion, regardless of their position on the outcome. While the senates are free to report vote distributions, they do so rarely, and even in these cases, the identity of judges in the majority and the minority is not revealed. Judges who vote against a decision can be identified only if they choose to publish a dissent. Dissenting opinions have been permitted since 1970, but they are rare. Of the 1,781 decisions issued between 1971 and 2002, dissents were published in only 115, or about 6 percent.[35] As a result of these procedural rules, which are similar in other European courts, systematic investigations of the voting record of individual European judges (as are typical of judicial scholarship in the United States) are generally impossible.

In most cases, European constitutional courts decide on the basis of the published record without oral arguments. In the period between 1983 and 1996, the FCC held oral arguments in only 7 percent of cases. The decision to hold oral arguments is made by the senate deliberating a case. Generally, oral arguments are held in politically sensitive or highly salient cases. However, in addition to the parties in a case, other interested parties, including the federal government, state governments, semipublic institutions, church organizations, and interest groups, are generally permitted to file amicus briefs.

One of the most distinctive features of the FCC's decision-making procedures is the role played by individual judges in the deliberative process.

---

[34] In other words, the challenged act is sustained in the event of a tie. Impeachment proceedings against the federal president or against federal judges, proceedings to determine the constitutionality of political parties, and decisions on the forfeiture of basic rights require a two-thirds majority.

[35] Statistics are available at www.bundesverfassungsgericht.de

When a judge is elected to the court, he or she is given responsibility for a particular legal area (called the *Dezernat*). Examples of such legal areas are freedom of association, labor law, international law, and tax law. These assignments carry great significance because judges automatically assume the role of rapporteur (*Berichterstatter*) for cases falling within their jurisdiction. The rapporteur is responsible for drafting a memorandum, called a "votum," that summarizes the legal issues involved in a case. The votum, which also includes a recommendation for decision, is circulated to all judges before the conference and becomes the basis of the court's deliberations.

Perhaps more importantly, the rapporteur is responsible for writing the court's draft opinion following conference deliberations. *Significantly, this is the case even if the rapporteur is in the minority.* Unlike the situation on the U.S. Supreme Court, there is thus no discretion in opinion assignment and no guarantee that a member of the majority will draft the court's opinion. The draft opinion is circulated and revised by the full senate in another conference before a final vote is taken. Conferences are held weekly, usually on Tuesdays, except in August and September, when the court is not in session.

DECISIONS

The court has a range of decisions available in disposing of a case. At the most basic level, the court can choose to find no constitutional violation or to raise constitutional objections to a government action (be it a statute, an administrative ruling, or a court decision). Beyond this basic distinction, the court has wide latitude in defining the scope and severity of its decisions, particularly when it finds constitutional violations. This variety is most easily explained with reference to decisions on the constitutionality of a law.

When striking down a statute, the court can declare the statute unconstitutional in its entirety, but it is also free to attack only specific provisions. In fact, as in Europe generally (Stone Sweet 2000:71), partial annulments are the norm. In addition, the court has two versions of an unconstitutionality ruling at its disposal. It can declare a law null and void (*unvereinbar und nichtig*) or merely incompatible with the Basic Law (*mit dem Grundgesetz unvereinbar*).[36] A law that is ruled null and void

---

[36] Originally, only a ruling of "null and void" was provided for in the FCCA. The "incompatibility" ruling was literally created by the court in its jurisprudence (Schlaich 1994:228).

ceases to have force immediately, while a law that is incompatible with the Basic Law can usually be applied pending a legislative revision (for a more detailed treatment, see Hesse 1995:285; Schlaich 1994:220ff.).[37] In such cases, the court increasingly provides for explicit deadlines by which legislative revision of the statute is supposed to be completed. Politically, an incompatibility ruling is significant since it allows the court to put other political actors on notice that it expects an issue to be addressed, but it spares these actors the immediate ramifications of the decision. As Donald Kommers has observed, "the practice of declaring a legal provision unconstitutional but not void is... used by the court to soften the political impact of its decisions" (Kommers 1997:53).[38] The Italian Constitutional Court makes use of a similar tactic to raise constitutional concerns without the immediate imposition of an annulment's consequences by announcing "that a legislative provision will be struck down as unconstitutional in future cases, if the legislature does not alter it beforehand" (Stone Sweet 2000:72).

CONCLUSION

The purpose of this chapter has been to provide the context for the remaining chapters by presenting an overview of the establishment and institutional structure of the Bundesverfassungsgericht in a comparative perspective. Like European constitutional courts more generally, the FCC is a specialized constitutional tribunal apart from the ordinary judiciary, and it exercises exclusive jurisdiction over constitutional questions. Since its creation more than fifty years ago, the court has become a central actor in the German political system and is widely regarded as one of the most significant judicial institutions in the world. As one prominent German legal scholar and federal judge has recently put it, "the Court, created specifically as the 'guardian of the constitution,' is precisely intended to ensure that the constitutional order defined by the Basic Law is realized in all respects" (Weber Fas 2002:217). Such a characterization, which is

---

[37] However, only criminal convictions based on an unconstitutional law can be appealed and may result in a retrial. All other administrative decisions based on an unconstitutional statute cannot be appealed and are not affected retroactively by the declaration of unconstitutionality (FCCA, paragraph 79; see also Hesse 1995:286; Schlaich 1994:226).

[38] In addition, the court can rule that a bill is unconstitutional only in specified circumstances or it can impose a particular interpretation on a statute. For a fuller discussion, see Kommers (1997).

typical of much legal scholarship, conceives of the court as an apolitical guardian towering above the turmoil of ordinary politics, fully able to control and constrain the actions of other institutions. The theory laid out in the previous chapter argues for a more qualified vision in which judicial power is conditioned by the political environment in which the court must act. It is now time to turn to a more systematic evaluation of this theory.

4

Transparency and Judicial Deference

The principal argument of this book, laid out in Chapter 2, takes off from the observation that the decisions of a constitutional court like the Bundesverfassungsgericht are not self-enforcing. Implementation of judicial decisions often requires the cooperation of other actors who may not wish to comply with a specific ruling, most importantly – for our purposes – legislative majorities. As a result, the incentives that legislators face in deciding how to respond to a judicial ruling take on central significance. The greater the pressure to implement a court's rulings faithfully, the more influential and effective a court will be. One important mechanism that creates such pressure for elected officials like legislators is the potential for a public backlash if they are perceived to flaunt a judicial decision. As I argued in greater detail in Chapter 2, two factors are central to this mechanism:

1. The degree of public support a court enjoys and
2. The likelihood that a sufficiently large number of citizens will become aware/convinced that a judicial decision has not been complied with if evasion is attempted (transparency).

As I stated at the end of Chapter 2, the second condition (transparency) is conditioned by a range of factors that work to decrease or increase the likelihood that citizens will become aware of evasive attempts by a legislative majority. Thus, transparency is generally higher in cases that are salient and attract more public attention. Because the level of public interest is already higher, it is more likely that citizens will become aware of a failure to comply with a decision than in cases that receive little public attention. A second crucial factor affecting transparency is the presence of organized groups that take an interest in seeing a decision implemented and have the resources and organizational capability to call attention to evasive maneuvers. As Epp (1998) has shown in detailed comparative case studies, should legislators choose not to comply with a decision, such groups can engage in media campaigns to raise awareness of the court's decision and the failure to implement it. They can also mount renewed legal challenges. As a result, it is more difficult to hide evasion than in situations in which outside groups take little interest in implementation. Finally, the nature of the issue presented in a case itself affects transparency. Transparency tends to be lower for a ruling that touches on a complex technical issue than for a decision on a relatively noncomplex issue (e.g., a procedural question). Because complex issues often touch on several policy areas at once and demand more complex technical responses, it becomes more difficult to establish convincingly whether a decision has been evaded. Less complex issues make it easier to do so.

The two conditions – the degree of public support and transparency – are part of the *political* (as opposed to the legal) environment in which a court must act. The model presented in Chapter 2 demonstrated that this political environment is central to the manner in which a constitutional court will exercise its powers and to the effectiveness with which it can constrain legislative majorities. Where public support is high and the environment is transparent, courts are in a strong position. Attempts at evasion are difficult to conceal and therefore become unattractive because they are likely to result in a costly public backlash (given the level of public support). Legislative majorities usually bow to judicial rulings and, as a result, judges are free to make aggressive use of their powers and to show little deference to legislative majorities. The influence of courts over public policy is high. However, where transparency or public support is low, courts find themselves in a weakened position. Evasion of unpleasant decisions becomes more attractive for legislative majorities since evasion is less likely to be caught and/or is less likely to result in a sufficiently costly public backlash even if it becomes widely known. In consequence, courts are less able to issue decisions that are politically costly for legislative majorities. Instead, to avoid defiance, judges begin to show greater deference to the interests of legislative majorities and to make less aggressive use of their powers. The result is that judicial influence over policy declines and legislative majorities are less constrained. This relationship between the court's political environment, the level of judicial deference to legislative majorities, and the effectiveness of courts is perhaps the most important implication of the argument presented in Chapter 2, and it was summarized in Observation 1:

Observation 1: If public support is central to the enforcement of judicial rulings, courts become more deferential and less powerful as the political environment becomes less transparent and as they are less likely to enjoy public support.

Importantly, this observation has a clear empirical implication for judicial behavior that lends itself to systematic testing. If Observation 1 is correct, the level of judicial deference – how aggressively a court makes use of its veto powers – will depend on the court's environment. Specifically, all else being equal, a court will be more likely to annul a statute when transparency and public support are high. It will be less likely to do so where either is low. The purpose of this chapter is to test this relationship through a systematic analysis of original data on decisions by the FCC on the constitutionality of state and federal legislation. Does the deference with which the FCC treats legislation vary with the court's political environment?

FOCUSING ON TRANSPARENCY

To test this relationship, we must first confront a challenge. As Observation 1 makes clear, both transparency and public support are crucial to the model's predictions (or, in more technical language, it is the *joint probability* of transparency and public support that determines the model's equilibria). Moreover, it is the *specific constellation of these factors for the particular case* confronting the court that is relevant. Ideally, we would therefore like to measure the ex ante likelihood of public support and transparency in specific cases and to test whether the German court is more likely to rule against a statute when this joint likelihood is high. The difficulty lies in measuring public support. Ex post, public opinion surveys typically ask only about selected landmark decisions (if they ask about the court's rulings at all). Moreover, reliable ex ante opinion polls that measure public attitudes on the myriad issues confronting the court are not available in a systematic fashion. As a result, constructing a direct measure of public support on particular issues confronting the Bundesverfassungsgericht for a large number of cases extending over a longer time period appears an extremely difficult if not impossible task.

Luckily, we can get some insight into public support for the German court from data on more general (diffuse) support for the FCC. Tables 4.1 and 4.2 show several different measures that compare public support for the Bundesverfassungsgericht to support for other institutions in

Table 4.1 *Trust in Public Institutions*

Institution	1982	1986	1990	1993
FCC	82%	85%	84%	73%
Bundestag	61%	74%	65%	44%
Federal government	59%	66%	61%	43%
Judiciary	74%	76%	69%	62%
Police	–	78%	83%	76%
Churches	67%	64%	62%	52%
Trade unions	53%	42%	44%	44%
Political parties	39%	45%	37%	23%
Newspapers	57%	51%	36%	42%

Note: Percentages are the proportion of respondents reporting that they trust an institution in response to the following question: "I am now going to read you a list of public institutions and organizations. Please tell me for each institution or organization whether you trust it, or whether that is not the case. How about...?"
Source: Emnid Institut (1995:56).

Table 4.2 *Opinion of Public Institutions*

Institution	1974	1985	1995	1999
FCC	47%	52%	36%	50%
Bundestag	49%	42%	24%	34%
Federal government	47%	39%	25%	25%
Bundesbank	42%	47%	32%	45%
Länd governments	35%	38%	21%	25%
Bundesrat	41%	43%	23%	32%

Note: Percentages are the proportion of respondents reporting that they have a "very good" or "good" opinion of an institution in response to the following question: "There are a number of institutions and organizations that are significant for political decision making in Germany. A few of them are listed on these cards. Could you arrange the cards on this sheet according to whether you have a good or a bad opinion of the institution?"
Source: Noelle-Neumann and Koecher (1997:812–13; 2002:710–11).

Germany. Several striking patterns emerge from these tables. The first is that regardless of whether we consider the number of respondents who trust the FCC (Table 4.1) or the number of respondents who have a "very good" or "good" opinion of the court (Table 4.2), the court seems to have the benefit of an exceptionally high level of support. This is especially true relative to other institutions of governance. With one exception (in 1974), more Germans have a good opinion of the court than of any other institution. Similarly, the FCC enjoys the highest level of trust among institutions. Moreover, the support that the court enjoys over the Bundestag, the federal government, and state governments is considerable. Particularly striking is the fact that the court even outperforms the Bundesbank – traditionally regarded as one of the most revered institutions in Germany.

The tables also suggest that support for the court is relatively stable over time. In the 1990s, there is a dip in support that may be related to controversial decisions in the *Soldier* and *Crucifix* cases (discussed in Chapters 1 and 2) that damaged the court's image. But by the end of the decade, support appears to have returned to its previous levels. Moreover, *even during the period in which support is lowest, the court still enjoys considerably higher support than the Bundestag, the federal government, or* Land *governments*. In other words, diffuse public support for the German court is generally very high. Even though diffuse support does not necessarily equal specific support on a particular issue, this exceptional level of support for the court suggests that where an open confrontation between the court and legislative majorities at the federal or state level develops, the broad public would be more likely to back the court.[1] That is, in terms of the graphical representation of the model's predictions in Figures 2.2 and 2.3, we are likely to find ourselves in the northern regions of the figures, where the likelihood of public support is high. As a result, the model's predictions about the court's level of deference will fundamentally turn on the transparency of the political environment.

Putting the same point differently, given that the German court enjoys extremely high support vis-à-vis other institutions, transparency becomes the crucial factor in the court's political environment. How likely is it that a sufficiently large number of citizens will become aware of an evasion attempt if a legislative majority chooses not to comply? If this likelihood is high, that is, if the environment is transparent, the court is in a strong position to assert itself vis-à-vis the legislature and will be more likely to make aggressive use of its powers, that is, to veto legislation. In areas in which transparency is low, evasion becomes more attractive and, hence, the court will be more deferential in its treatment of legislation. In short, while measuring public attitudes toward a large number of cases is practically impossible, we can make use of the fact that diffuse public support for the FCC is high and stable over time to focus the empirical test on

---

[1] In the next chapter, we will consider data gathered in interviews with German legislators. These data clearly reveal that German legislators share the assessment that the broad public would back the FCC in a confrontation with the legislature.

the second factor: transparency. Thus, the general relationship that is predicted by the model presented in Chapter 2 and that we will test in this chapter is the following:

Proposition: The greater the likelihood that the environment in which the FCC is acting is transparent, the less deferential to legislative majorities the court will be.[2]

HYPOTHESES

In order to test this proposition, we need to translate the general expectation that the court will be more aggressive as its environment becomes more transparent into concrete hypotheses. The fact that transparency is a function of several different factors – discussed earlier and in Chapter 2 – helps us to do so. Consider first the impact of public awareness of a decision. Legislative majorities at the federal and state levels are less constrained in resisting rulings that linger in obscurity and generate little public interest. On the other hand, transparency – and therefore the threat of losing public support for evasion – is likely to be higher in cases that enjoy a greater degree of public awareness. As a result, the model would lead us to expect that the court will be more aggressive in highly salient cases:

Hypothesis 1: Ceteris paribus, the FCC will be more likely to veto legislation in cases for which potential or actual public awareness is higher.

The presence of organized groups that may call attention to evasive maneuvers is another significant factor that impacts transparency. Organized groups that would like to see a judicial annulment of a statute implemented make it more difficult for legislative majorities to resist because they increase transparency. Such groups have the means and a clear incentive to draw public attention to attempts at evasion. In other

---

[2] The argument presented earlier shows intuitively why greater transparency translates into less deference. The comparative statics results of the model also demonstrate that this relationship holds. Recall that an increase in the likelihood that the environment is transparent can only induce a switch from an equilibrium in which the FCC does not censor the bill to an equilibrium in which it does. The reverse relationship is never possible. That is, all else being equal, if the court's behavior changes as the environment is more likely to be transparent, the court will only become less deferential. This result is clearly reflected in Figures 2.2 and 2.3: For any given level of public support, as the likelihood of transparency increases (i.e., as we move to the right), we are more likely to see a judicial annulment, never the reverse.

words, they provide an ally for a court that is inclined to veto a statute and therefore make the court less deferential. This leads to the following hypothesis:

> **Hypothesis 2:** Ceteris paribus, the FCC will be more likely to veto legislation when outside groups that provide political support for an annulment are present.

Finally, the complexity of the issue at stake is a third factor that influences the transparency surrounding a decision. The less complex a policy area is, the easier it will be for citizens to determine whether a decision has been respected. This is the case because the implications of a noncomplex decision for policy are more straightforward. For example, compliance with a decision that declares life imprisonment without the possibility of parole unconstitutional is easier to monitor than compliance with a decision that touches on the interrelationships between various provisions of the tax code. Where citizens can more readily determine whether the constitutional court's decision has been faithfully implemented, legislators must be more acutely aware of the potential for a public backlash should they not conform to the court's ruling. Consequently, one would expect the court to be more aggressive in policy areas that have this characteristic:

> **Hypothesis 3:** Ceteris paribus, the FCC is more likely to veto legislation the less complex a policy area is.

These three hypotheses, which correspond to the three components of transparency that we have outlined, are designed to capture the impact of transparency on judicial deference. They are the primary focus of the empirical test. However, recall that the model also predicts that the court will be more deferential on issues that are of central concern to the legislative majority, since the legislature is more likely to resist attempts at annulment in such cases (Observation 3 in Chapter 2). The expectation that the interests of legislative majorities condition judicial deference leads to a final hypothesis (given that, in the German case, we are dealing exclusively with parliamentary systems in which the cabinet or government must be supported by a parliamentary majority, we can equate the legislative majority with the government):

> **Hypothesis 4:** Ceteris paribus, the FCC will be less likely to veto legislation in cases in which the government/legislative majority has a particular interest in sustaining a law.

THE DATA

As discussed in the previous chapter, the FCC has broad jurisdiction and issues decisions in a wide range of proceedings, from reviewing lower court verdicts, to ruling on the constitutionality of political parties, to reviewing federal and state laws. Given the theoretical focus on the relationship between the court and legislative majorities, not all of these decisions are relevant for an empirical test of our hypotheses. Instead, we focus exclusively on those cases in which the court rules on the constitutionality of *legislation*, either at the federal or the state level. To perform the empirical test, I therefore use original data on all 329 decisions issued by one of the two senates of the Bundesverfassungsgericht on the constitutionality of a federal or state statute in the twelve-year period between 1983 and 1995.[3]

The theoretical model and the hypotheses implied by the model focus on the fact that the court is likely to be more aggressive in making use of its veto powers when the environment in which it is acting is transparent. Thus, the dependent variable is suggested directly by the theoretical argument: Does the FCC annul a statute or not? The dependent variable is a binary variable capturing the court's decision. It is coded 1 for cases in which the court declared a federal or state law (or part thereof) unconstitutional. It is coded 0 if the court dismissed a constitutional challenge against a statute (either by declaring the statute constitutional or by dismissing the case as inadmissible).[4]

---

[3] Thus, the dataset does not include unpublished chamber decisions (see Chapter 2). Recall that these decisions raise no new constitutional issues, must fall clearly under the court's established precedent, and may not declare a statute unconstitutional. In addition, I exclude cases in which the court reviews a lower court verdict, not a statute. Given that we are interested in legislative–judicial relations, doing so makes sense. However, as a robustness check, I have also performed the analysis reported here when including decisions on the constitutionality of lower court verdicts. The results are robust to this inclusion.

[4] This approach of operationalizing judicial deference, for purposes of statistical analysis, as a binary coding of judicial decisions is also consistent with the approach taken by scholars studying the U.S. Supreme Court. For example, Caldeira (1986:1215) has employed rates of annulment as a reasonable proxy for the degree of judicial deference. Naturally, a binary coding obscures aspects of a decision that may be important for assessing the degree of judicial deference exhibited by a court. In particular, the tenor, reasoning, and orbiter dicta of a decision may be crucial. Nevertheless, in the absence of reliable criteria for coding these more complex attributes of judicial decisions, and given the close fit between this variable and the predictions of the model, which also focus on the decision to annul, this approach makes sense in the current context. In the next chapter, I will use interview data to explore the concept of judicial deference in a richer setting.

The Data

Hypothesis 1 focuses on the level of public awareness of a case. Testing this hypothesis thus requires a measure that captures the degree of public awareness of a decision. Unfortunately, for some of the same reasons that make it difficult to generate direct measures of public support in particular cases, the degree to which citizens are aware of cases confronted by the court is difficult to measure systematically for a large number of cases. Public opinion surveys, for example, typically ask only about selected landmark decisions. For current purposes, I employ two measures to capture the degree of public awareness of a case. The first is a proxy variable that codes whether a case is accompanied by oral arguments. Some explanation is necessary for using this variable as an indicator of public awareness. The court holds oral arguments rarely. Of the 329 decisions in the data set, oral arguments were held in only 44. Cases involving oral arguments are usually cases of great significance, and the level of public interest is considerably higher than in ordinary cases. The opening ceremonies of oral arguments are videotaped, and excerpts are generally shown during the nationwide evening newscasts. As a consequence, citizens are more likely to be aware of a case that involves oral arguments than of a case that does not. As a second indicator of public awareness, I include a variable that counts the total number of amicus curiae briefs filed in a case by interest groups, lower courts, or governments. As scholars studying the U.S. Supreme Court have argued, more intense outside participation by organized interests suggests that a case is more significant and is likely to generate more public interest (Caldeira and Wright 1990; McGuire and Caldeira 1993; Spriggs and Wahlbeck 1997).

Hypothesis 2 is concerned with the impact that organized outside interests have on transparency. Organized groups or institutions that have the ability and the incentive to monitor compliance with a decision and to call public attention to attempts to evade a ruling can act as allies for the court should it decide to annul a statute. To measure whether the court enjoys such outside political support, I code the substance of amicus curiae briefs filed in a case. Specifically, this variable is coded 1 if an interest group has filed a brief arguing that the challenged statute is unconstitutional. I also code this variable 1 if another government (i.e., not the government whose statute is being reviewed) has filed a brief to indicate that it believes the statute to be unconstitutional. The presence of either kind of brief indicates that the court has outside support by a political actor who has an interest in monitoring the response to the court's decision if the court notes a constitutional violation. If no such brief exists, the variable is coded 0.

A test of Hypothesis 3, which focuses on the fact that transparency is likely to be lower in highly complex cases, requires a variable that captures the complexity of the policy area that a case touches on. For this purpose, I use a binary variable that classifies the primary policy area involved in each case as "complex" or "noncomplex." The following policy areas were classified as complex: economic regulation, state-mandated social insurance (unemployment, health, and retirement insurance), civil servant compensation, taxation, federal budget issues, and party finance. These policy areas are complex in several ways. First, they generally involve questions that concern several policy areas at once. For example, a certain action (say, raising the standard of living for low-income families) could be accomplished through changes in economic regulation or through a change in social insurance provisions. These policy areas are also complex in that they tend to involve technical regulatory questions. Finally, they all tend to raise questions of revenue and resource allocation. The following policy areas were coded as noncomplex: institutional disputes, family law, judicial process, individual rights, asylum rights, and military conscription. All of these policy areas are less complex in that they typically involve questions that do not have direct or immediate connections to other policy areas. They also tend not to involve revenue questions directly. Finally, they often involve procedural questions, which are easier to monitor.[5]

Finally, Hypothesis 4 requires measures that capture the substantive interest of the government/parliament whose statute is being challenged in a particular case. (Recall that because we are dealing exclusively with parliamentary systems, in which the cabinet must be supported by a legislative majority, we can usefully treat the government and the associated legislative majority as one entity.) There are two variables that I employ for this purpose. A straightforward measure of a government's interest in a case is the substantive content of a brief filed by the government, as well as the decision on whether to file a brief at all. Filing a brief and taking an official position on a case commit both institutional and

---

[5] It should be noted here that the classification of policy areas into complex and noncomplex issues areas is concerned with how easy decisions in these areas are to monitor, not with how far-reaching these decisions are. For example, a decision that mandates that illegal immigrants are granted a full review of their case before being returned to their country of origin can have extremely far-reaching consequences (for the judicial system, the education system, and the economy). But it is noncomplex in the sense that it is relatively easy to establish whether or not detained immigrants are granted such review or not.

reputational resources. One would not expect such an investment unless the government concerned has an interest in the outcome of a case. The first variable therefore indicates whether the government whose statute is being challenged has filed a brief to argue in support of the challenged law. Of course, in some cases, a government may no longer have an interest in seeing a statute upheld (or may even have an interest in seeing it struck down). To capture this possibility, the second variable is coded 1 when the relevant government has filed a brief arguing that the challenged statute is unconstitutional. If both variables are coded 0, the government has not filed a brief.

Like all models, the model presented in Chapter 2 necessarily abstracts away from many of the precise details of the German case. In testing the model, we therefore want to introduce several control variables to account for features that may affect the level of judicial deference but are not explicitly treated in the model. Perhaps the most important of these concerns the federal structure of Germany. The model concerns the relations between a legislative majority and a court, and it does not draw a distinction between levels of government, that is, between relations between the court and legislative majorities at the federal level as opposed to relations between the court and majorities at the state level. However, in testing the model empirically by considering state and federal legislation, it is probably desirable to distinguish between these two situations.

One reason to do so is that the power to resist or evade judicial rulings may not be equal for legislative majorities at the different levels. The Bundestag and the federal government comprise the highest legislative and executive authorities, and they face no higher level of government that can force compliance. They have at their disposal federal ministries with control over considerable means that can be deployed in evading a decision. Moreover, the Bundestag can make major changes to the institutional structure of the FCC through simple legislation. State parliaments and governments may be more constrained in their ability to evade decisions of the FCC. First and foremost, legislative majorities at the state level must contend with the federal government, which may try to employ its leverage in forcing compliance with judicial decisions. (For example, faced with evasion of constitutional court decisions by the regions, the Russian government in 2001 passed a law to force regional compliance.) Despite these limitations, state parliaments and governments have some power to resist the court's decisions, as the *Crucifix* decision discussed in Chapter 1 illustrates (BVerfGE 93,1). That decision declared a Bavarian school ordinance requiring the display of a crucifix in all elementary school rooms unconstitutional. Backed by massive public protest against the verdict, the Bavarian government refused to abide by the court's decision and finally passed a new statute that keeps crucifixes in schoolrooms. To capture any differences that may arise as a result of the different capabilities of legislative majorities at the state or federal level, we will control for the institution with which the FCC is interacting.

In addition, I control for a particular institutional feature of the German court. Recall from the previous chapter that the German court is divided into two senates with separate personnel and jurisdiction. As a result, I control for any differences in judicial behavior that might arise due to jurisdictional or personnel differences between the two senates.

ANALYSIS AND RESULTS

Given the binary nature of the dependent variable, I use a logit model to analyze the effects of these independent variables on the court's decision. The parameter estimates in a logit model estimate the impact of an independent variable on the log-odds ratio, which can easily be transformed to calculate a predicted probability of observing a ruling of unconstitutionality for various combinations of the independent variables. A positive coefficient for an independent variable implies that an increase in the value of this variable raises the probability of an annulment (and vice versa for a negative coefficient). For example, a positive coefficient for the variable indicating that a decision is made by the Second Senate would mean that this senate is more likely to rule against a verdict or a piece of legislation than the First Senate.

The hypotheses provide clear expectations about the signs of the estimated coefficients. Hypothesis 1 implies that the estimated coefficient of the variable indicating whether oral arguments were held will be positive and that the likelihood of an unconstitutionality ruling will increase with the number of briefs filed. Hypothesis 2 leads to the expectation that the coefficient on the variable indicating that the court has outside political support will be positive. According to Hypothesis 3, the court becomes more deferential in complex policy areas, so the estimated coefficient of this variable should be negative. Finally, Hypothesis 4 implies that the estimated coefficient for the variable indicating that the government in question alleges that no constitutional violation has taken place should be negative, while the coefficient for the variable indicating that the government perceives a constitutional violation should be positive. I have no particular expectations about the signs of the control variables.

The results are presented in Table 4.3. Model 1 represents a first cut at the data. The model includes all of the variables designed to test Hypotheses 1–4, as well as control variables for federal laws and decisions made by the Second Senate.[6] A quick look at the estimated coefficients confirms that the results are overwhelmingly consistent with the expectation that the FCC will be more aggressive in using its veto powers in environments that are more likely to be transparent. The first two variables (oral arguments and the number of briefs filed) both have the expected sign, and the coefficient for oral arguments is highly significant. The coefficient for the number of briefs filed, however, does not attain statistical significance. In part, this may be due to collinearity between this variable and the variable indicating whether the court enjoys outside political support for an annulment ($r = .64$; the highest correlation between any other two variables is $r = .31$). Excluding the variable indicating outside support from Model 1 reveals that the number of briefs becomes highly significant ($p < .01$), while the coefficients of all other variables retain their levels of significance and approximate size. In other words, the results strongly suggest that the court is less deferential in cases in which public awareness is higher.

The data also provide unambiguous support for the expectation that the court will be more aggressive in the presence of organized outside interests that increase transparency because they have an incentive to call attention to evasion attempts. The coefficient for the variable indicating that an interest group or a government (other than the government in question) has filed a brief asserting that the challenged statute is unconstitutional ("Political Support for Unconstitutionality") is highly significant. Similarly, the court is more likely to make use of its veto powers in policy areas that are less complex. In short, the results provide clear support for Hypotheses 1–3. The FCC appears to be systematically more likely to annul a statute in political environments that are more likely to be transparent.

The variables used to measure the preferences of the government whose legislation is under review produce more ambiguous results. The variable indicating that the government concerned has filed a brief in opposition

---

[6] The results reported are also robust to excluding controls for the Second Senate and for federal laws. Excluding these variables does not change the significance level of the other variables, nor does it affect the size of coefficients in a meaningful way.

to the statute is significant and has the expected sign. However, the decision to file a brief in support of a statute appears to have no statistically discernible effect on the likelihood of an annulment.[7] Thus, support for Hypothesis 4 is much more mixed than the results indicating the impact of transparency. Interestingly, the two control variables indicating federal laws and decisions made by the Second Senate are statistically indistinguishable from 0. Thus, it does not appear that there are systematic differences in behavior between the First Senate and the Second Senate despite differences in personnel and jurisdiction. Moreover, based on this evidence, federal and state laws appear to receive equal treatment at the hands of the court. Table 4.3 reveals that Model 1 yields considerable improvements in prediction over a null model. Compared to the prediction of the modal category as a baseline, the model reduces error by about 28 percent.

CONTROLLING FOR THE LEGAL ENVIRONMENT

Although the results so far are encouraging, there is an important complicating factor that we need to explore. The model presented in Chapter 2, and the hypotheses that we have derived from the model and are testing here, focus on the impact of the court's political environment (specifically, the transparency of the environment). This focus on the political influences on judicial decision making does not imply that legal or constitutional influences are irrelevant (in the model in Chapter 2, such considerations are part of the preferences of the players; that is, a court that has genuine constitutional objections to a law is a hostile court and derives disutility from seeing a statute implemented).

The possibility that the legal or constitutional features of a case are relevant to the court's decision is significant because it raises a potential question about one of the central findings. The results indicate that the FCC is more likely to rule against a statute when an interest group or an outside government files a brief in opposition to a challenged statute. This result is consistent with the argument that outside support increases transparency and thus provides support for Hypothesis 2. But there is also an alternative hypothesis that could explain the finding. When it is

---

[7] One possible explanation for this finding is that a government's decision to file a brief may be endogenous to its expectations about the outcome of the case, leading it to file such briefs overwhelmingly in cases it expects to lose. Unfortunately, this possibility cannot be investigated given the current data.

Table 4.3 *Results of Logit Regression*

Variable	Model 1		Model 2		Model 3	
Oral arguments held	0.963	**	0.979	**	0.962	**
	(0.39)		(0.40)		(0.40)	
Number of briefs filed	0.002		0.002		−0.001	
	(0.06)		(0.06)		(0.06)	
Political support for	1.582	***	1.588	***	1.576	***
unconstitutionality	(0.40)		(0.40)		(0.40)	
Judicial support for			0.065			
unconstitutionality			(0.28)			
High court support for					0.484	
unconstitutionality					(0.51)	
Complex policy area	−0.505	*	−0.511	*	−0.532	*
	(0.29)		(0.29)		(0.30)	
Affected govt. claims	0.556		0.556		0.520	
constitutionality	(0.40)		(0.40)		(0.40)	
Affected govt. claims	1.389	*	1.382	*	1.23	
unconstitutionality	(0.80)		(0.80)		(0.82)	
Federal law	−0.303		−0.304		−0.305	
	(0.33)		(0.33)		(0.33)	
Second Senate	−0.075		−0.069		−0.089	
	(0.31)		(0.31)		(0.31)	
Constant	−1.344	**	−1.383	**	−1.322	**
	(0.52)		(0.59)		(0.52)	
Number of cases	329		329		329	
Percent correct	77.51%		77.81%		77.81%	
Reduction of error	28.14%		28.65%		28.65%	
−2 log likelihood	343		342.9		341.8	

Note: ***significant at $p < .01$, **significant at $p < .05$, *significant at $p < .10$ (one-tailed test). Robust standard errors appear in parentheses.
The dependent variable is the decision of the court (coded 0 if constitutional, 1 if not).

plausible that a statute conflicts with legal or constitutional requirements, it is probably more likely that there will be an interest group or a government filing a brief to say so. In other words, the fact that an outside group has filed a brief challenging a statute may be a function of the underlying legal situation. Thus, the fact that the court is more likely to annul a statute under these circumstances may not necessarily be the result of the outside political support such a group offers, but may simply be a function of the fact that the statute actually conflicts with constitutional requirements. Can we rule out this alternative explanation?

In Models 2 and 3, I present two alternative ways to try to rule out this alternative explanation by controlling for the legal environment in which the court is acting. Both models rely on the same underlying logic. The rules of procedure of the FCC (Paragraph 22(4)) allow the court to request legal briefs by the highest federal and state courts on the legal and constitutional issues that confront the court in a given case. The court makes use of this right frequently, requesting such briefs in 115 of the 329 cases in the dataset. Moreover, in cases of concrete judicial review, in which a lower court refers a statute to the FCC, the lower court must file a detailed brief to explain why it believes a statute to be unconstitutional.

These lower court briefs provide a convenient way to control for the legal environment surrounding a case. Interest groups and governments are likely to be motivated primarily by the partisan political issues involved in a case. Lower court judges, on the other hand, presumably have lower political stakes in the outcome of a particular case. Moreover, they are trained lawyers familiar with constitutional requirements and reasoning and with the FCC's jurisprudence. As a result, one would expect that the tenor of a brief filed by a lower court would provide a more accurate assessment of the objective legal situation confronting the court than a brief filed by political actors like interest groups or governments.

Model 2 applies this logic by including a control variable ("Judicial Support for Unconstitutionality") that is coded 1 if any lower court (including the highest federal and state courts, but also ordinary lower courts that refer a statute) has filed a brief asserting that the challenged statute is unconstitutional. Importantly, the variable turns out to be statistically insignificant. More importantly, the parameter estimates of all the other variables, including the indicator of outside political support, are robust to the inclusion of this control. Levels of statistical significance do not change, and the size of other coefficients changes only marginally. In Model 3, I refine the control variable. One possibility is that ordinary lower courts are simply not particularly good at judging the constitutional issues confronting the FCC. What if we restrict our attention to the opinions of the highest federal and state courts that are requested by the FCC? In Model 3, I include a control variable ("High Court Support for Unconstitutionality") that is coded 1 if one of these highest courts files a brief asserting that the challenged statute is unconstitutional. Once again, the results are unambiguous. All other variables are robust to the inclusion of this variable. In particular, the presence of outside political support continues to exert a highly significant impact on the likelihood of an annulment even when we control for the legal environment. In short, the results strongly suggest that it is the fact that organized political interests raise the level of transparency that exercises a powerful influence over the court's decision-making process and increases the likelihood of an annulment.

SUBSTANTIVE IMPACT

The results provide strong support for the hypothesis that factors that increase the transparency of the political environment surrounding a decision will raise the aggressiveness with which the FCC exercises its veto powers. However, given the nature of logit coefficients, the *substantive* impact of transparency on judicial deference is difficult to interpret by inspection. The estimated coefficients do not *directly* report the effect of the variable on the likelihood that the court will declare a statute unconstitutional. Moreover, since the logit model is nonlinear, the substantive impact of each variable also depends on the values of the other independent variables. One convenient way to address these problems and to illustrate the substantive impact of the independent variables is to use the estimated model to calculate *predicted* probabilities of an unconstitutionality ruling under different scenarios. These predicted probabilities can then be used to gauge the substantive impact of a variable. For example, how much more likely is the court to rule against the constitutionality of a statute if it enjoys outside political support? How does this impact vary across cases that are complex and noncomplex? Figures 4.1 and 4.2 illustrate the impact of the three main variables that were designed to measure the impact of the transparency surrounding a case: oral arguments, outside political support, and complexity.[8]

Figure 4.1 shows how the complexity of the issue area and the presence of outside political support for an unconstitutionality ruling affect the predicted probability of an annulment in cases in which oral arguments are held. As the figure shows, the impact of both conditions is substantively significant and particularly dramatic for outside political support. In the environment that is least likely to be transparent – a case in a complex issue area in which the court has no outside political support – the predicted probability of an unconstitutionality ruling is a mere .36. As we move to the most transparent environment – a noncomplex issue with outside support for an annulment – the predicted probability more than doubles

---

[8] To create the graphs, it is necessary to establish a reasonable baseline probability from which the impact of the other variables can be evaluated. Here I have set variables that are not being manipulated at their median. Alternatively, all other variables could be held at their mean. Doing so produces essentially the same results.

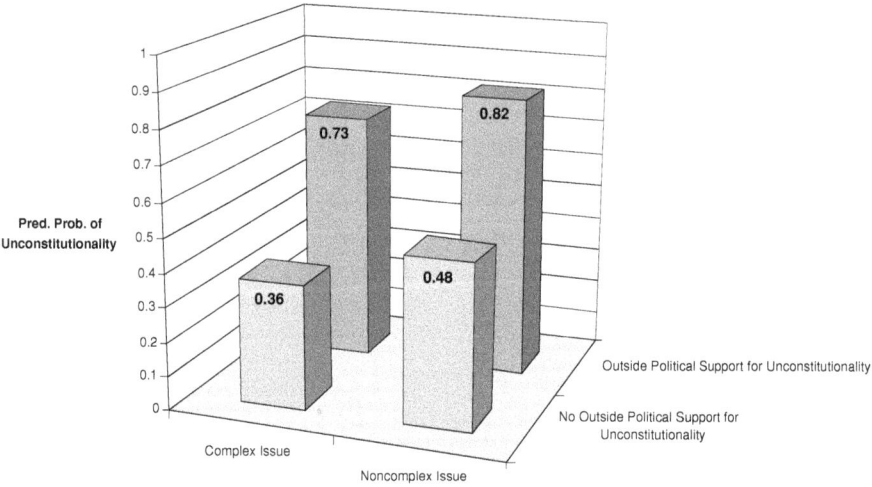

Figure 4.1. Impact of Outside Political Support and Complexity (Oral Arguments Held).

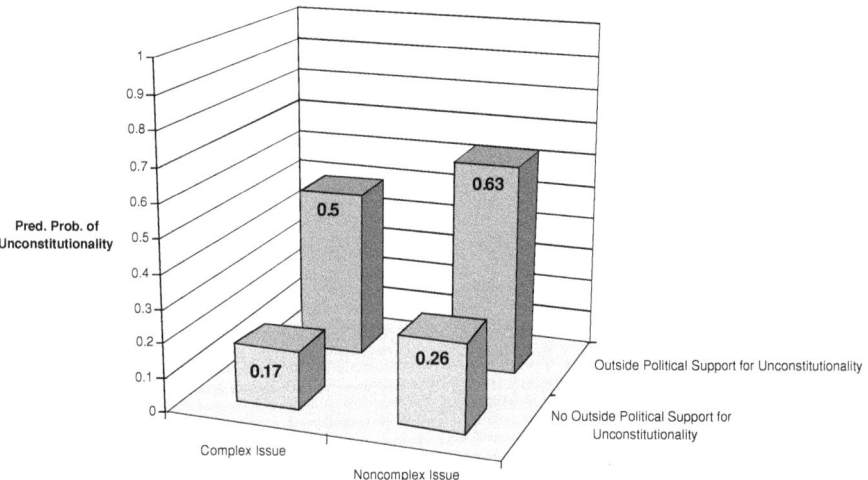

Figure 4.2. Predicted Impact of Outside Support and Complexity (No Oral Arguments Held).

to .82. More generally, the court is approximately more than 20 percent more likely to veto legislation involving a noncomplex issue than a complex issue. The impact of outside political support is even more pronounced. When an outside interest group or government files a brief in support of an annulment, the court is more than 85 percent more likely to veto the statute than when such outside political support is not present,

Conclusion

In Figure 4.2, the same impacts are illustrated for cases in which the court does not hold oral arguments. The figure reveals the same pattern: Cases that occur in a more transparent environment are much more likely to result in an annulment than cases that occur in a nontransparent environment. Looking at the two figures, we can also see that the proxy variable we have employed for public awareness of a decision (oral arguments) has a significant impact on the predicted probability of a judicial veto. In cases in which the court holds oral arguments, the court is, on average, about 70 percent more likely to annul a statute than in cases in which no oral arguments are held.

In short, the data strongly support Hypotheses 1–3, which capture the impact of transparency on the court's level of judicial deference. The court is substantively much more likely to make use of its powers when the environment in which it is acting is transparent. Even when controlling for the legal environment, the FCC is much more likely to veto a statute when public awareness of a case is high, when a noncomplex issue area is involved, or when the court has outside political support.

CONCLUSION

Perhaps the most important implication of the theoretical argument presented in Chapter 2 is that the level of judicial deference and the effectiveness of a constitutional court depend on the court's political environment, specifically on public support and transparency. In this chapter, we have tested this implication. Given the high degree of public support for the FCC, this test has focused on the impact of transparency. A systematic analysis of more than 300 decisions by the FCC on the constitutionality of federal and state laws has produced unambiguous support for the argument. When we control for the legal environment of a decision, political factors that decrease transparency – lack of public awareness, lack of outside political support, and complexity of the issue involved – significantly reduce the likelihood that the FCC will annul a statute.

While these results provide support for the argument, they also invite additional investigation. The dependent variable classifies cases according to the decision of the court as either constitutional or unconstitutional. While this measure is tied directly to the model presented in Chapter 2 and provides a reasonable approach to measuring judicial deference, it is a relatively blunt instrument. For many decisions, mere categorization of unconstitutionality or constitutionality does not capture more subtle but crucial aspects that are likely to be of significance for the legislative reaction to a case. Such details may involve a variety of dimensions. How significant is the law under review in terms of its impact on the budget, the political capital the government has riding on it, and broader consequences? If it is not a complete annulment, which part of the law was thrown out? Is it a minor detail or a major provision?[9] How narrowly is the decision written? Finally, what principles are being established in the decision, and how important are these principles likely to be in the future? A few examples can illustrate the point.

In September 1992, the Second Senate issued a seminal decision dealing with the size of standard tax deductions for natural persons (BVerfGE 87,153). A long-established principle of taxation in Germany, going back to the origins of German income taxation in the nineteenth century, holds that only disposable income may be taxed. Specifically, the minimum amount necessary for subsistence (*Existenzminimum*) must be left tax-free (see also BVerfGE 61, 319). The question facing the court in this case was whether the standard tax deductions in effect after 1978 had been sufficiently large to meet this standard. This was especially questionable in light of the fact that the average level of welfare benefits provided by the *Länder* (an implicit measure of the *Existenzminimum*) exceeded the deductions. The senate ruled that the provisions of the tax code limiting the deductions to an amount below the average welfare payment were indeed unconstitutional. However, the Second Senate wrote the decision in such a way as to severely qualify the immediate impact of the decision, thereby making it considerably easier for the federal government to swallow. It ruled that the decision would not be retroactive, that is, that tax assessments that had been made on the basis of the unconstitutional limits would not be revised, and that citizens were not entitled to refunds, even if they could still legally contest their tax assessments (BVerfGE 87:178ff.). Moreover, the court ruled that the unconstitutional provisions could continue to be applied for up to three years until the legislature had passed a revision. It is clear that these two concessions changed the impact of the decision on the government (and particularly on the budget) in significant ways that are not captured by the simple classification unconstitutional.

A second example comes from the FCC's party-finance jurisprudence. In 1986, the Second Senate ruled on the constitutionality of a new

---

[9] This is particularly important because complete annulments of laws are extremely rare. This is true not only for the FCC but seems to hold more generally as well. For example, the French Constitutional Council also tends to invalidate parts of bills rather than an entire statute (Stone 1992).

Conclusion

party-finance law that had been passed in 1983 (BVerfGE 73,40). Although the senate sustained the bulk of the law, it declared unconstitutional a provision that allowed tax-free donations to political parties up to specified percentages of annual income. The basis of the decision was that such a scheme would privilege the wealthy and therefore violate the guarantee of equal political influence for all citizens. However, the court also ruled that a fixed upper limit on tax-free donations as high as DM 100,000 – a huge sum – would be constitutional. This concession essentially eliminated any impact that the annulment of the percentage clause might have had. Although this case shows up as an unconstitutional ruling in the data set, it is clear that its substantive impact was largely mitigated by other aspects of the decision.

This discussion suggests a conclusion. The statistical evidence presented in this chapter provides clear and considerable support for the theory. Transparency appears to play a systematic and sustained role in the decision making of the FCC, and we can trace its implications as patterns in the aggregate decisions of the court over time. However, as the examples suggest, the impact of judicial decisions may turn not only on whether a statute is sustained or annulled, but also on details that are not easily quantified. It would therefore be desirable to supplement the statistical analysis with qualitative evidence that will allow a more detailed and context-sensitive examination of the decision-making process of the FCC and of the deliberations of legislators in reacting to judicial rulings. This is the task to which I turn in the next two chapters.

5

From the Inside Looking out

Judicial and Legislative Perceptions

In the previous chapter, I provided systematic statistical support for a central implication of the theory presented in Chapter 2. This implication focuses on the fact that if the potential to lose public support for evasion represents a key enforcement mechanism for judicial decisions, the Bundesverfassungsgericht will be more aggressive in using its veto powers the more transparent its political environment is. The evidence was overwhelmingly consistent with this prediction. The court is considerably more likely to annul legislation when public awareness of a case is high, when the court enjoys outside political support for an annulment, and when the issue involved is noncomplex and easy to police. Although critical, this relationship between transparency and judicial deference constitutes only on aspect of the theoretical argument. In this chapter, we explore other implications of the theory. Before I outline these implications, a few remarks about the approach taken in this chapter are useful.

Methodologically, we change tracks in this chapter. Instead of analyzing data statistically, we will consider qualitative evidence – specifically, interviews with judges of the FCC and members of the Bundestag. What makes such qualitative evidence particularly relevant? Rational choice theories (like the one presented here) posit that actors are conscious decision makers who act in ways that they believe will maximize their welfare as they perceive it. In other words, the *subjective perceptions* of the actors whose behavior is being explained constitute a crucial ingredient in rational choice approaches. In modeling an interaction, we are therefore concerned to capture the most salient features that actors believe are relevant. That is, as a noted game theorist has put it, a formal model is "an abstract summary of the players' actual perceptions of the complicated situations they are in" (Rubinstein 1991:917). As a result, assessing how

Judicial and Legislative Perceptions

well a model maps up to the "players' actual perceptions" is one way to evaluate the adequacy of a rational choice explanation.

A closely related reason for considering qualitative evidence consists of the central role played by *anticipatory reactions* in rational choice arguments. Rational choice explanations focus on strategic interdependence. Because the outcome of an interaction depends on the joint behavior of multiple actors, each actor attempts to anticipate what other actors may do and adjusts her own strategy in light of these expectations. As a result, the expectations that actors have about what would happen if they chose to do something other than what they do are essential to understanding how they act. Using more technical language, "off-equilibrium path behavior" is significant to sustaining equilibrium path actions. For example, the expectation that a decision to annul a particular statute may be ignored by the legislature may persuade judges to uphold the statute despite their preference for vetoing it. Because counterfactuals that reside in the minds of the actors but are never realized are so significant for rational choice theories, evidence that allows us to understand the subjective perceptions and beliefs of actors is especially relevant.

This chapter focuses on three central features and implications of the model that are tied very closely to the subjective perceptions of judges and legislators and can therefore be explored usefully using qualitative evidence:

1. In the model, the potential for losing public support for evasion acts as the enforcement mechanism for the Bundesverfassungsgericht. Is the threat of a public backlash a primary motivating factor for legislators in the real world? Do judges believe that the support they enjoy is crucial to their authority?

2. The formal model treats public support as an exogenous parameter, but a natural extension of the argument, presented at the end of Chapter 2, implies that judges will be concerned to maintain public support and that this concern influences the court's decisions. Do judges worry about maintaining support? And do anticipations of how decisions may affect support have an impact on their deliberations?

3. The formal model implies that the costs to legislative majorities of complying with a ruling impact the actions of judges and legislators. As the political costs of compliance increase, legislative majorities are more likely to resist. Anticipation of resistance by judges implies that as political costs increase, judges become more deferential in their treatment of legislation. Do legislators consider the political costs of compliance

Judicial and Legislative Perceptions

when deciding how to react to a decision? Do judges anticipate legislative reactions, and are they more deferential when the costs of compliance for legislative majorities are high?

In this chapter, we will explore these three aspects of the argument. The chapter is based on one-on-one interviews with three law clerks, ten judges of the Bundesverfassungsgericht, and eight key members of the Bundestag. Among the legislators interviewed were a deputy faction chair of the main government faction (CDU/CSU), the chair and vice-chair of the judiciary committee, the chair of the domestic policy committee, and a former minister of justice who served in the government of Helmut Kohl between 1992 and 1996. Because these legislators are directly involved in the crucial stages of the policymaking process, they are particularly relevant for understanding how legislative majorities respond to judicial rulings.

The internal deliberations of the FCC and, to a large extent, of the Bundestag are closed to outside observance (thus, party faction meetings and even parliamentary committee meetings are usually closed to the public). To allow judges and legislators to discuss their experiences openly and candidly, I agreed to use quotations only in ways that would prevent identification of particular persons. All quotations are therefore assigned to "a judge of the constitutional court" or "a clerk" or "a member of the Bundestag." To allow the reader to follow respondents across quotations, each interviewee has been assigned a number. For example, quotations from J1 ("Judge 1") belong to the same judge throughout the text. Since the majority of my interviewees were male, I use the pronoun "he" regardless of the gender of the quoted source to protect anonymity.

An important issue in elite interviewing concerns the question of whether interviews should be tape-recorded. I suspected that a running recorder would put judges and legislators on their guard. Like H. W. Perry in his seminal project on the certiorari process of the U.S. Supreme Court, I therefore decided not to record the interviews.[1] Instead, I took notes and wrote an extended summary immediately following each interview. The average duration of an interview was forty-five minutes to one hour. Like Perry, who followed the same procedure, I soon discovered that with a little practice, one becomes proficient at remembering important

---

[1] Several judges and legislators insisted that conversations not be taped when I approached them about interviews. Others expressed relief during the interviews that "you are not like one of those reporters who always have to tape everything."

quotations verbatim. Therefore, I treat the statements as direct quotations. As Perry puts it, "there may be a misplaced 'and' or 'the,' but the important words are the informant's own" (1991:10).[2]

PUBLIC SUPPORT AND JUDICIAL AUTHORITY

The model posits that the threat of a backlash against governing majorities that choose not to comply with a judicial decision is a driving force that lends authority to decisions of the FCC. Do legislators and judges accord as much importance to public support? In Chapter 3, we briefly reviewed an episode that suggests that at least during the court's early development, broad public support was an important resource for the court. During the confrontation that developed between the court and the Adenauer administration over the court's pending decision on the constitutionality of a German contribution to the European Defense Community in late 1952, the Adenauer government considered various attacks on the institutional integrity of the court in order to influence its deliberations. Only the perception of overwhelming public opposition to the government's actions persuaded Adenauer to abandon these plans.

In the previous chapter (see Tables 4.1 and 4.2) we saw that the FCC continues to enjoy tremendous support among German citizens and that its support exceeds that of any other public institution. Donald Kommers has argued that this support is crucial because "today, politicians would risk their reputations by tampering with [the FCC's] authority or independence" (1994:486). The interviews strongly suggest that the overwhelming number of judges shares this assessment. They perceive the court's support as a shield that protects the institutional integrity of the FCC against governing majorities. As two judges put it in responses that are typical:

The court has such authority in the public mind that no politician could afford to threaten its independence. (J10,4)

At the moment, things are so settled that it would be difficult to make any changes...the support of the press has provided the court with a great cover

---

[2] The names and positions of all those interviewed are listed in Appendix A. The questionnaires, which consisted exclusively of open-ended questions, are reprinted in Appendix B. For each quotation, the number following the respondent ID identifies the question to which the response refers. For example, (J6,5) indicates that the quotation comes from judge 6 in response to question 5. Where no question is indicated, the remark was made in general conversation.

in public opinion. Anyone who wants to shake up the FCC has to expect a storm of protest. (J2,4)

Interestingly, the second judge focuses on not only the importance of public support, but also the mechanism by which this support is activated: potential media coverage. Public support may function as a "latent" resource that can be brought to bear through media influence (as in the controversy surrounding the European Defense Community).

But is respect for the court's formal independence sufficient? The linchpin of the theoretical model presented in Chapter 2 is that respect for the institutional integrity of a court is not equivalent to respect for its *decisions*. While open attacks on the court's structure may not be politically feasible, governing majorities may evade decisions while leaving the structure of the court untouched. One judge immediately seized on this issue when asked about threats to the court's institutional integrity:

I don't think there is much of a threat to the institutional framework. That's been settled in a manner that is satisfactory for everyone. Another question is how the court can maintain its position and get respect from the legislature and the other courts. That is something that is tricky... sometimes the legislature just doesn't act on the decisions, and the court has no troops to enforce them. (J8,4)

While the distinction between respecting the formal institutional structure of a court and faithfully implementing the court's decisions is central to the argument, the same underlying mechanism can solve both problems: the threat of a public backlash against legislative majorities that choose to challenge a court in either manner. The interviews reveal that the judges agree that support is vital to their authority in particular cases. The general consensus among the judges appears to be that decisions are respected when there is sufficient public support for the court and politicians must fear a loss in public support for noncompliance. When asked about the consistently high level of public support for the court and whether this support mattered, several judges responded:

The court has no enforcement power, so it is dependent on the loyalty of the legislature and the government. In part that depends on political culture, of course, but it also depends on the esteem that the court enjoys in public opinion and among citizens. In the final analysis it has to be the case that no one can afford to circumvent the court or to ignore it. (J1,5)

The public trust is incredibly important. That's something I think about every day. The court doesn't have any enforcement power, no army and no police force, thank God. It only has its authority, in the end nothing but the authority to write on a piece of paper. There has to be a certain commitment to the constitutional order among the public without which the court cannot function. (J6,5)

It is crucial that public opinion is behind the court so that politicians can't afford to ignore the decisions. (J10,5)

In short, the emphasis that the model places on public support as an enforcement mechanism for judicial decisions appears to square well with how judges think about what lends authority to their decisions. What about the other institution in this interaction? Do members of the Bundestag consider public support and the potential for a backlash as crucial factors in explaining how legislative majorities choose whether to comply?

As in the case of the judges, the answers left little doubt. When asked about factors that influence how the Bundestag approaches FCC decisions, the legislators I interviewed all focused on the importance of public opinion. Politicians seem to be acutely aware of the public's esteem for the court. They are also aware that the court enjoys higher *relative* support in the public mind than the Bundestag. As a result, legislators believe that a public confrontation with the court would be costly electorally. Consider a few typical responses:

One just can't ignore that the court... enjoys tremendous trust among the general public. In a confrontation, the broad public would stand behind the court. (MdB2,7)

There is not a single deputy here who thinks it would be advisable to move against the court. A serious confrontation would just create a public discussion in which one could easily get a bloody nose. (MdB4,7)

No other institution has as much trust in the population. Recently that has been disturbed a little [referring to the *Crucifix* and *Soldier* verdicts], but the FCC still enjoys tremendous public esteem. Anyone who would try to brush aside the court or to limit its competencies would have enormous problems. (MdB7,7)

Of course, public opinion is also important. In a case of conscious and willful disobedience the public would take the side of the court. The public trust in the court is higher than that in the Bundestag.... In any serious confrontation, the public would rally around the court, provided the court doesn't ruin its esteem through decisions that the public no longer understands. (MdB1,6)

The last two quotations raise a subtle and fascinating issue. As I argued in Chapter 2, the centrality of public support is a double-edged sword. On the one hand, it can furnish a powerful enforcement mechanism for judicial decisions. On the other hand, it may impose a significant constraint on judicial behavior. The need to retain sufficient public support places boundaries on the judges' freedom to act and may influence their deliberations and decisions. Before we explore this issue in more detail in the next section, however, there is another aspect of public support as an enforcement mechanism that we need to consider.

A central implication of the theory is that while public support can provide a powerful enforcement mechanism for judicial decisions, this mechanism also has a flip side that limits judicial power. If there is little public support for a decision or if the environment surrounding a decision is such that evasion is unlikely to become widespread public knowledge (i.e., if transparency is low), the threat of a public backlash diminishes and the court's position vis-à-vis legislative majorities is weakened. One judge immediately seized on this flip side in discussing cases that generate little public interest:

> You know, the court has issued many decisions that were never complied with, for example about the treatment of civil servant pensions. And there really isn't anything the court can do about that. If no one else takes an interest in it, that's just the way it is going to be. And of course the court has to be worried about that, that a tradition of ignoring the court isn't established.... The civil servant [taxation] decision is now more than fifteen years old and clearly should have been complied with by now. (J4)

It is useful to consider the decision that concerned the judge in a little more detail. It was issued in 1980 and dealt with the taxation of civil servant pensions (BVerfGE 54, 11). Traditionally, civil servants in Germany do not participate in the general state-mandated retirement insurance plan. Instead, they are paid a pension after retirement. Because these pensions are not based on direct employee contributions, they are subjected to full income taxation. Regular retirement benefits, in contrast, derive in part from employee contributions and, as a result, are only partially taxed. The percentage subject to taxation was fixed in the 1950s. Since then, increases in life expectancy and in the level of retirement benefits have substantially increased the proportion of benefits paid beyond an individual's contribution. Nevertheless, the taxed percentage of benefits has remained constant.

During the 1970s, several civil servants brought constitutional complaints against this arrangement. They argued that full taxation of their pension benefits constituted a violation of the equal treatment clause (Article 3 of the Basic Law) since ordinary retirement benefits were subject to limited taxation even though, in practice, these benefits (like pensions) did not derive primarily from taxed employee contributions. The court's ruling is a classic example of judicial restraint. Issuing an admonitory decision, the court rejected the complaints of the civil servants, arguing that for the fiscal years during which the contested taxes were assessed (1969–70), the differential treatment of retirement benefits and pensions was not sufficiently severe to constitute a constitutional violation. At the same time, the court stated:

> A constitutional analysis of the extent of the privileged tax status of retirees vis-à-vis retired civil servants must conclude that due to changes in circumstances, this privilege has now reached proportions that make a correction necessary...the legislature is therefore obliged to take steps towards a correction. (BVerfGE 54, 34ff.)

The court explicitly declined to give instructions on how such a correction should proceed (i.e., whether retirement benefits should be subjected to increased taxation or whether taxes on pensions should be reduced). Although the federal government convened a commission to advise the government and the Bundestag on possible revisions, the tax code was not changed. After a decade of delay, civil servants filed a second constitutional complaint claiming that the Bundestag had failed to comply with the decision. In 1992, the court dismissed the new challenge with the explanation that "legislative delay" was not "unreasonable" given the "complexity" of the issue (BVerfGE 86,369).[3] By 2003, the retirement system still had not been revised.

The quotation from judge 4 clearly suggests that for the judge, the fact that "no one else takes an interest in it" goes a long way toward explaining why the Bundestag has so far chosen not to act on the court's demand for a revision of the tax code. But do members of the Bundestag share this assessment? The interviews strongly suggest that legislators also perceive little public interest in and support for implementing this particular decision, and that this lack of public interest is largely responsible for their failure to act:

> No one is interested in civil servants anyway. Citizens generally think that civil servants are too well off already. There aren't very many people who are going to be upset if that decision is ignored. (MdB8,6)

Talking about the same decision, another deputy used even stronger language, noting that the public was not only unconcerned about this issue,

---

[3] The decision by the court to dismiss the renewed challenge may well provide an instance of the "legislative supremacy equilibrium." Expecting continued defiance, it is plausible that the court chose to dismiss the challenge in strategic anticipation of the government's likely reaction.

but that crucial constituencies were worried about what would happen if the Bundestag complied:

> The taxation of retirement benefits is politically unpopular anyway. It would be very hard to get across to the average retired person that they would have nothing to fear from that.... It's just hard to explain that the normal retiree would have nothing to fear. But of course those are all extra-judicial considerations. But nobody wants to touch that. That's just going to make trouble. (MdB3,7)

In other words, the interviews strongly suggest that members of the Bundestag are acutely aware of the degree of support for the court and that this support explains their willingness to comply with decisions. But the interviews also reveal the other side of the coin: When public support or interest is low and there is little threat of losing support, legislators feel much less constrained by judicial rulings. The fact that "no one is interested in civil servants anyway" explains (at least in part) why legislators have felt little pressure to comply with this decision. Another judge echoed this same sentiment in stressing that, given the level of public support for the court as an institution, evasion of decisions occurs only when public interest in a specific decision is low:

> [To ignore a decision], that can only be done in secret. If that were to happen with a decision in which the public takes an interest, there would be an outcry by the press and the public. That just wouldn't be sustainable. That only works when things are at stake that don't really interest the public. (J5,6)

In summary, the interviews with legislators and judges leave little doubt about the centrality of public support to the authority of the FCC. Judges clearly believe that public support for the court provides a shield against potential threats to the institutional framework of the court and also generates pressure for compliance with judicial decisions. Similarly, legislators are candid about the fact that the potential for a public backlash is a primary motivating factor in complying with FCC decisions. When a decision – such as the civil servant taxation decision – generates little public interest, legislators are much more readily persuaded to resist the court. In other words, the subjective perceptions of the actors about the decisive role of public support for judicial authority strongly support the theoretical argument.

PUBLIC SUPPORT AS CONSTRAINT ON JUDICIAL BEHAVIOR

The formal model presented in Chapter 2 treats public support as an exogenous parameter. At the end of Chapter 2 I extended the logic of the model, arguing that if public support is vital to judicial influence, the dynamics of support may affect how judges do their work. If judges believe (and, as the previous section shows, the interviews strongly suggest that they do) that public support is crucial to their influence, a concern for maintaining or building such support may have an impact on their behavior. Considerable research on the foundations of public support (see the extended discussion in Chapter 2) suggests that two factors are particularly important in driving support for courts and thus are most likely to attract judicial attention:

1. Public support for courts depends on the perception that a court is an impartial, apolitical actor.
2. In the long run, public support for courts depends on satisfaction with the specific decisions of the court. A court that consistently rules against prevailing public attitudes undermines its support.

Among the judges interviewed, these two views of the source of public esteem for the court predominated. When asked about the origins of public esteem, several judges insisted that public trust is maintained and enhanced by an impartial approach to cases. In this view, the court must be perceived to be acting on principle, and cannot be suspected of following public opinion or the wishes of particular political parties too closely:

It's good to have a certain "line of credit" in public opinion, but that is not something that one can consciously be on the lookout for. It's part of our job to be unpopular, and we can afford to be. If one just echoes majority views, one only destroys the court's legitimacy in the long run. (J9,5)

Similarly, other judges replied:

I think that the impartial fulfillment of the court's task is most important. If you look too quickly at how others are going to react, you'll just hurt yourself in the long run... the loser must be able to say: That wasn't a political decision, I can understand this... to look too closely at the public mood doesn't get you very far. The court cannot just be another player in the game. That would endanger the esteem it enjoys. It must be outside the political process and define its boundaries; it cannot get involved in the process itself. (J1,5)

We're dependent on enjoying the public's trust. I think that the court generates such trust by being incorruptible and impartial. A parliament or the army, they can get away with a black sheep. But if we have only one corrupt judge, the court is finished. We have to be an example of integrity. (J5,5)

Judicial and Legislative Perceptions

For other judges, the second dimension of public support – sensitivity to public opinion – came to the fore. While these judges usually acknowledged the importance of principled, impartial decision making, they expressed the belief that judges need to be sensitive to public opinion more directly and that a concern for public attitudes plays a role in judicial deliberations. For many of these judges, the particular experiences of the *Soldier* and *Crucifix* decisions, which generated massive and widespread opposition, seem to have driven home the conviction that the court is constrained by prevailing attitudes:

Without public trust, the court can't do its job...that plays a role in deliberations...you have to think pretty carefully before making a decision that you know is going to meet great resistance from the population. On the other hand, one can't look directly at opinion polls. (J4,5)

Of course that doesn't mean that you follow public opinion or pay homage to the spirit of the times, but there has to be a certain sensitivity for the capacity of the public to accept decisions. Take for example the *Crucifix* or the *Soldier* verdicts...you just can't do something like that too often...one has to be aware of the fact that current public feelings and standards derive from a tradition, and one has to respect that. (J6,5)

The court has to be careful not to "take off," as one says in modern German. Decisions like the *Crucifix* and *Soldier* verdicts really make you think....One cannot cross the tolerance threshold of the public; otherwise, the court loses its authority. One has to stay within a framework that is understandable for the broad public. (J7,5)

There cannot be a long-running divergence between the views of the public at large and the jurisprudence of the court. The court must be carried by a consensus of the citizens...it's important to take care that a decision does not hit on a weak spot in public consensus...you shouldn't set off an explosion in the San Andreas fault....The *Crucifix* verdict, for example, just completely misread public opinion in Bavaria. Every citizen has certain ideas about what the Basic Law is supposed to guarantee, and you can't depart too far from that. The decisions have to be understandable and acceptable. (J8,6)

In discussing the impact of public attitudes, one judge referred to the court's seminal decisions on abortion policy to illustrate. The Bundesverfassungsgericht first ruled on abortion policy in 1975. In 1974, the SPD–FDP coalition had passed a new abortion statute to liberalize the fairly restrictive West German abortion policy. The new law decriminalized abortion during the first twelve weeks of pregnancy (thus removing the threat of punishment), provided that a woman had undergone abortion counseling. Immediately following passage of the law, the CDU Bundestag faction, together with a number of state governments, initiated an abstract judicial review proceeding arguing that the new law was incompatible with the Basic Law's guarantee of human life in Article 2.

In a landmark decision, the court declared the major provisions of the law unconstitutional and laid down specific instructions for a legislative revision (BVerfGE 39,1). By a vote of 5 to 3, the court's First Senate held that any abortion statute based on time phases, that is, on the stage of the pregnancy, violates the Basic Law. Moreover, the senate ruled that the Basic Law also prohibits the Bundestag from declaring that abortion is legal under certain circumstances. To be constitutional, an abortion statute must specify that all abortions are *in principle* illegal. Exemptions in which abortion is still illegal, though not punishable, can be made for certain "indications," including medical, eugenic, or serious "social" reasons. The ruling, and the "indication solution" it provided, ran directly contrary to the legislative intentions of the governing coalition. Nevertheless, the government passed a new abortion bill conforming to the court's decision. The decision would define West German abortion policy until German unification following the crumbling of the Berlin Wall and the demise of the East German regime in the fall of 1989.

East German policy, which allowed abortion on demand during the first trimester of pregnancy, was completely at odds with the West German provisions. The problem of reconciling this liberal abortion law with the more restrictive Western policy became a major issue that could not be resolved during the negotiations over unification. As is often the case when a seemingly intractable issue threatens to hold up fundamental agreement, a decision was made to postpone discussions over abortion policy: It was agreed that a newly elected Bundestag would resolve the issue following unification. The Bundestag did in fact attempt to tackle this problem expeditiously in an abortion law passed in 1992. The new statute was based on a time-phase solution that combined compulsory abortion counseling with decriminalization of abortion during the first trimester. After undergoing counseling, women would be able to obtain an abortion without fear of punishment after a three-day waiting period. The law thus clearly ran contrary to central principles of the 1975 decision. Again, the statute was referred to the FCC in an abstract review proceeding by 249 CDU deputies and the Bavarian government. The FCC issued its ruling in 1993, declaring important provisions of the new statute unconstitutional (BVerfGE 88,203). Specifically, reaffirming its 1975 decision, the court ruled that any provisions of an abortion statute declaring an abortion "not illegal" (as the new law did for first trimester abortions) would be incompatible with the state's obligation to protect human life.

At least formally, abortions would have to be labeled "illegal" under all circumstances.

However, and more importantly, the court also qualified and revised its 1975 ruling in a crucial respect. The earlier ruling had explicitly demanded criminal sanctions for abortions that do not meet the requirements for the indicated exemptions. In its new decision, the court held that "suspended" punishment for nonindicated abortions following counseling is constitutionally permissible during the first trimester, provided that certain criteria for the counseling process have been met. In practice, this meant that the court had come to accept a time-phase solution, a clear and fundamental shift of ground from the earlier ruling. A new abortion law was passed by the Bundestag in 1995. The legislature largely followed the court's prescriptions, although there are important areas in which the court's demands were essentially disregarded.[4] In order to prevent another abstract judicial review proceeding, the new law was based on a compromise between the major parties that ensured that the law would not be referred to the court in another abstract review proceeding (Vanberg 1998b). One judge (who participated in the decision) explained the court's shift from its position in the 1975 decision with reference to public opinion:

There are significant differences between the 1975 and 1992 decisions. The differences can largely be explained by the desire to find a solution that would be acceptable to everyone.... That was a very conscious effort, we were looking for such a solution. Of course, the court didn't take an opinion poll, but public attitudes did play a role. (J7,5)

Survey data gathered before the 1975 and 1992 decisions, respectively, confirm that the court's judgment was indeed in line with the solution preferred by a plurality of citizens (including women) in each case (Emnid Institut 1992:75; Noelle and Neumann 1974:245).

The fact that judges are sensitive to public opinion has also not gone unnoticed by legislators. One member of the Bundestag seized on another example to make his point. Traditionally, German asylum law, which is rooted in the Basic Law, has provided broad access to asylum for political refugees. Moreover, the FCC has interpreted these provisions expansively.

---

[4] As one member of the Bundestag who participated in drafting the law told me during an interview, "the court had demanded that we provide additional sanctions for relatives that pressure a woman into an abortion. So we included some passages in that law that take care of this pro forma. But we never expected that this would change anything in practice.... It was only formal compliance, and that is what we were aiming for" (MdB3).

In late 1992, the major parties in the Bundestag (the CDU/CSU, SPD, and FDP) agreed to an "asylum compromise" to regulate a considerable influx of asylum seekers. In part to guard against an annulment by the FCC (which appeared a genuine possibility in light of the court's liberal asylum jurisprudence), the compromise was enshrined in the Basic Law as a constitutional amendment. Nevertheless, the constitutionality of the amendment was challenged before the FCC.[5] Faced with overwhelming public support for a restriction of asylum rights and a compromise worked out among all the major parties, the court upheld the constitutionality of the amendment (BVerfGE 94,49). One legislator referred explicitly to this decision and concluded that the judges had been influenced by their political environment:

Judges do have political considerations. In the back of their minds they seem to have the question: What are the political consequences of this decision?... The asylum decision, for example, is one in which I think the court accommodated public opinion. (MdB8,2)

Another member put it even more strongly:

It's a fairy tale to believe that [the judges] only look at the constitution and at previous decisions. They are well aware of the public mood... the public mood is very important for the judges. (MdB3,2)

In summary, the interviews reveal that almost all judges believe that impartiality (and the perception of impartiality) is crucial to the legitimacy of the court. In addition, there is considerable, though not unanimous, agreement among them that prevailing public opinion does set certain boundaries on the freedom of the court to act. As J6 put it, when it comes to ruling against prevailing attitudes, "you just can't do something like that too often." Both requirements can act as constraints on judicial behavior that judges must take into account. Moreover, at least in principle, the two requirements may clash. The need to be impartial and consistent may sometimes require taking actions that are highly unpopular, as in the

---

[5] The FCC has (limited) authority to review the constitutionality of constitutional amendments. Article 79(3) of the Basic Law rules out amendments that abolish federalism and the participation of state governments in federal policymaking or that alter the principles asserted by Articles 1 and 20 of the Basic Law (the principle of human dignity and the designation of Germany as a "democratic and social federal state"). The court itself asserted even broader authority to review the constitutionality of constitutional amendments for their consistency with principles of natural law in its early landmark decision in the *Southwest* case (BVerfGE 1,14). See also Hesse (1995:292).

Soldier cases, in which well-established freedom-of-expression jurisprudence clashed with the seeming judicial endorsement of an emotionally laden insult to members of the military. As a result, judges may find themselves in a delicate *political* balancing game (as opposed to *legal* balancing of competing legal claims).[6]

More fundamentally, if public opinion imposes constraints on the court's freedom of action, it also places limits on its countermajoritarian abilities. While the FCC may be able to get away with a *Crucifix* decision once in a while, it is unlikely that it can consistently play the role of "minority protector" without dissipating the public support on which it relies so heavily.[7] Insofar as judges feel the need to respond to prevailing public attitudes, the FCC is a much more political body than is commonly acknowledged – not only because its judges are political appointees, but because the court must live in a strategic environment in which the support it enjoys is crucial. I return to this issue in the concluding chapter.

EVASION AND THE COSTS OF COMPLIANCE

Public support and the threat of a public backlash for failure to comply with a judicial decision comprise one aspect of the calculus faced by legislators under the model presented in Chapter 2. As we saw in the first section, legislators are worried about this potential. But the model also makes a prediction about the impact of a second factor: the costs of compliance. As the costs of complying with a judicial decision grow, legislative majorities will be increasingly willing to resist a ruling and to engage in evasive maneuvers. The model further predicts that this greater willingness to resist leads judges to anticipate the costs of their decisions for legislative majorities and induces them to be more deferential in

---

[6] Of course, such balancing requires judges to recognize that the need to be impartial and the need to be sensitive to prevailing opinions are in conflict. At least in some cases, this may not be the case. As one judge remarked with respect to the *Soldier* decisions: "We thought: 'We have said this a thousand times.' We just didn't recognize that this sentence would provoke a special reaction" (J2,4).

[7] In earlier work, Donald Kommers found considerable support for the proposition that specific decisions of the court find approval among opinion leaders (see 1976:266ff.). Moreover, in the one case for which data are available (Television case BVerfGE 12,205), support for the decision by opinion elites is closely reflected by public support generally. Insofar as Kommers's surveys tap responses to specific decisions post hoc, however, they do not make it clear whether the court convinced elites, and therefore found acceptance, or whether it was sensitive to prevailing opinions when deciding the case in the first place.

cases in which a judicial veto would be particularly costly for governing majorities.

Perhaps the most important general cost of compliance that governing majorities must bear is the budgetary impact of a decision. There are a number of reasons that make financial considerations particularly fundamental. Decisions that demand additional outlays (e.g., by mandating the expansion of a program) or diminish available revenues (e.g., by annulling a tax code provision) threaten the government's budgetary plans. Compliance requires raising funds (via increased taxes or deficit spending) or cutbacks in other areas. Therefore, the budgetary impact creates a direct link between compliance with a decision in one area and the policies that can be pursued in other areas. Moreover, the causal connection between compliance with a decision and the induced adjustments in other policy areas is indirect and affords some discretion to legislative majorities (e.g., where do you cut?). As a result, blaming the adverse consequences of diminished financial maneuver room on the court may prove difficult. (For example, abolishing the death penalty in response to a judicial decision can easily be blamed on the court since the causal connection is relatively clear. Convincing a particular constituency that the government has just cut the group's favorite program against the government's wishes because an unrelated court decision has had a budgetary impact is likely to be a much harder sell.) All of these considerations suggest that compliance with a decision that has significant financial implications is particularly costly.[8]

The model would therefore lead us to expect that legislative majorities are more inclined to avoid compliance with decisions that have large financial implications. The interviews strongly support this expectation. When asked in an open-ended question about considerations that influence the legislative reaction to a decision, all Bundestag deputies targeted the financial impact of a decision (in addition to the impact of public opinion). There was unanimous agreement that a ruling is more likely to be ignored or compliance with it delayed if it imposes considerable additional expenses or leads to a shortfall in revenue. Consider these statements:

First of all, all parties basically agree that the decisions of the FCC must be respected. When that doesn't happen once in a while, it is usually a question of money. Usually, there will be cross-party agreement that we need to find a way of getting around a decision without ignoring it openly or explicitly. (MdB1,6)

---

[8] Adding further to the significance of the financial impact in the German case is the fact that the Basic Law imposes rigid requirements for incurring public debt, which further restricts the German government's financial maneuvering room.

Of course, it is also important whether or not there is public pressure and whether or not it is going to cost money. If it requires a financial outlay, it is postponed. (MdB5,6)

The most important consideration is budgetary. The majority will just say, "We can't afford that or don't want to spend the money on it." (MdB7,6)

The financial aspects are very important. Those [decisions that are not implemented] are mostly cases that would cost a lot of money. And then, of course, there is the question [of] how high public pressure is. (MdB8,6)

Referring specifically to examples of noncompliance in the civil servant taxation case and another decision that mandated additional child-care funding for civil servants with more than two children (BVerfGE 81, 363), two legislators responded:

In those cases, there was a broad consensus in the Bundestag that the fiscal possibilities played a very important role. The financial resources that would be necessary were so large that these decisions were never implemented but only remained on paper. (MdB4,6)

In cases like the taxation of pensions, the financial aspects of the cases are naturally of great importance. Something like that, you try to avoid getting to for as long as possible, especially if the coffers are empty.... Fiat iustitia, pereat mundus or pereat fiscus ["Let justice be done though the world may perish," author's note], you just can't do that. (MdB6,6)

Thus, consistent with the model's implications, the interviews suggest that financial considerations loom large in legislative reactions to judicial decisions.[9] Decisions that require additional financial outlay are more likely to be put off or not to be complied with than those that do not. A key implication of the model is that judges will not be oblivious to this fact. In particular, the model predicts that judges will anticipate such potential evasion and will moderate their decisions in an attempt to reduce the costs imposed on legislative majorities. (Thus, the court upholds legislation that it would like to veto in the legislative supremacy equilibrium precisely because it anticipates evasion.)

---

[9] Judges also seem to believe that the financial costs of compliance play an important role in legislative reactions to decisions. For example, one judge stated with reference to a recent labor law decision: "A new law has now been passed that practically still has all the provisions we struck down last time, only this time they are more carefully hidden. All the professors who looked over the bill said that immediately. That was disobedience with the justification that otherwise they would be short of money" (J5,6).

The interviews strongly suggest that such anticipatory reactions play an important role in judicial deliberations. When asked in open-ended questions about the impact of political considerations on deliberations, virtually all judges and law clerks raised the importance of financial consequences. One clerk put it most bluntly:

When these kinds of cases come up [involving financial questions], the professional politicians tend to talk about how much money things are going to cost, and that intimidates the judges. They are left a little helpless.... (C1)

Most judges also candidly discussed the fact that in cases involving the potential for large financial outlays or shortfalls for the federal government, financial considerations loom large:

Fiat iustitia, pereat mundus – that's not something a constitutional court can afford to practice. How the other branches are going to react to a decision does play a role. Take, for example, the issue of taxing married couples. Millions of DMs depend on that. It's possible to do great harm there, and that's something the court has to avoid. (J4)

Especially in cases that have an impact on the budget, the court goes out of its way to avoid any economic or budgetary turbulence. (J7,3)

The court practices great restraint. You can't just ruin public finances or social insurance with your decisions. But of course, one must also point to injustices.... (J10,3)

You realize that you're not just deciding about a single case but about incredibly large sums of money. We have a lot of respect for the budget authority of the Bundestag. That's an area where we are pretty careful. And most of the time unconstitutionality isn't intentional, it's just carelessness on the part of parliament. Then you really need to ask yourself, is this issue worth constraining the budget powers of the Bundestag for the future?... For example, in the decisions about how to treat the debts of the former East German agricultural collectives, that was always in the backs of our heads. If we had made a different decision there, that would have really burdened public finances. (J5,8)

The last quotation raises a particularly interesting issue. The judge seems to struggle with the impact that financial considerations have on the court's deliberations. Curiously, he attempts to justify the court's deference in cases with financial implications by pointing to the fact that legislators may infringe on constitutional constraints *unintentionally*. But of course, if one were to accept the argument that the constitutionality of a statute depends on the state of mind of legislators when passing the law, a major justification for the entire institution of constitutional review by an independent court would be undercut.

In the formal model presented in Chapter 2, the only method the court could use to avoid a legislative–judicial conflict was to dismiss a case or to rule in favor of the government. In fact, this method does seem to be employed by the FCC, as the statistical evidence in the previous chapter suggests. Similarly, the court's refusal to entertain the renewed challenge to the Bundestag's failure to act on the civil servant taxation decision reviewed in the previous section may be an example. One judge discussed another prominent example in the interviews. During the late 1980s, a number of citizens mounted constitutional challenges against various taxes collected on the basis of real estate and other property. The constitutional violation these citizens alleged was that real estate was, for all practical purposes, subject to reduced taxation vis-à-vis other property because the evaluation of real estate for taxation purposes relied on assessments completed in 1964, adjusted by 40 percent in 1974. As a result of inflation and changes in demand, by the 1980s real estate was severely undervalued compared to other types of property, which were evaluated at market prices. In inheritance cases, for example, the amount of inheritance tax to be paid could depend radically on the form in which the property was inherited, even if its market value was essentially the same. Rather than confront the issue, the First Senate, which was dealing with these cases, dismissed all of them (e.g., BVerfGE 74,182 and BVerfGE 89,329). As one judge who participated in the decisions reported in an interview, these dismissals were directly motivated by considerations of the political costs of ruling in favor of the complainants:

there was one judge involved who was a financial expert. [This judge] told us that if we touched the evaluation business, the entire Federal Republic would end up in hell's kitchen. It would be better not to decide the issue and just let it be. (J4)[10]

Within the confines of the model, a court that wishes to avoid a potential confrontation only has the option of upholding the legislature's action. The statistical evidence and the interviews provide support for the conclusion that the FCC does employ this strategy. But of course, dismissing a complaint is a crude all-or-nothing method. If we extend the logic of the argument, we might expect that in situations in which evasion or a legislative–judicial conflict is a possibility, the court may attempt to pursue other avenues to reduce the costs of its decisions without

[10] In 1995, a taxation case that also touched on the unequal evaluation of property was brought to the Second Senate. In a seminal decision, the Second Senate declared the differential treatment unconstitutional (BVerfGE 93,121).

upholding a challenged statute it wishes to annul. In other words, in the real world, the tools available to the FCC for reducing the costs of its decisions are more likely to comprise a continuum than a dichotomous choice.

In fact, the FCC seems to have developed several techniques that allow the court to have its proverbial cake and eat it, too, that is, to note constitutional violations while reducing the costs of its decisions for legislative majorities. One such tool is to declare a law incompatible with the constitution instead of declaring it void. Importantly, such a ruling does not have retroactive force, and it generally allows the continued application of the statute that has been struck down until a legislative revision has been passed. In essence, the Bundestag is put on notice that it is going to have to address a certain concern, but it is spared the immediate consequences of the decision and is granted a grace period in which to adjust the policy. Especially in taxation decisions, this practice is common (e.g., BVerfGE 87,152; BVerfGE 93,121).

A second tool that can reduce the costs of a decision is the use of "insofar" clauses. In issuing a decision, the court will occasionally declare a statute to be in violation of the constitution insofar as it applies to a particular set of circumstances but not otherwise (Schlaich 1994:221f.). The model would lead us to expect that the court would use both tools to reduce the costs of its decisions to legislative majorities. In a similar vein, scholars of the FCC have speculated that the court consciously employs both tools in politically delicate situations to reduce the impact of decisions (e.g., Kommers 1997:53). My interviews largely confirm this hypothesis. Consider the following remarks by judges:

There are innumerable cases, especially where financial outlays or taxes are concerned, in which one could easily bankrupt the state. The court has found ways to dampen the impact of its decisions in such cases, for example by declaring a law incompatible or setting a deadline for revision... there are always enormous sums involved. There is a tendency to be very careful in those cases. (J8,4)

In my experience, one tries to mitigate the political consequences of decisions.... The incompatibility ruling... [is] a key to achieving this. The court reduces the impact of its decisions by this method. It also uses "insofar" sentences to do this. (J10,3)

As an aside, let me point out that in void and incompatible rulings, the "insofar" clause often plays an important role. It restricts the incompatibility to a certain class of people or situations and thereby reduces the impact of the ruling. A law is then only unconstitutional in a certain type of situation. That limits the impact of a decision. (J4)

There are several ways to deal with the potential for disobedience.... Of course, you try to write decisions in such a way as not to make them retroactive, and you leave the legislature some time to revise the statute. Sometimes you can write in a deadline by which a law has to be revised in order to place greater pressure on the legislature. (J5,6)

While judges employ both techniques in an effort to reduce the political impact of their decisions, they do not view these tools as purely defensive mechanisms. In many cases in which the court allows further application of an unconstitutional statute, it will also provide a deadline for legislative revision. If the deadline is not met, the court usually instructs lower courts to solve cases they confront on a case-by-case basis. Several judges suggested that such deadlines can be used as part of a carrot-and-stick approach. Allowing continued application of a law reduces the costs of a decision for governing majorities and furnishes the legislature with some room to maneuver during a grace period (the carrot). But the deadline for revision increases transparency by establishing a definite date by which a legislative reaction is expected and creates the threat of decentralized lower court action if the deadline is not met (the stick). As a result, the pressure for compliance increases. As several judges reported:

A lot of times, the court has to set a precise deadline for revision or nothing at all will happen. (J8,4)

The potential for disobedience or defiance does play a role, but not necessarily in the defensive sense that one thinks "we have to be careful here" but more in an offensive sense: "We have to write it in such a way that they have no choice but to obey".... We already knew from the pension case that simple demand for legislative revision can be without effect. So we set a deadline for legislative revision and ruled that if the legislature did not act by then, the lower courts would solve the problem on a case-by-case basis.... Most of the time, the legislature is so bothered by the uncertainty of what lower courts might decide that it gets to work. (J2,6)

In fact, several judges were quick to point out that the civil servant pension decision discussed earlier had a blemish: It did not feature a deadline for legislative revision (J2, J6).

To summarize, this section has established several important points. First, legislators consider the political – and especially financial – costs of abiding by FCC decisions, and these costs affect their willingness to comply. As the model predicts, judges anticipate these legislative calculations. They consider the financial consequences of their decisions, and they tend to be more deferential in cases that have large budgetary consequences than in cases that do not. The judges may exhibit such deference by upholding statutes when striking them down would generate substantial costs for a governing majority. They have also developed more subtle tools, including the incompatibility ruling, which allow them to reduce the political costs of their decisions while still noting constitutional violations. These findings are consistent with a central implication of the model, namely, that the cost to legislative majorities of complying with judicial decisions affects the deference and the influence of the FCC.

CONCLUSION

In this chapter, we have considered qualitative evidence for three central aspects of the theory laid out in Chapter 2. Interviews with judges, legislators, and court clerks reveal that the experiences and subjective perceptions of these actors conform well to the model. The model moves public support for the court to the fore in explaining what drives compliance with judicial decisions: The threat of a public backlash against legislative majorities that flout judicial rulings provides the key enforcement mechanism for the court. The interviews with judges and legislators demonstrate that these actors also perceive that such public support plays a vital role in explaining the authority of the FCC. Moreover, the interviews provide strong support for two central implications of the theory. First, a concern for sustaining public support for the court influences judicial deliberations. Most importantly, judges candidly discuss the fact that sensitivity to prevailing public attitudes and opinions has an impact on judicial decision making. Second, we explored the implications of the model for the effect of political costs on compliance. Specifically, the model predicts that legislators will be more willing to evade the court on issues that are politically costly, and that the court will (as a result of anticipating greater legislative opposition) be more deferential on issues that are central to the interests of governing majorities. The interviews again revealed that both implications of the model comport well with the subjective experiences of German judges and legislators.

Together with the statistical evidence presented in the previous chapter, we thus have considerable support for the model. There is strong evidence that the interactions between the FCC and the Bundestag are conditioned by the political environment in which these two institutions interact. In the next chapter, we will consider a case study that illustrates the dynamics of the model in a concrete policy area before returning to a broader discussion of the argument, the evidence, and its implications in the final chapter.

APPENDIX A: AFFILIATIONS OF INTERVIEWEES

Judges, law clerks, and Bundestag deputies were interviewed in various German cities between May 1997 and June 1998. Several judges and law clerks were interviewed twice.

Judges Interviewed (Court Tenure and Senate Affiliation in Parentheses)

Professor Dr. Ernst-Wolfgang Böckenförde (1983–95, Second Senate)
Professor Dr. Thomas Dieterich (1987–94, First Senate)
Professor Dr. Hans Faller (1971–83, First Senate)
Professor Dr. Konrad Hesse (1975–87, First Senate)
Frau Renate Jäger (1994–2006, First Senate)
Professor Dr. Paul Kirchhof (1987–99, Second Senate)
Professor Dr. Hans Hugo Klein (1983–96, Second Senate)
Herr Konrad Kruis (1987–99, Second Senate)
Herr Dr. Jürgen Kühling (1989–2001, First Senate)
Professor Dr. Alfred Söllner (1987–95, First Senate)

Law Clerks Interviewed

Herr Dr. Brede (Judge Jentsch)
Herr Dr. Häußler (Judge Seidl)
Herr Petz (Judge Seidl)

Bundestag Deputies Interviewed (Party Affiliation, Committee Assignment, and Bundestag Tenure in Parentheses)

Herr Horst Eylmann (CDU, Chair of Judiciary Committee, MdB since 1983)
Frau Sabine Leutheusser-Schnarrenberger (FDP, Minister of Justice 1992–6, MdB since 1990)
Herr Dr. Jürgen Meyer (SPD, Member of the Judiciary Committee, MdB since 1990)
Herr Dr. Wilfried Penner (SPD, Chair of the Domestic Policy Committee, MdB since 1972)

Appendix B

Frau Cornelia Schmalz-Jacobsen (FDP, Member of Domestic Policy Committee, MdB since 1990)
Herr Dr. Rupert Scholz (CDU, Senior CDU member of Judicial Selection Committee, Minister of Defense 1988–9, MdB since 1990)
Herr Ludwig Stiegler (SPD, Vice-Chair of Judiciary Committee, Member of Judicial Selection Committee, MdB since 1980)
Frau Ute Vogt (SPD, Member of Domestic Policy Committee, MdB since 1994)

APPENDIX B: BUNDESTAG QUESTIONNAIRE

The following questionnaire was used for the Bundestag interviews. The order of the questions was sometimes changed if a response to a particular question raised issues directly related to a later question and therefore made it desirable to move a question up. Similarly, in some interviews some questions were omitted if the respondent had already answered the question in the context of another response.

1. In the United States, the political question doctrine allows the Supreme Court to avoid politically controversial decisions. On the whole, the Supreme Court has acted with some restraint vis-à-vis Congress. Does the Bundesverfassungsgericht also practice the appropriate level of judicial self-restraint or is it too active?

2. What de facto means can be employed by the other institutions of governance, that is, the Bundestag, the Bundesrat, and the federal government, to influence the decisions of the constitutional court or to correct them after the fact?

3. How important are constitutional arguments in the deliberations of the committees? In other words, does the presence of the constitutional court have important anticipatory consequences for legislation?

4. Through the accumulated jurisprudence of almost fifty years, the constitutional court has concretized many of the articles of the Basic Law. Is the jurisprudence of the court fairly lucid and predictable, so that it is possible to anticipate possible review of a bill by the court?

5. How important is the abstract judicial review proceeding, or the threat of a suit in Karlsruhe, as a means for the opposition to influence policy? I am thinking in particular of the third reading of the revision to the law on paragraph 218. In the Bundestag debate, speakers of both large parties explicitly argued that one advantage of the agreed-upon compromise was that because of bipartisan support, a new suit in Karlsruhe could

be avoided. A speaker for the Greens argued that the Greens had been excluded only because they could not threaten a suit.

6. Alexander Hamilton argued in the Federalist Papers that the Supreme Court would always be dependent on the executive and legislative [branches] to enforce its decisions. In the history of the Supreme Court, it has repeatedly happened that decisions have not been enforced. Similar things have happened to the constitutional court – for example, in the question of the taxation of pensions and retirement benefits and in the question of child benefits for civil servants with large families. What factors are important in the manner in which decisions by the court are approached by the Bundestag?

7. Since the disputes between the Adenauer government and the court in the early 1950s, no serious attempt to restrict the powers of the court has been made. Moreover, the major parties seem to be fairly worried about losing a case in Karlsruhe. What explains this remarkable respect for the constitutional court?

8. Do you feel that the accumulated jurisprudence of almost fifty years is becoming increasingly restrictive for the Bundestag or is there still sufficient flexibility?

9. The FCC imposes certain constraints on the majority. At the same time, it can be very useful to a government coalition, for example to control *Länder* governments or to bring a constitutional dispute to a close. Do you view the court primarily as a useful or as a constraining institution for the governing majority?

10. In light of the recent dispute surrounding the appointment of Professor Papier to the court, some have argued that the appointment process has become more politicized. Do you think that is true?

APPENDIX C: COURT QUESTIONNAIRE

The following questionnaire was used for the interviews with judges of the constitutional court. The order of the questions was sometimes changed if a response to a particular question raised issues directly related to a later question and therefore made it desirable to move a question up. Similarly, in some interviews some questions were omitted if the respondent had already answered the question in the context of another response.

1. Could you tell me a little about what your area of expertise (*Dezernat*) at the court was?

Appendix C

2. What do you consider to be the most important decisions in which you took part while at the court?

3. In his essay "Bundesverfassungsgericht and Staatsraison," Professor Hans Klein has argued that the court backs away from decisions that have politically unacceptable consequences through the use of ad hoc interpretations, especially in budgetary matters. As examples, he mentions the decision about the challenge to the 1961 Bundestag elections and the decision on the revenue tax. I would like to ask whether this analysis is correct in your view, and if so, whether you can think of any examples from your own experience at the court.

4. After the court was created in 1951, it had to fight for its independence from the executive and especially the justice department, an effort in which judge Leibholz played a crucial role. Even so, there were subsequent occasions on which the independence of the court was threatened, for example in the debate about changes in the election mode for judges in 1956. Are such threats to the independence of the court still relevant today, and is the preservation of independence something about which judges worry consciously?

5. The court enjoys tremendous trust among German citizens; it usually finishes first or second among the public institutions of the FRG. Do you think this public trust is important for the court, and is the maintenance of that trust something that the judges worry about?

6. In the debates surrounding the U.S. Constitution, Alexander Hamilton argued in the Federalist Papers that the Supreme Court is in a fairly weak position since it must rely on the executive for the enforcement of its decisions. Several times during its history, the Supreme Court has encountered an unwillingness to enforce its decisions, notably in the decision concerning racial segregation in schools. The constitutional court as well has run into this difficulty, for example with respect to its decision concerning the taxation of pensions and retirement benefits. Is the potential for defiance by the executive something that enters into the deliberations of the court?

7. The Supreme Court, as the highest court in a common law system, is more dependent on precedent in its rulings than traditional continental European courts. Is precedent an important factor in the Bundesverfassungsgericht's jurisprudence?

8. Looking through the opinions of the court, one gets the impression that the court has particularly exercised judicial restraint in the areas of foreign policy and public finance. Is that impression correct, and if so, what makes these two fields special?

9. During the early years of the court's existence, it happened that members of the government or the Bundestag would directly contact judges at the court about current cases. For example, Justice Minister Dehler and Staatssekretaer Lenz drove to Karlsruhe to discuss the suits against the European Defense Community with Court President Hoepker-Aschoff. Is such direct contact still something that happens today?

10. I would like to ask you about the last party finance decision. In its 1992 decision, the court overrruled several precedents on party finance, especially its 1986 decision. The dissenting opinion written by Judge Boeckenfoerde in 1986 became a large part of the majority opinion in 1992. Could you tell me what your hunches are about what had changed in those six years to bring about that reversal?

11. Do "political facts," like the majority with which a bill was passed, influence the deliberations of the court?

12. It seems that political parties worry about losing a case at the court. Helmut Schmidt once said: "My government has been overruled in Karlsruhe several times, and that is not something one takes lightly." Do you think that observation is correct, and if so, why do you think parties are so worried?

6

Pushing the Limits

Party Finance Legislation and the Bundesverfassungsgericht

A central implication of the theory developed in Chapter 2 is that legislative majorities in the Bundestag will be strongly tempted to evade judicial decisions that touch on interests that are fundamental to the parties, and that this temptation is particularly strong whenever public support or transparency is low.[1] The theory further implies that judges of the FCC anticipate this potential for evasion and adjust their behavior in two ways. First, they will be sensitive to the preferences of legislative majorities and employ methods to reduce the costs of their decisions. Second, when they choose to annul a statute, they will try to increase the transparency surrounding the decision to generate greater pressure for compliance.

In the previous chapter, we found considerable evidence for the various components of this argument. Legislators reported that the costs of a decision affect their response to a judicial decision, and judges discussed a number of strategies they employ to reduce the political costs of their rulings. In this chapter, I illustrate these interactions in greater detail through a case study of the interactions between the Bundesverfassungsgericht and Bundestag in a particular policy area: public financing of political parties. This case study is particularly valuable because it traces the dynamics of the often contentious relationship between the FCC and the Bundestag as they interact repeatedly over the same issue. In the interests of parsimony and theoretical clarity, the theory – and in particular the formal

---

[1] Formally, as α (the parameter that indicates the value placed by the legislature on the policy under review) increases, only the Contentious and Judicial Self-Censoring Equilibria survive. In the Contentious Equilibrium, the court annuls the statute but the legislature evades the decision. In the Judicial Self-Censoring Equilibrium, the court upholds the statute despite its preference for an annulment because it anticipates evasion and does not believe that it can prevail in a confrontation with the legislature.

model – focuses on the interactions between legislative majorities and judges over a particular bill. But the logic of the argument extends readily to a more dynamic situation. Most importantly, as court and legislature interact repeatedly over similar policies, information about the preferences of both sides, as well as experience with what works and what does not, accumulates. For example, as legislative reactions to previous decisions reveal that majorities are committed to protecting certain policies, we might expect judges to take greater account of legislative preferences in their decisions or to make more transparent demands to increase the pressure for compliance. The case study demonstrates in a concrete example how such adaptation takes place.

At the outset, I must make it clear that this case study is not concerned with providing a normative evaluation of the FCC's party finance jurisprudence. I do not address the question of whether the decisions by the FCC and the responses by the Bundestag are right or desirable in some deeper sense. While the appropriateness or wisdom of the court's jurisprudence constitutes an interesting field of study in its own right, I am concerned to evaluate the extent to which the theoretical framework advanced here provides a useful way of understanding the interactions between the Bundestag and the FCC in a crucial policy area. Therefore, I leave the normative issue aside and pursue a more limited aim: I want to make a plausible case that, in fact, the court's decisions have been subject to consistent evasive efforts by legislative majorities, and that this fact has affected the jurisprudence of the court in ways predicted by the theory presented in Chapter 2.

Two reasons make party finance an especially attractive policy area for this kind of illustration. First, party finance is a crucial policy area. The resources that are available to political parties, as well as the conditions under which these resources are made available, go to the heart of the democratic process. They determine, in part, how flexible the party system is and how responsive established parties have to be to new challenges. The manner in which public money is distributed can also have an impact on the power distribution within established parties (see Alexander 1989; Alexander and Shiratori 1994; Landfried 1994; von Arnim 1993, 1996). As a result, the constitutional constraints that structure public financing of political parties take on special significance. How effectively can these constraints be enforced by the FCC?

Second, party finance exhibits several of the characteristics that should be associated with attempts by legislative majorities to evade costly high court decisions. Because public financing of parties provides resources that can be crucial to parties as they compete for office, protecting and expanding such funding is likely to be a core concern for established parties. Moreover, party finance is a policy area in which most parties are likely to share, at least to some degree, the same preferences – in particular, the desire to minimize the possibility of external challenges to established parties. Hence, an important organized interest – the parliamentary opposition – that would have an incentive to police compliance with a decision is unlikely to provide effective control. As a result, evasion of high court decisions that seek to limit the privileges of established parties will be an attractive alternative for a legislative cartel composed of governing parties and the opposition. Hans Herbert von Arnim, for example, has documented extensively that legislative coalitions at the federal and state levels in Germany make use of this coincidence of interests between the opposition and the majority to reduce the likelihood of public scrutiny by amending party finance legislation at the last minute and by passing the bills without scheduled debate or immediately before parliamentary recess (von Arnim 1993, 1996, 2002).[2]

In short, party finance is the kind of policy area in which we are most likely to encounter the Contentious or the Judicial Self-Censoring Equilibria predicted by the model. And as we will see, since the Bundesverfassungsgericht first ruled on party finance, legislative majorities have consistently attempted to evade decisions that sought to establish constraints on public financing of political parties. The FCC, in turn, has reacted in ways that are consistent with the argument presented in Chapter 2. On the one hand, the judges have tried to increase transparency. As particular aspects of their decisions were ignored, they increasingly provided for specific policy prescriptions in their decisions, thus increasing pressure for compliance. On the other hand, the judges have been sensitive to the preferences of legislative majorities. They have been careful to temper their decisions by making important concessions to established parties that reduce the costs of those decisions and therefore reduce the potential for a direct legislative–judicial confrontation.

---

[2] For example, the most recent party finance law in Germany was introduced in parliament on April 16, 2002. It was referred to committee without the customary debate on April 17. It was reported out of committee on April 19 and passed by parliament on the same day. By cross-party agreement, debate on the bill had been limited to one hour (von Arnim 2002). This three-day legislative process contrasts with a legislative process that, on average, takes well over four months in Germany (Martin and Vanberg 2004).

PARTY FINANCE IN GERMANY

One distinguishing characteristic of post–World War II German democracy is the financial support granted to political parties from public funds. The founding fathers of the Federal Republic rejected the notion of direct public support for political parties.[3] Nevertheless, West Germany was the first industrialized Western democracy to introduce direct public financing (1959), and the level of public support remains among the most generous in the world (Nassmacher 1989:238; von Arnim 1996:188).[4] Ironically, a 1958 decision by the FCC may well have been a contributing factor in the establishment of public funding (BVerfGE 8,51). The case originated in an abstract review proceeding initiated by the SPD government of Hesse, which had petitioned the court to review a 1954 addition to the tax code that made it possible for individuals to make a tax-deductible contribution of up to 5 percent of their income to political parties. Companies could donate up to 2 percent of their annual revenue and enjoy the same tax privilege.

In its decision, the court invalidated this provision. Coupled with a progressive tax system, the court argued, any tax deduction calculated on the basis of a percentage of income privileges wealthy donors. Due to higher marginal tax rates, the same contribution to a party would require a lower donation by wealthier citizens than by donors with a lower marginal tax rate. Therefore, the tax provision gives rise to unequal treatment that violates the constitutional guarantee of equal citizen influence (BVerfGE 8,51:69). Moreover, because contributions are "less expensive" for wealthier donors, the provision privileges political parties that appeal to wealthier constituencies and therefore violates the principle of equality of opportunity for parties (BVerfGE 8,51:66). Significantly, however, the court also noted in an orbiter dictum that the Basic Law contains no constitutional provisions explicitly prohibiting direct public funding of political parties for election purposes (BVerfGE 8,51:62f.). Thus, the court concluded, public funding of parties was constitutionally permissible for

---

[3] The topic was not even debated in the Parliamentary Council. Hesse Minister-President Georg August Zinn, a leading figure in the constitutional convention, later reported that "the proposition that the parties should be supported by the state was absolutely unimaginable to us back then" (quoted in Dübber 1970:97).

[4] Only Costa Rica (1954) and Argentina (1955) had introduced direct public financing earlier. Other Western democracies soon followed the German example, including the Scandinavian countries in the late 1960s, the Netherlands in 1972, and Italy in 1974 (von Arnim 1996:78f.).

some purposes, provided that such funding did not violate the principle of equality of opportunity (BVerfGE 8,51:65). The Bundestag (led by the CDU/CSU) wasted no time in responding to this decision. In the federal budget for fiscal year 1959, 5 million deutsche marks (DM) were allocated as direct subsidies to political parties. In 1962 these subsidies were raised to DM 20 million, and they ballooned to DM 38 million by 1964.

These developments set the stage for a series of interactions between the FCC and the Bundestag about the general and specific nature of public subsidies to political parties. These interactions can be grouped usefully into three sets of decisions and the legislative reaction to each. The first set consists of two initial decisions issued by the court in 1966 and 1968. The second set consists of two decisions issued in 1986. The third set consists of the decision issued in 1992. The remaining sections of this chapter demonstrate that the theoretical framework presented in Chapter 2 can illuminate our understanding of each of these decisions, the legislative responses to them, and the changes in the court's jurisprudence over time.

THE COURT'S INITIAL APPROACH TO PARTY FINANCE

In a position they have since given up, the SPD opposed the early increases in public funding for political parties and voted against the 1964 expansion.[5] Reacting to the exploding subsidies that were pushed through the Bundestag, the SPD government of Hesse once again initiated an abstract judicial review proceeding to test their constitutionality. The decision in this case, issued in 1966, provided the Bundesverfassungsgericht with the first opportunity to establish the constitutional standards that would govern the nature of public financing of political parties. The court took the opportunity to impose restrictions on the kind of funding that would be permissible by attempting to establish several fundamental principles.

First, the court ruled that a general public financing scheme for political parties violates the constitutional principle of the free formation of public opinion and the public will. The only form in which public money could

---

[5] See the Bundestag debate on April 15, 1964 (fourth legislative period, plenary session 122), especially the statements by Herbert Wehner. As will become apparent shortly, the SPD quickly relented in its opposition to public finance. During the 1980s, the Greens once again opposed the public finance laws. However, like the SPD before them, they have also abandoned this stance.

be granted to parties would be as reimbursement for certain campaign expenses:

> [I]t is not permissible to grant public subsidies to political parties for their general political activities. It is constitutionally justifiable, however, to reimburse political parties for the necessary expenses of an appropriate election campaign, provided the principle of the independence of political parties from the state and the principle of equality of opportunity can be observed. (BVerfGE 20,56:113)

Second, the court held that campaign reimbursement, if granted, could be restricted. Specifically, public funds would not have to be extended to any party, no matter how insignificant, that competes in an election. At the same time, the court was quick to point out that such a restriction could not be too stringent. In particular, access to public funds could not be tied to clearing the electoral threshold that restricts entry into the Bundestag to parties that secure at least 5 percent of the vote. As the opinion states, any "cutoff must lie considerably below the five percent threshold required for the allocation of seats" (BVerfGE 20,56:118). Finally, the court established a principle dubbed the "relative upper limit": Public funds allocated to a party may not exceed the funds that the same party generates from private donations and membership dues (BVerfGE 20,56: 102).

In response to this ruling, the Bundestag in July 1967 passed the Political Parties Act after a cross-party agreement had been worked out between the CDU, SPD, and Liberals.[6] Two components of the bill dealing with direct public funding of political parties are of interest. First, the parties interpreted the court's ruling that only the "expenses of an appropriate election campaign" could be "reimbursed" in such a way as to preserve, essentially, the nonspecific public subsidies to the parties that had been declared unconstitutional.[7] The law provided for DM 2.50 to be paid for every eligible voter in a Bundestag election. The total amount thus

---

[6] Article 21 (3) of the Basic Law obligates the Bundestag to pass such a Parties Act to regulate the status of political parties and the requirement that they publicly declare the source of their funding. The Bundestag had delayed passing this act for eighteen years because the major parties, in particular the CDU/CSU, feared the implications of imposing clear restrictions on their financial activities (Bösch 2001; Heidenheimer 1957; Landfried 1994; von Arnim 1996).

[7] Pinto-Duschinsky (1991:186) states: "The intent of the Constitutional Court was nevertheless evaded by the Bundestag from 1967 onward in two important ways. First, the Parties Law of 1967 stretched the definition of 'campaign' expenditures. It was argued that party organizations must prepare for an election campaign over a period of years. Thus, expenditures that may have appeared to be routine actually needed to be categorized as campaign items. The 'campaign only' provisions were

Table 6.1 *Electoral Performance of Parties below 5 Percent in 1957–1965 (Percent of List Votes [Zweitstimme])*

Party	1957 Bundestag Election	1961 Bundestag Election	1965 Bundestag Election
GB/BHE	4.6	–	–
DP	3.4	–	–
GDP	–	2.8	–
DRP	1.0	0.8	–
NPD	–	–	2.0
DFU	–	1.9	1.3
FU	0.9	–	–
Others	0.6	0.2	0.3

Source: Schindler (1994:36f.).

determined would then be divided proportionally in response to the election's outcome. Furthermore, the money would be disbursed in payments stretched out over the legislative period prior to an election in anticipation of long-term preparations for a campaign.[8]

Another important dimension of the scheme created in the 1967 Parties Act concerns the restrictions placed on the receipt of public funding. Recall that the FCC had explicitly ruled that any public financing scheme could not be used to entrench the position of established parties and stifle attempts at outside competition. The court had therefore stated that any restriction on receiving public funding must lie "considerably below the five percent threshold required for the allocation of seats." In drafting the Parties Act, the parties represented in the Bundestag fixed this cutoff level at 2.5 percent. At first sight, this cutoff may appear to represent a sincere attempt to follow the instructions of the FCC; 2.5 percent is only half of the support necessary to receive seats in the legislature. However, consider Table 6.1, which displays the electoral performance of parties that missed the 5 percent threshold of representation in the three most recent elections before the Parties Act was passed (Bundestag elections of 1957, 1961, and 1965).

---

  expanded on these grounds to include considerable payments for party organization between elections...."

[8] Thus, the total amount of public funding would be independent of voter turnout. Moreover, parties could receive 10 percent of their anticipated amount in the second year of the legislative period, 15 percent in the third year, 35 percent in the fourth year, and the remainder following the election. Should the amount disbursed prior to the election exceed the de facto amount a party would be entitled to, excess payments would have to be returned.

Several things about this table are striking. The only parties that exceeded the 2.5 percent cutoff in the three federal elections prior to passage of the Parties Act were the GB/BHE, the Deutsche Partei (DP), and the Gesamtdeutsche Partei Deutschlands (GDP). The last party, in fact, had emerged out of the fusion of the GB/BHE and the DP in 1961. In response to the poor showing in the election of 1961 (compared to the performance of the two parties since 1949), the newly formed GDP dissolved, as most members joined the CDU/CSU and did not even compete in the 1965 election (see Boldt 1993:382; Fenske 1994:289f.). The parties that remained relevant after 1965 are the remaining parties in the table. Most significant are the parties of the radical right. After the election of 1961, the Deutsche Reichspartei (DRP) fused into the Nationaldemokratische Partei Deutschlands (NPD) (see Fenske 1994:295). The three previous elections, as well as a series of *Land* elections, had demonstrated that the support of the new party hovered around 2 percent. Similarly, other parties, including the pacifist Deutsche Friedensunion (DFU) polled somewhere around 1 percent. All of these parties would be excluded from public funding under the Parties Act by the 2.5 percent restriction.

In light of this political environment, it appears plausible that the choice of 2.5 percent in the Parties Act of 1967 was motivated, at least in part, by the desire of the established parties to disadvantage challenger parties. The FCC had ruled that public funding could not be restricted to parties in the Bundestag and that, as a result, any cutoff would have to be "considerably" lower than the electoral threshold. According to the court, the only legitimate purpose of a cutoff could be to discourage splinter parties that would run solely in order to receive public funding (BVerfGE 20,56:118). Given the prevailing political situation, the 2.5 percent cutoff did not meet this standard. Effectively, it served to restrict funding to the established parties (and those parties knew that it would do so). Furthermore, the cutoff eliminated public funding for several parties that were serious contenders in the sense of not running solely in the hope of receiving public funds. In short, the legislative response to the court's first attempt to establish certain constitutional principles in the area of party finance seems to have been characterized by attempts at evasion:

- The financing scheme was only loosely connected to actual campaign expenses
- Disbursement of public funds was, in practice, restricted to established parties.

The Court's Initial Approach to Party Finance

Not surprisingly, several small parties immediately brought an Organstreit proceeding against the new statute. Several aspects of the decision issued by the FCC in response to these challenges in December 1968 are interesting. First, the court invalidated the 2.5 percent threshold imposed on the 1967 statute. Given the average turnout in Bundestag elections, the judges argued, meeting the 2.5 percent cutoff would require a party to gather at least 835,000 votes. Demanding this kind of support as proof of a party's seriousness was unjustifiable. Instead, the court directed the legislature to drop the threshold to 0.5 percent (BVerfGE 24,300: 342). However, in a crucial component of the decision, the judges validated the general financing scheme established in the Parties Act by declaring the lump-sum payments made to parties stretched out over a legislative period in proportion to the election results constitutional. By doing so, the court, for all practical purposes, dropped its earlier insistence that only the "necessary expenses of an appropriate election campaign" could be "reimbursed" (von Arnim 1996:83). While making this concession, the court also tried to impose some restrictions on the future development of these subsidies. In particular, it held that the level of subsidies (as determined by the 1965 election) could only be increased in order to keep up with inflation. Therefore, "clear limits to the future development of campaign-cost reimbursement" had been established (BVerfGE 24,300:339).

The development from the 1966 to the 1968 decision is broadly consistent with the expectations derived from the theoretical framework. Recall from the discussion in Chapter 2 that evasion becomes more attractive and easier to achieve the less transparent an issue becomes. As a consequence, I argued, judges can try to increase the transparency of their rulings in order to create greater pressure for compliance. The changes from the 1966 to the 1968 decision fit this pattern. The requirement that the cutoff must lie "considerably below the five percent threshold required for the allocation of seats" is not very transparent and made the attempt to evade the 1967 statute fairly safe. In 1968, the judges explicitly remedied this deficiency of the earlier ruling by providing a highly transparent ruling: The cutoff could not exceed 0.5 percent. Given this explicit statement by the court, any future revision to the Parties Act could easily be checked to ascertain whether the court's ruling had been implemented in this respect. Similarly, the explicit limitation of the size of the "public finance pie" to the real value of subsidies granted for the 1965 election is fairly transparent.

At the same time, the theory leads to the expectation that on issues that are vital to the interests of governing parties, the court will make concessions that reduce the costs of its decision to those parties. Again, this seems to have been borne out by the 1966 and 1968 decisions. After experiencing the evasive attempts in response to the 1966 decision, the FCC tempered its 1968 decision by accepting the legislature's interpretation of reimbursement of necessary campaign expenses as allowing for general subsidies that are only tangentially linked to campaign expenses and could be paid continuously throughout a legislative period. Second, in establishing the upper limit to the size of this "pie," the court used the 1965 election campaign. Choosing this particular year as the benchmark constituted a significant compromise because the subsidies granted for that campaign had been relatively high (see von Arnim 1996:84). Both of these concessions made the decision significantly easier to swallow.

LEGISLATIVE RESPONSE TO PARTY FINANCE II AND THE 1986 DECISIONS

Despite the attempt to provide more transparent constraints and to take account of the preferences of the parties, the court's decision did not create effective boundaries to the growth of public support for political parties. Nor did it ensure that parties not represented in the Bundestag would not be systematically disadvantaged vis-à-vis the established parties by unequal access to public support. While bowing to the court's most transparent demands, the parties in the Bundestag quickly engaged in new evasive attempts to secure continuing and increasing access to public funds. In revising the Parties Act, the established parties did incorporate the court's demand for a 0.5 percent cutoff. Similarly, direct public subsidies to political parties remained relatively constant in real terms for a number of years following the 1968 decision. Figure 6.1 displays the direct federal subsidies granted to political parties since 1962 in constant 1991 deutsche marks.[9] The variation in payments is created by

---

[9] The data on party finance are taken from the work of Hans Herbert von Arnim. Von Arnim is one of the preeminent authorities on German party finance. He has repeatedly served as an expert witness in legislative hearings on the subject. In 1992 he was appointed by the president, Richard von Weizsäcker, to a six-member commission to advise the Bundestag on a revision of party finance statutes following the FCC's most recent party finance decision (BVerfGE 85, 264). In several books, he has amassed data on financial support of political parties, Bundestag factions,

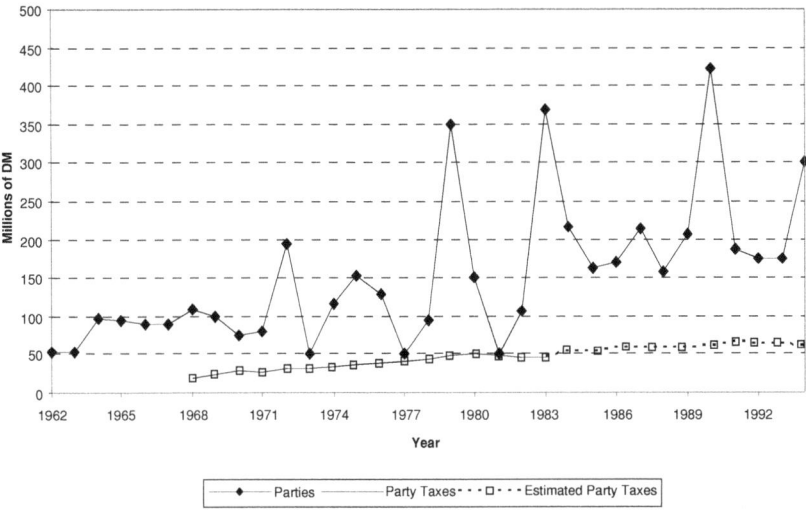

Figure 6.1. Public Financing of Political Parties (Federal Level) (in 1991 Deutsche Marks).

the disbursement of funds throughout legislative periods, with the largest amounts being disbursed following a federal election. (The "party taxes" that appear in Figure 6.1 are special contributions imposed on parliamentary deputies by their parties and are paid out of deputies' salaries. They are discussed in more detail later.)

However, while complying with the court's most transparent demands, the parties turned to other avenues to gain access to public money. In particular, a legislative coalition of the CDU/CSU, SPD, and FDP followed up the revisions to the Parties Act by transferring money and responsibilities from the party organizations to other institutions affiliated with the parties. Beginning in 1969, funding for the party factions in the Bundestag was increased significantly, paid staff positions for Bundestag deputies were created, and the foundations maintained by the established parties received growing subsidies.

Consider the funding for factions and Bundestag staff first. Figure 6.2 displays the total amount of federal funds devoted to the support of

---

Bundestag staff, and party foundations (von Arnim 1993, 1996). The nominal deutsche mark amounts provided by von Arnim were converted into real terms (with 1991 as basis year) using the price index provided by the German Federal Statistical Office (available at http://www.statistik-bund.de). The data displayed in Figure 6.1 can be found in von Arnim (1996:120ff).

Party Finance Legislation and the Bundesverfassungsgericht

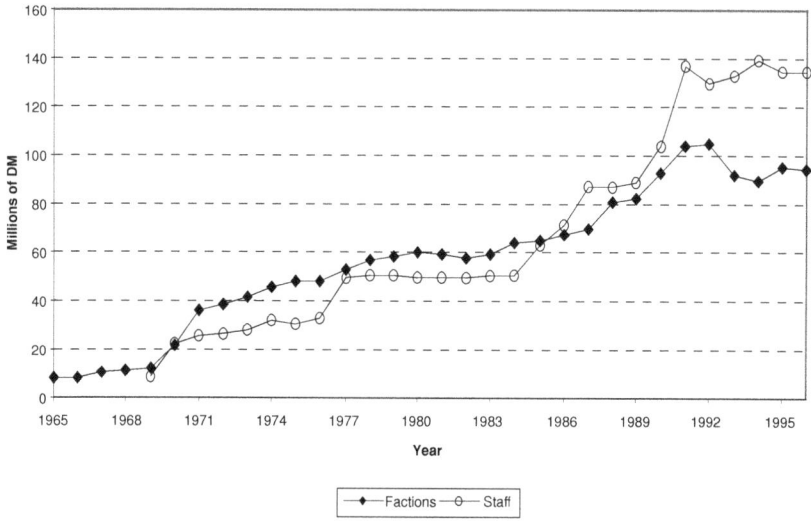

Figure 6.2. Public Funding of Bundestag Factions and Staff (in 1991 Deutsche Marks).

Bundestag factions and staff between 1965 and 1996.[10] The years immediately following the court's 1968 decision mark a dramatic increase in the amount of real resources assigned to the factions. This growth has continued over time. The year 1969 is also the first year in which paid Bundestag staff positions were introduced, and the staff budget has consistently expanded since then. Nor is this growth an artificial product of changing assembly size. Until German unification in 1990, the size of the Bundestag remained relatively constant. The pattern in Figure 6.2 remains equally strong if one considers per deputy spending. The suspicion that these developments were a reaction designed to evade the court's attempts to limit public funding of political parties seems plausible. As von Arnim has concluded, "in the search for new means of securing public financing, the party factions, party foundations, and Bundestag staff became a target. The flip-side of the legal and statutory limitation of party finance in the narrow sense was therefore a tremendous growth of public money devoted to factions, party foundations, and staff" (1996:135; see also Dübber 1970:103).

In addition to passing the "interocular trauma test," there are several concrete indications that faction and staff funds are being used in part

---

[10] The raw data can be found in von Arnim (1996:139ff.,180).

as an indirect means of financing the activities of political parties. The subsidies to factions are listed and paid as lump-sum amounts in the federal budget. The factions are not required to account for the use of their funds, making it extremely difficult to determine how the subsidies are being spent (Landfried 1994:101; von Arnim 1996:156). Several studies have estimated that as much as "50 percent of the public subsidies to factions are being used to cover the continuing operating expenses of the parties" (Landfried 1994: 101; see also Schleth 1971). For example, faction funds are routinely employed to commission and pay for opinion surveys before and after elections (*Der Spiegel* 1995 [Nr.8]:39).

The same is true of resources allocated for Bundestag staff. It is extremely difficult to ascertain how staff funds are being used. However, in addition to the dramatic increases in resources devoted to staff since 1969, a drastic shift is apparent in the allocation of staff to duties in the Bundestag itself and to duties in the various electoral districts. While only one-third of staff members were employed in district offices in 1969, this proportion rose steadily to close to two-thirds by 1991 (see Schindler 1994:1283). These staff members are almost certainly being used (at least in part) for campaign and party-related work. At a conference on party finance, Heiner Geißler, former deputy faction leader of the CDU/CSU, explicitly labeled the distinction between the parliamentary and party duties of Bundestag deputies as a "lie of political life" (quoted in von Arnim 1996:185; see also Hirsch 1981).

It seems fairly apparent that the use of faction resources and staff budgets for such purposes is incompatible with the spirit of the FCC's attempts to limit the growth of public funding for political parties. This conclusion is reinforced by statements by the FCC itself, which has explicitly noted in a series of orbiter dicta that the use of faction resources noted previously is unconstitutional (Landfried 1994:102; von Arnim 1996:150). In its 1966 decision, the court had announced:

If parliaments were to grant subsidies to party factions in amounts not justified by the needs of the factions, such subsidies would constitute a hidden form of party finance and an abuse in violation of the constitution. (BVerfGE 20,56:105)

Naturally, the sticking point is to give concrete meaning to the phrase "amounts justified by the needs of the factions." In doing so, the court has insisted that subsidies granted to party factions can only be used to "coordinate" the parliamentary work of the faction and, in particular, to draft bills and to keep faction members informed. In other words, subsidies to the factions can only be used to cover the administrative costs of the factions' legislative activities. They cannot extend to broader purposes, like campaign work. This argument was reasserted by the FCC in 1989, when the court dismissed a complaint by an independent Bundestag deputy who had initiated a proceeding against his exclusion from the faction funds. In ruling against Thomas Wüppesahl, the judges argued that "faction subsidies are earmarked for the financial support necessary to achieve coordination of parliamentary work.... In the case of an independent deputy, there is no such need for coordination, and hence no right to equal financial treatment" (BVerfGE 80,188:231). However appealing this may be as an ideal conception of the use of faction subsidies, the previous discussion makes it clear that this argument belies political reality. The subsidies granted to the factions are by no means used exclusively for parliamentary work, but are in fact employed to finance general political activities. I will return to the court's toleration of this evasive maneuver shortly.

A second set of institutions that has been targeted by the established parties in their attempts to circumvent the restrictions placed on direct party financing by the FCC consists of the various political foundations affiliated with the established parties. All the major parties have established such foundations. The link between the foundations and the parent parties is extremely close, largely created via the boards of the foundations, which are made up predominantly of senior party officials. For example, Pinto-Duschinsky has documented that in the 1982–4 period, 55 percent of the board members of the FDP foundation were FDP members of the federal or state governments or parliaments. For the SPD foundation, the number was 53 percent, for the CDU foundation 85 percent, and for the CSU foundation 64 percent (1991:197).

After the FCC had invalidated general subsidies for "political education" paid to political parties and restricted direct funding of parties to reimbursement of campaign expenses, general subsidies paid to the political foundations for political education appeared with the 1967 budget. It seems "reasonable to suppose that this marks a simple 'reallocation' of resources, and that the CSU decided to establish the Hanns-Seidel-Stiftung in 1967 in order to qualify for these funds" (Landfried 1994:103). Similarly, Pinto-Duschinsky has concluded:

A significant role of the party foundations in Germany has been to permit the parties to circumvent regulations and Constitutional Court rulings that apply to them but not to nonparty bodies, for the *Stiftungen* are able to escape party status. The party foundation device is the most significant method of evading restrictions that apply to political parties but... it is not the only one. (1991:233)

Legislative Response to Party Finance II and the 1986 Decisions

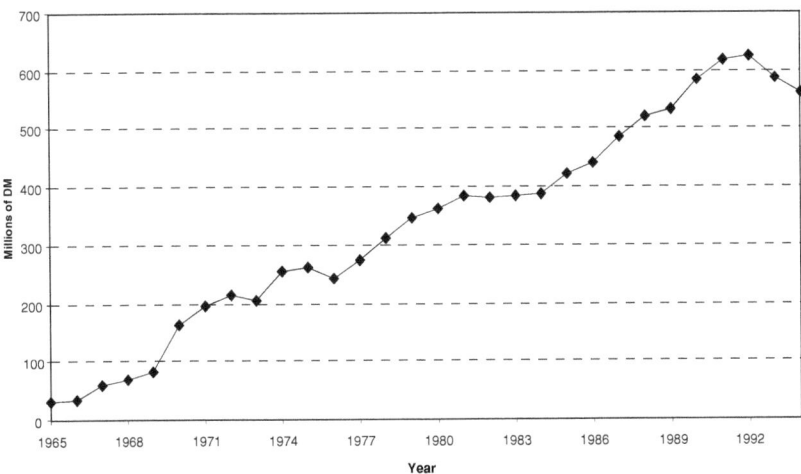

Figure 6.3. Public Financing of Party Foundations (Federal Level) (in 1991 Deutsche Marks).

Figure 6.3 displays federal subsidies paid to the party foundations between 1965 and 1994.[11] Again, a dramatic increase following the FCC's 1968 decision limiting direct party funding is evident.

As in the case of the factions, there is considerable evidence that funds allocated to the foundations are being used to finance indirectly the activities of their parent parties. In connection with a constitutional challenge to foundation funding by the Greens, the Bundesrechnungshof (Federal Accounting and Auditing Office) conducted an audit of the foundations for the period 1981–3. Even during this limited period, the audit uncovered several instances of indirect party financing. For example, in 1982, the FDP foundation extended several short-term loans exceeding DM 1 million to the party on extremely favorable terms. When the Rechnungshof undertook the audit, the interest on the loans had not been paid (see Landfried 1994:105). Similarly, the auditors determined that the foundations had consistently commissioned and paid for opinion surveys before and after state and federal elections. The results were passed on to senior party officials (Landfried 1994:106; Pinto-Duschinsky 1991:222). Finally, the foundations had bought and distributed campaign literature and taken out newspaper advertisements for their parent parties. The Rechnungshof was unable to establish to whom the various materials had been sent because the foundations had kept no records (Landfried 1994:108).

[11] The raw data can be found in von Arnim (1996:167).

In addition to circumventing general limits on the amount of public resources at the disposal of political parties, the transfer of funds to factions, staff, and foundations has the effect of circumventing the FCC's demand that newly established parties should not be unduly disadvantaged vis-à-vis parties represented in the Bundestag by lack of access to public funds. Funds for factions and Bundestag staff are obviously conditioned on having cleared the 5 percent threshold in the previous federal election. Moreover, the parties have restricted foundation funds to parties that have been represented in the Bundestag for at least two legislative periods (von Arnim 1996:175). After unsuccessfully challenging funding of party foundations in the FCC (more on that later), the Greens established their own foundation in 1987 after they had returned to the Bundestag for their second legislative period. Especially small parties like the FDP and the Greens may derive considerable competitive advantages vis-à-vis challenger parties from the availability of these funds to established parties (Pinto-Duschinsky 1991).

In the early 1980s, all the established German parties found themselves in dire financial straits. Almost all parties had accumulated considerable debts (Landfried 1994:60). Moreover, the Flick scandal, involving substantial illegal donations to the established parties, had broken in the early 1980s and dried up another (although illegal) source of party finance.[12] Finally, a new challenger party, the Greens, had emerged and was beginning to gain substantial electoral support. All these factors combined to place great pressure on the established parties to secure additional funding. Following the Flick scandal, Federal President Carl Carstens appointed a commission of experts to propose new changes to party finance regulations (Schneider 1989). In response to the commission's report, the Bundestag in 1983 passed a new Parties Act that expanded public financing of political parties. While many significant changes were made in this revision, I will only mention two here. First, the campaign reimbursement amount was raised to DM 5 per eligible voter (it had been raised from the original DM 2.50 to DM 3.50 in 1974). This increase (which constituted an increase in real terms) shows up clearly in Figure 6.1.

Second, the Bundestag resurrected the possibility of making tax-deductible contributions to political parties of up to 5 percent of an individual's income (or 2 percent of revenue for companies). Recall that the

---

[12] For a detailed account, see Blankenburg et al. (1990) and Landfried (1994). The scandal that erupted in late 1999 surrounding illegal contributions to the CDU may yet eclipse the Flick scandal in political significance.

Legislative Response to Party Finance II and the 1986 Decisions

FCC had declared such an arrangement unconstitutional in 1958. In order to balance out the obvious unconstitutionality of the provision in light of the court's jurisprudence, an additional procedure was introduced that would compensate parties that could not attract donations from wealthy sponsors for advantages enjoyed by parties that could. The "equal chances scheme" (*Chancenausgleich*) involved an incredibly complex set of calculations that determined additional direct public payments to be made to parties to neutralize the indirect public financing of parties that could attract higher donations via the larger tax breaks afforded to wealthy donors.[13]

In 1986, the FCC issued decisions in two cases brought by the Greens against the Parties Act of 1983 as well as against the general funding scheme for the party foundations. These cases provided the court with an obvious opportunity to reassert the limits it had imposed on party finance and to attempt to counteract some of the evasive attempts by the parties. At the same time, the court found itself in an especially weak position. As pointed out earlier, the financial situation of the established parties was precarious in the early 1980s, and the expansion of 1983 had been motivated in large part by this financial need. Thus, the issue under review was especially important to the established parties at the time. In this situation, the model would lead us to expect that the judges of the court should be particularly inclined to be accommodating vis-à-vis the interests of parties. The decisions are indeed consistent with this expectation.

While nominally adhering to the principles of its earlier jurisprudence, the FCC accommodated itself to political reality and upheld the Parties Act of 1983 as well as the funding scheme for political foundations in all relevant respects. Three aspects of the court's two decisions are particularly interesting. The first concerns the deductibility of donations to political parties. The only provision of the new law declared unconstitutional by the court was the allowance of a tax-deductible donation of up to 5 percent of annual income. The court reasserted the principle of its 1958 decision (reiterated repeatedly since then) that such a provision would be incompatible with the constitutional guarantee of equal political influence for citizens because wealthier donors would enjoy advantages that

---

[13] The details of the provision are not important here. For an example that demonstrates the complexity of the process, see Landfried (1994). Even the president of the Bundestag stated that he could not understand the particulars of the *Chancenausgleich* (Bundestag Drucksache 11/2007).

the average taxpayer could not. However, in a passage that seems almost comical, the court went on to state that "keeping this in mind, the senate regards tax-deductible donations of up to DM 100,000 as constitutionally unobjectionable, while donations above that limit are incompatible with the principle of equal citizen influence" (BVerfGE 73,40: 79,84). Thus, the court gave back with one hand what it had just taken away with the other. It managed to stick nominally to its established principle while upholding, for practical purposes, the intent of the law. In practice, a limit of DM 100,000 on tax-deductible contributions would have the same effect as the 5 percent limit declared unconstitutional (Blankenburg, Staudhammer, and Steiner 1990:928; Landfried 1994:82; von Arnim 1996:65).[14] The parties, as a result, could not expect to be hurt by the decision in their efforts to generate donations.

The FCC also held fast to its principle that at most half of a party's income could be generated from public revenues (the "relative upper limit") (BVerfGE 73,40: 96). But once again, it watered down the impact of that principle through two explicit accounting procedures. First, the court asserted (without further explanation) that the payments parties received out of the equal chances scheme could be counted as *private* income of the parties for purposes of determining the relative upper limit, even though these payments were made directly out of the federal budget. Second, the court ruled that "party taxes," which consist of special contributions that parties traditionally impose on their deputies in the Bundestag and in Land parliaments, could also be counted as private income (BVerfGE 73,40: 100).

These party taxes are not trivial income for parties. In a survey of Bundestag deputies in 1988, Landfried determined that CDU/CSU deputies were paying, on average, DM 920 to their party every month, SPD deputies DM 1,492 per month, and FDP deputies DM 988 per month. In the period 1968–83, party taxes at all levels constituted about 10 percent of total revenues for the CDU, 9 percent for the SPD, 8 percent for the CSU, and 7 percent for the FDP (Landfried 1994:98f.).[15] The fact that the court allowed these taxes to be counted as private income seems

---

[14] The average annual salary of a German employee at the time was DM 40,000 (see Judge Ernst Wolfgang Böckenförde's powerful dissent).

[15] Since the Parties Act of 1983, party taxes are no longer listed separately in the financial records of the parties, but are lumped in with membership dues. The party taxes are displayed in Figure 6.1 (for the years following 1983, the figure displays von Arnim's estimate of the taxes. For the details of how this estimate was derived, see von Arnim 1996:122).

Legislative Response to Party Finance II and the 1986 Decisions

especially strange since party taxes appear to be unconstitutional in light of the court's own jurisprudence, as the Federal President's commission had pointed out (Schneider 1989:225). For example, in its 1975 decision on parliamentary salaries, the court had ruled:

> The salary [paid to deputies] is solely intended to secure their standard of living. It may not be used for other purposes; for example, to contribute towards the financing of factions or parties or campaign expenses. (BVerfGE 40,296:316)

Moreover, because they are paid out of deputies' salaries that are determined by parliament itself, these party taxes are also unlike private donations because it is likely that parties are already taking the party taxes into account when determining deputies' salaries (Landfried 1994:99; von Arnim 1996:316). Finally, these contributions are not truly voluntary because they must be paid by a deputy in order not to hurt his or her standing in the party and to retain the seat. Nevertheless, the FCC allowed parties to count both of these sources of income, which derive directly from public funds, as private income, thus making it easier for parties to avoid the relative upper limit.

Finally, the court dismissed the Greens' challenge to the funding of political foundations. The court argued that the work of the foundations constitutes an "independent set of tasks worthy of public support, separate from the political parties, and independent of the work undertaken by political parties" (BVerfGE 73,1: 37). In addition, the court asserted that there was no evidence to suggest that foundation money was systematically being employed to support the work of political parties. In light of the various improprieties uncovered by the Bundesrechnungshof in the audit undertaken in connection with this case, this conclusion appears to be hard to sustain. The audit revealed loans made to parties on favorable terms, commissioning of opinion surveys for the parties, newspaper advertisements, and purchase of campaign materials by party foundations. Nevertheless, the court chose to ignore the report by dismissing its contents as "isolated events." Given that the audit covered only a two-year period, there is, of course, little reason to think that these are only isolated events. As Landfried has concluded in her study, "the court's depiction of the work of the foundations... is unrealistic and trivializes the misuses uncovered by the Auditing Office" (1994:110).

The unambiguous overall conclusion that emerges from the two 1986 decisions is that the FCC (for whatever reason) effectively decided to tolerate and even legitimize the evasive responses to its earlier decisions that had attempted to impose some restrictions on public financing of political parties. As von Arnim concluded, "with the verdict of 1986, the court had, for all practical purposes, capitulated" (1996:66).[16] Similarly, Blankenburg et al., commenting on the 1986 verdicts, write:

> The persistent noncompliance with existing legal rules had finally paid off... it is plain to see that the court has in fact sanctioned the practices that parties had employed illegally in the past, blatantly contradicting its own former jurisprudence. While in its earlier rulings the FCC had consistently tried to defend citizens' democratic participation against self-styled party rule, at last it submitted to the powerful realities of the "representative absolutism" and party oligopoly by adapting its jurisprudence to the parties' unconstitutional practices. (1990:928)

This development appears clearly consistent with the theory developed in Chapter 2: The court reacted in a predictable way to a set of circumstances in which evasion and defiance of costly decisions would be highly likely. The financial need of the parties and the stake of the parties in having the Parties Act sustained loomed especially large in 1986. We would therefore expect the court to be even more constrained in this second set of decisions than it had been in 1968. The decisions are consistent with this expectation. Instead of risking a confrontation, the court was careful not to tread too closely on the interests of established parties.

THE REVISION OF 1988 AND THE 1992 PARTY FINANCE DECISION

In response to the 1986 verdict and emboldened by the FCC's lenient treatment, the parties in the Bundestag once again revised the Parties Act. While making some changes to the equal chances scheme, they also introduced a so-called base amount (*Sockelbetrag*) to be paid to parties as a subsidy for their continuing organizational expenses. This fixed amount was to be paid to any party gathering at least 2 percent of the votes in a federal election, and increased public finance by about DM 17 million annually (Landfried 1994:66). Finally, the parties changed the tax code to allow tax-deductible donations to political parties of up to DM 60,000, and increased the disclosure limit for donations to DM 40,000 (i.e., only donations over DM 40,000 would require public disclosure of the source of the donation). Once again, the Greens brought suit against the new statute to the FCC. In April 1992, the Second Senate issued a sweeping decision in the case. This decision is interesting in many respects. Most

---

[16] See also Landfried (1994:80).

The Revision of 1988 and the 1992 Party Finance Decision

importantly, it marks a clear return by the court to its earlier jurisprudence, in which it had combined transparent demands with considerable concessions to the parties in order to induce compliance.

The court's decision contains four principal holdings. First, the court declared the equal chances scheme and the base amount unconstitutional (BVerfGE 85,264: 294ff.). Second, it declared the DM 60,000 limit on tax-deductible donations to political parties unconstitutional, asserting that the equality of citizens in the political process demands that any tax privileges must be such that the majority of citizens can take advantage of them, implying a much lower limit on tax-deductible contributions (BVerfGE 85,264: 312). Third, the judges declared the public disclosure limit of DM 40,000 unconstitutional and ordered disclosure of any donations from one source that total more than DM 20,000 in one calendar year (BVerfGE 85:264: 325).

Finally, the court abandoned its long-established principle that parties could be reimbursed only for campaign expenses. Acknowledging that party finance had de facto developed into a system of public subsidies for the general activities of political parties, the court declared that such a funding scheme would be constitutional. At the same time, the court tried to impose explicit restrictions on such funding. Most importantly, to ensure that parties would remain responsive to citizens' demands, the court ruled that public funds granted to a party must be explicitly tied to a party's electoral support and its ability to generate private donations and membership dues (BVerfGE 85,264: 265). Toward the same end, the court also reasserted its long-established principle that at most half of a party's revenues could be derived from public subsidies ("relative upper limit"). Finally, in order to limit the future growth of public finance, the court declared that the real value of the total average amount of public subsidies received by the parties in the years 1989–92 constitutes an absolute upper limit on the amount of public subsidies that may be granted ("absolute upper limit") (BVerfGE 85,264: 265).

Several aspects of this decision are interesting from the theoretical perspective developed here. First, in trying to place limits on party finance, the court concentrated on *simplifying* the regulations. It dropped the ambiguous distinction between campaign and other expenses. Instead, it established two principles that would govern the amount of public money a party could receive: the relative and absolute upper limits. Given a certain set of accounting procedures (more on that later), both principles are fairly transparent and can be checked relatively easily. One way to interpret the court's decision is therefore as an attempt to bring greater transparency to party finance. Greater transparency, in turn, would create greater pressure for compliance.

Second, in simplifying the constitutional constraints on party finance in this manner, the FCC also made significant concessions to the political parties that made the decision easier to swallow. As in the 1986 decision, the court continued to permit parties to count party taxes as private revenue in calculating the relative upper limit (BVerfGE 85,264: 289), thereby reducing the "bite" of that particular principle. As Landfried concluded, "the judges of the Second Senate neglected to ensure that the principle of the independence of parties from the state is not watered down by a party-friendly definition of 'private revenues'" (1994:343). Moreover, in calculating the baseline amount for the absolute upper limit, the court explicitly included payments from the equal chances scheme and the base amount even though both had been declared unconstitutional (BVerfGE 85,264: 291). As a result, the decision did not demand a reduction in the total amount of public revenue available to the parties. Similarly, the court did not order the parties to return any of the payments that had been deemed unconstitutional. Both constitute important concessions to the interests of the established parties.

To summarize, the 1992 FCC decision displays the same combination of tactics already evident in the 1968 decision. On the one hand, the court strove to impose simpler and more transparent constraints on public funding schemes (general funding subject to the relative and absolute upper limits), thereby making evasion more difficult to hide. On the other hand, the judges incorporated important concessions in interpreting the meaning of these constraints. The concessions the court granted radically reduced the cost of the decision to the established parties (the generous calculation of the upper limit and the accounting rules for the relative limit) and thereby reduced the potential for a legislative–judicial confrontation.

The legislative response to the 1992 verdict is also interesting on several dimensions. As it did in the wake of the 1968 decision, the Bundestag broadly followed the most transparent of the court's directions. Thus, the upper limit of DM 230 million was adopted, and a procedure was put into place to ensure that this limit is not exceeded in future years (it was raised to keep up with inflation in early 1999). Under the new law, the total amount of a party's subsidies is determined by its ability to generate votes in federal, state, and European elections and by its donations and membership dues (see von Arnim 1996:98f.).

However, once again, the parties included several provisions that seem to evade the court's decision where that decision is less transparent. Most importantly, the new law still provides, for all practical purposes, for a base amount. The base amount was preserved by a provision that posits that parties receive an additional DM 0.30 for the first 5 million votes gathered above the subsidy of DM 1 per vote generally.[17] In practice, this provision means that parties continue to receive a certain fixed base amount (which favors small parties). The constitutionality of this provision was so questionable that fifteen SPD members of the Bundestag publicly stated their constitutional objections and refused to vote for the law (BTD 12:16448f.). The federal president also voiced his concerns about constitutionality and signed the new law only after a considerable delay.

Moreover, the parties set the upper limit for tax-deductible contributions at DM 6,000 (DM 12,000 for a married couple). This amount exceeds the amount proposed by the federal president's commission of experts (formed to advise the Bundestag after the 1992 decision) by a factor of 3. In its 1992 decision, the court had declared that the maximum tax-deductible amount must be low enough to allow the average taxpayer to make such a contribution (BVerfGE 85,264: 265). Guided by the fact that the only tax provision the court had sustained in the 1992 decision provided for tax-deductible contributions of up to DM 1,200/DM 2,400,[18] the commission proposed a limit of DM 2,000/DM 4,000 (von Arnim 1996:73). One important motivation in expanding the tax-deductible limits beyond these recommendations to an amount that clearly cannot be taken advantage of by an average taxpayer may well have been the desire to ensure that the party taxes would qualify as tax-deductible (von Arnim 1996:74).[19] In short, while bowing to the FCC's clearest demands, there seems to be at least some prima facie evidence that the established parties have again attempted to evade important aspects of the court's decision. A renewed challenge to the party finance

---

[17] The latest revision of the party finance law (see von Arnim 2002) preserves this bonus payment. Parties receive Euro 0.70 for each vote with a bonus of Euro 0.15 for the first 4 million votes captured.

[18] BVerfGE 85,264: 316: "The provision of paragraph 34g EstG ... conforms to constitutional demands. The legislator could reasonably suppose that in fiscal year 1984 a donation of DM 1,200/DM 2,400 was reachable for the average wage earner."

[19] In addition, because tax-deductible contributions are rewarded with a 50 percent public subsidy under the new law, this limit ensures that the party taxes are also subsidized.

law, brought by communal voter associations, was dismissed by the court in 1998 (BVerfGE 99, 84).[20]

CONCLUSION

As the case study in this Chapter has demonstrated, the interactions between the Bundesverfassungsgericht and the Bundestag over party finance are consistent with the expectations derived from the theory advanced in Chapter 2. Party finance is a policy area in which all established parties have strong common preferences. Moreover, given these congruent preferences, an important "watchdog" that can call attention to legislative evasion – the parliamentary opposition – is missing.[21] As a result, the argument would lead us to expect that legislative majorities will attempt to evade decisions that run contrary to their preferences. As the evidence has shown, virtually from the outset, legislative majorities in the Bundestag have done so. They have consistently tried to evade FCC decisions that limit their access to public funds, bowing to the FCC's most transparent demands while devising other means of circumventing the restrictions imposed by the court. The judges of the Bundesverfassungsgericht, in turn, have also responded in ways that the theory leads us to expect. As the extent of evasion in response to early decisions became apparent, they attempted to increase pressure for compliance by increasing the transparency of rulings (e.g., by directing that parties garnering at least 0.5 percent of the vote must be eligible for public funds). Moreover, in imposing constraints on party finance, the judges have been careful to make considerable concessions to the established parties that temper the cost of their decisions and reduce the potential for a legislative–judicial conflict. As the model would lead us to expect, these concessions were particularly

---

[20] Communal voter associations had challenged the new law because the court's 1992 decision had directed the Bundestag to consider local voter associations in any revision of the party finance law, but the Bundestag's revision continued to exclude these associations from all funding. In response to the CDU funding scandal that broke in 1999, the Bundestag passed a new party finance law in 2002. However, the law retains all of the relevant provisions of the 1992 law discussed earlier. In addition, the new law has further restricted access to public finance by increasing the number of votes required by minor parties to qualify for funding (von Arnim 2002).

[21] In addition, many other interest groups in Germany, which often have close ties to the political parties and must maintain productive working relationships with the parties to preserve their influence on other issues, may not have a strong interest in calling attention to evasive maneuvers on an issue that unifies all established parties.

Conclusion

pronounced when the financial need of parties was most acute during the 1980s. In short, the theoretical argument of Chapter 2 usefully illuminates the history of party finance in Germany.

The previous three chapters have provided considerable support – statistical as well as qualitative – for central implications of the theoretical model. It is now time to step back and evaluate the broader implications of the argument for our understanding of the Bundesverfassungsgericht as well as for constitutional courts around the world.

7

Prudent Jurists

Around the world, courts with the power to declare legislative and executive actions unconstitutional are playing a more and more prominent role. Establishing a constitutional court to act as the guardian of the constitution is often seen as a necessary part of making a transition to democracy (Howard 1993; Schwartz 2000; Widner 2001). Thus, in one of the most sweeping waves of democratic transition in history, each of the newly democratic states in Eastern Europe chose to include judicial review in its new constitutional order (Elster, Offe, and Preuss 1998:102). Nor is the influence of courts limited to new democracies. In countries where constitutional review has been a part of the political process for decades, courts appear to be playing a more and more active role (e.g., Shapiro and Stone 1994, 2002; Stone Sweet 2000). The reach of courts extends even beyond the nation-state. Supranational courts like the ECJ that can rule on the validity of national legislation are growing increasingly influential (Alter 2001; Mattli and Slaughter 1998; Stone Sweet and Brunell 1998). It is perhaps not surprising that scholars have begun to speak of a "globalization of judicial power" (Tate and Valinder 1995) and a "judicialization of politics" (Stone Sweet 2000).

Given these trends, understanding how courts interact with legislative majorities and other institutions of governance is of central importance in understanding politics in constitutional democracies today. And yet, comparative political scientists have traditionally devoted surprisingly little attention to studying courts. Partly in response, a considerable literature on the impact of judicial institutions on the political process has emerged over the past two decades.[1] A major purpose of this literature has been to

---

[1] It would be impossible to cite all the works that deserve mention here. Some of the most prominent and most recent contributions are Blair (1981), Brewer-Carias

"bring the courts back in" by demonstrating the impact of constitutional courts on policy. Careful case studies of issue areas as diverse as abortion, privatization, and university organization reveal that policy is often made in a complex interaction between legislative majorities and judicial actors (Landfried 1984, 1988; Stone 1992; Stone Sweet 2000). Nor have scholars stopped at analyzing specific outputs of courts. Instead, considerable theoretical effort has gone into tracing how legislative majorities accommodate themselves to the potential interventions of a court ex ante and how the mere availability of judicial review transforms the legislative process (see Landfried 1992; Stone 1992; Stone Sweet 1998; Vanberg 1998a, 1998b). The widely shared conclusion that emerges from this literature is that courts are exercising tremendous influence in shaping political outcomes in European democracies. Consider Stone Sweet's judgment, which is representative:

> The work of governments and parliaments is today structured by an ever-expanding web of constitutional constraints. In a word, European policy-making has been *judicialized*. Constitutional judges routinely intervene in legislative processes, establishing limits on law-making behavior, reconfiguring policy-making environments, even drafting the precise terms of legislation. The development of European constitutionalism has also infected the European Union. The European Court of Justice, the constitutional court of the Union, has fashioned a kind of supranational constitution, and this law binds governments and the parliaments they control. (2000:1)

The seminal contribution of this literature has been to call attention to the importance of judicial institutions and to demonstrate the very real effect of "judicialization" on the political process. But the traditional approach to studying European courts also leaves open central questions. Most importantly, the picture that emerges from this literature appears one-sided. By and large, scholars have treated courts as exogenous constraints to which legislative majorities must adjust in pursuing their policy agenda. In other words, with only a few notable exceptions (e.g., Epstein et al. 2001; Staton 2003; Volcansek 2000), the characterization of legislative–judicial interactions that sustains much of this literature – as suggested by the tenor of the preceding quotation – conceives of courts as unconstrained actors that are able to impose their preferences on other policymakers. Yet the accounts in of the previous chapters challenge this assumption. They demonstrate that courts are, at least in certain

(1989), Cappelletti (1989), Holland (1991), Landfried (1984), Shapiro (1981), Stone (1992), Stone Sweet (2000), Tate and Vallinder (1995), and Volcansek (2000).

circumstances, constrained and that their political environment may shape their decisions.

What differentiates the theory presented in this book is that I focus on this second aspect: the need for courts to adjust to their environment. The linchpin for the argument is the observation that formally, at least, constitutional courts occupy a weak position. Because they rule directly on the validity of legislation, they must often rely on legislative majorities to abide by, and sometimes even to carry out, their decisions. This dependence on the very institutions the court is intended to control gives rise to a potential compliance problem. How can courts successfully constrain legislative majorities when – as is often the case – legislative majorities oppose a judicial ruling? The central argument I have made is that a principal enforcement mechanism for judicial decisions in advanced democracies consists of public support for a court (and its decisions) and the concomitant threat of a public backlash against elected officials who fail to heed judicial rulings. If elected officials who refuse to be bound by the rulings of a court must fear loss of public support, powerful incentives for compliance emerge.

While other scholars have highlighted the potential compliance problem and the central role that public support can play in generating judicial authority (e.g., Canon and Johnson, 1999; Gibson et al., 1998), this book has focused on developing a detailed account of the implications of this enforcement mechanism for the interactions between constitutional courts and legislatures, for judicial behavior, and for the ability of judges to constrain legislative majorities. By focusing on the conditions under which public support can bring effective pressure to bear on legislative majorities (transparency) as well as the foundations of public support for courts, the argument in this book demonstrates that the jurisprudence of a court and its de facto ability to constrain legislative majorities depend on more than the legal issues surrounding a case, the constitutional text, or the judges' preferences. They also depend on the constellation of public support, the level of public awareness, the interests of political parties, and the presence (and preferences) of organized interest groups.

This simple, parsimonious theoretical approach yields a surprisingly rich theory of legislative–judicial interactions that is consistent with a wide range of observed interactions between courts and legislatures. More importantly, the theory predicts the circumstances under which we should expect to see each type of interaction. Where courts enjoy considerable public support and transparency is high, courts will be powerful actors to whom legislative majorities will largely be forced to defer. Where courts have little support or transparency is low, legislative majorities will generally not be constrained by the presence of a court. And in environments characterized by intermediate levels of support and transparency, we may observe open conflict between a constitutional court and governing majorities.[2]

A fundamental conclusion of the argument is therefore that the ability of a court to shape policy and to issue decisions that are opposed by legislative majorities depends on the court's political environment. While not denying that constitutional courts are significant and powerful actors under certain circumstances, the theory thus cautions us not to overinterpret judicial successes in some areas to assume that courts are *universally* able to constrain legislative majorities. In other words, the argument qualifies the one-sided picture that emerges from much of the current literature. Because the power of a constitutional court depends on the court's political environment, courts will not be equally powerful under all circumstances. Across countries and across time, the power of institutionally identical courts will vary, depending on the political context. Even for the same court at one point in time, influence is likely to vary across issue areas.

In emphasizing the constraints placed on constitutional courts, the argument mirrors an exchange that has been prominent in the literature on transnational courts, in particular the ECJ. Over the past decade, scholars have debated the extent to which the ECJ is able to constrain national governments in circumstances in which these governments would prefer not to cooperate with European law. Some scholars have emphasized the constraints imposed on the ECJ by the threat of noncompliance (Carrubba 2003; Garrett 1995; Garrett and Weingast 1993), while others have, much in the tradition of scholars working on European courts at the national level, characterized the ECJ as a largely unconstrained actor that can drive the process of European integration (Alter 1998, 2001; Mattli and Slaughter 1998; Stone Sweet and Brunell 1998). The principal difference between the approaches that emphasize the constraints confronting the ECJ and the approach taken here consists in the mechanism that is assumed to enforce compliance. Because the ECJ is a transnational court, scholars who highlight the problematic nature of compliance have generally sought to ground the authority of the ECJ in the interests that member states have in their ongoing relationships. As a result, explanations of

---

[2] Of course, these statements are always relative to the intensity of judicial and legislative preferences. See Chapter 2.

noncompliance focus on the interests of member states, not on public support or transparency.[3]

While the need to maintain public support and the limits imposed by transparency define boundaries to judicial power, it is important to note that the argument does not imply that constitutional courts are powerless paper tigers or that judicial decisions are determined mechanically by the preferences of other actors and by public opinion. Under the right circumstances – when public support for the court is sufficiently high and compliance is relatively easy to monitor – high courts can be powerful forces in moving policy in directions not favored by governing majorities. And *within* the constraints imposed by the implementation problem, a wide variety of considerations may shape judicial decisions, including jurisprudential reasoning and judicial policy preferences. In other words, the power of courts to enforce constitutional boundaries and to constrain governing majorities can be substantial, but it is limited. It depends on the ease with which citizens can verify compliance, and it depends on the willingness of citizens to lend support to a court by punishing those who ignore its decisions.

BEYOND GERMANY

The previous chapters have provided considerable evidence for this argument with respect to the German FCC. But the argument applies more generally to any situation in which the need to retain sufficient public backing is an important dimension of the decision calculus of legislators in deciding how to respond to judicial decisions. In fact, notable features of the argument appear consistent with the experiences of prominent courts around the world. Consider the relationship between public opinion and judicial rulings. Extensive research suggests that (isolated examples to the contrary notwithstanding), even the U.S. Supreme Court – often regarded as the most powerful court in the world – does not deviate systematically from prevailing public opinion (Bickel 1962:23; Marshall 1989:97; McCloskey 1994:208; McGuire and Stimson in press; Mishler and Sheehan 1993, 1994; Norpoth and Segal 1994). Similarly, Volcansek has stressed that public opinion appears to impact judicial deliberations in Italy (Volcansek 2000:148f). Some scholars have linked this tendency for courts to be

---

[3] The one exception is Carrubba (2003), who considers public support as an enforcement mechanism for ECJ decisions but who does not explore the impact of transparency on the efficacy of this mechanism.

attuned to public sentiments directly to the issue at the center of the analysis presented here:

> For even if given the opportunity to do so, a court cannot attempt for long to reverse a clear political trend. By doing so, it would risk exhausting the reservoir of public respect and destroying the consensus in favor of judicial resolution of political issues on which its influence and above all the assurance of compliance with its decisions depend. (Blair 1981:256)

Perhaps the most interesting implication of the theory from a comparative point of view is that the impact of constitutional review will vary across courts, across time, and even across issues for the same court. Not all courts benefit from the level of support that the U.S. Supreme Court and the Bundesverfassungsgericht enjoy. And even courts that do have considerable support must act on an array of issues characterized by different constellations of support for particular decisions and by varying levels of transparency. As a result, constitutional review, even if exercised within the same formal institutional framework, will not provide an equally effective check on the power of executives and legislative majorities in all circumstances.

The process of democratization underway in the former Communist nations of Eastern Europe provides a useful testing ground for this hypothesis. As Schwartz (2000) has documented in an extensive, careful study, the experiences of the new constitutional courts have varied widely. Some, like the Hungarian Constitutional Court, have become powerful institutions. Others, like the Russian Constitutional Court, suffered direct attacks on their independence and have been much less successful in establishing significant constraints on the governments they are intended to control.[4] Why do some courts succeed and others fail? The theory laid out here may help us to understand this variation.

For example, to the extent that public support for courts varies across Eastern Europe, courts with the same institutional structure should be more or less influential, depending on the support they enjoy. In fact, this expectation is consistent with observations by prominent commentators on the Eastern European courts. Thus, Schwartz conjectures that for the successful courts, "the constitutional courts' standing with the general public ... is remarkably high.... This public esteem may help to explain why there has been no systematic defiance of these courts in the countries

---

[4] Thus, Aleksandr Solzhenitsyn has concluded that "the [Russian] Constitutional Court is a mere plaything" (Solzhenitsyn 1997).

under discussion" (Schwartz 2000:237). Similarly, Orkeny and Scheppele (1996:83) have called attention to the fact that the support enjoyed by one of the most powerful constitutional courts in Eastern Europe, the Hungarian Constitutional Court, exceeds support for the political branches. Conversely, in explaining the failure of some courts, Schwartz has pointed to the relative weakness – in terms of popular support – of these bodies vis-à-vis other institutions:

> One fair inference from this sample is that while a constitutional court cannot ultimately prevent a determined and powerful authoritarian regime – particularly when, as in Kazakhstan, Belarus, Romania, and Armenia, that regime has wide popular support – it can put a finger in the dike to gain time and put some pressure on a weaker style of authoritarianism. But that is probably all it can do. (2000:227)

In short, the argument made here holds out considerable promise in helping us understand the experiences of Eastern European courts. In fact, some scholars have already begun to develop systematic theoretical accounts of the authority of constitutional courts in Eastern Europe that emphasize the importance of public support (Epstein et al. 2001).

In addition, investigating the success of the theory in accounting for the Eastern European experience makes it possible to test aspects of the theory that could not be adequately evaluated in the context of an established democracy like Germany. Perhaps the most interesting dynamic prediction of the model (summarized in Observations 5 and 6 in Chapter 2) is that the observable interactions between constitutional courts and legislative majorities may have a "curvilinear" relationship: Initially, little conflict between court and legislature is observed as a court finds itself in a weak position to oppose a legislature (the Judicial Self-Censoring Equilibrium). As a court gains public support, it becomes bolder in asserting itself vis-à-vis the legislature, even when it expects occasional noncompliance (the Contentious Equilibrium). Finally, the court may establish so much support that it is able to effectively constrain legislative majorities under most circumstances (the Separation-of-Powers Equilibrium). The development of the U.S. Supreme Court over the course of the nineteenth century appears consistent with this pattern (Carrubba and Rogers 2003; Friedman 2003; Graber 1998). The new democracies in Eastern Europe, where courts are undergoing precisely this development, provide a unique opportunity to investigate the dynamic aspects of the interactions between constitutional courts and legislative majorities, and to gain a more detailed understanding of how courts do (or do not) develop their authority. It is now time to step back and consider the broader normative implications of the findings.

BROADER NORMATIVE IMPLICATIONS

A conventional, widely shared view of courts conceives of them as judicial bulwarks that provide a countermajoritarian influence in democratic political systems otherwise designed to enhance majority control over the policymaking process. This "guardian vision" of courts has a long tradition (de Tocqueville 1835/1988:103ff.; White 2000), and it is often self-consciously asserted by those who must draft constitutions.[5] Konrad Adenauer's remarks during the Constitutional Convention that wrote Germany's Basic Law, quoted in Chapter 1, reflect this vision well:

> Tyranny by a single person is not the only form of dictatorship. Tyranny by a parliamentary majority is also possible. And we want to furnish protection against such tyranny in the form of a constitutional court. (PRD, second session:25)

The normative commitment underlying this vision of courts as countermajoritarian institutions raises fundamental philosophical questions about the nature of democracy and the role of various institutional arrangements, including constitutional courts, in realizing a particular ideal vision of democratic government (Dahl 1989; Powell 2000). But it also suggests a more immediate, practical question: *Can courts effectively act as countermajoritarian institutions that enforce constitutional constraints on governing majorities?* The underlying assumption of the guardian vision is that the answer is "yes." The central conclusion that arises from the analysis offered in this book suggests a more ambiguous answer. The power of constitutional courts is considerable but constrained. The judges who serve on these courts cannot afford to consider only the constitutional text, legal principles, or their own preferences. Because implementation of judicial decisions is potentially problematic, judges must take into account the likely reactions of other actors to decisions by the court. They must be responsive to the interests of governing majorities, and they cannot rule consistently against prevailing public sentiments. In other words, the argument presented here challenges the descriptive assumptions about the abilities of courts that underlie the guardian vision. Constitutional courts cannot always restrain the exercise of political power by legislative majorities, and they are not likely to function consistently as countermajoritarian institutions.[6]

---

[5] In turning to constitutional courts, constitution writers in Eastern Europe were similarly motivated by the desire to protect political minorities (Schwartz 2000:258n48).

[6] This conclusion mirrors the one reached by Gerald Rosenberg (1991) in his careful empirical analysis of the ability of U.S. courts to shape policy in opposition to prevailing political majorities.

Not surprisingly, the *normative* judgment one passes on this need for courts to remain sensitive to the interests of governing majorities and to public opinion depends, at least in part, on what one thinks democratic and constitutional politics *ought to* be. Adherents to the guardian vision tend to be wary of placing too much power in the hands of elected officials and favor arrangements that provide a role for courts to actively police constitutional boundaries. Observing what they perceive as excessive deference to legislative majorities, some proponents of the guardian vision have argued for more vigorous judicial supervision. Thus, Riker and Weingast conclude that courts are not sufficiently aggressive in protecting minority rights that do not receive adequate consideration through regular democratic channels:

Judicial deference to legislatures, as past actions of legislatures clearly reveal, leads to policies that compromise the rights of minorities.... Our perspective, therefore, provides a more complete underpinning of the proposition that judges should not defer to legislative decisions regarding rights of any kind. (1988:399f.)

One interpretation of the results found here concludes that such calls for a more aggressive countermajoritarian role for courts rest on a "hollow hope" (Rosenberg 1991). The argument and the evidence strongly suggest that courts cannot consistently live up to the guardian vision. Courts may, in Schwartz's words, "put a finger in the dike to gain time" (2000:227), but they cannot effectively resist clear popular trends. In this sense, the results are likely to be uncomfortable for those who believe that "constitutional provisions should be designed to work against precisely those aspects of a country's culture and tradition that are likely to produce most harm through that country's ordinary political processes" (Sunstein 1991:385) and who regard the primary role of courts as providing a countermajoritarian check on the will of governing majorities.

There is, however, another way to view the results. Reacting to what they perceive as the increasing influence of courts on democratic politics, some scholars have argued that the increasing activity of constitutional courts is an indication that courts are no longer practicing the appropriate level of judicial restraint. These scholars tend to view courts as unaccountable and undemocratic "substitute legislatures" that are increasingly able to dictate their preferences to policymakers who possess more direct democratic legitimacy (see Holland 1991; Landfried 1984, 1992). These criticisms, of course, also draw on a long tradition, going back to the French Revolution, of democratic mistrust in a "government of judges" (Cappelletti 1989; Stone 1992). The current study suggests that such fears of unaccountable and unconstrained judicial influence may be overdrawn. For those who favor political arrangements that increase the responsiveness of policy to currently prevailing moods, and who are suspicious of placing constraints on directly accountable policymakers, the findings should be encouraging. Constitutional courts pose less of a threat to such a vision than is commonly supposed.

All of this is not to say that constitutional courts are not influential policymakers. Undoubtedly, they can exercise considerable sway over policy, but their ability to do so is contingent and constrained. It is contingent on the threat of a public backlash against elected officials who ignore or evade rulings, and therefore judges must be sensitive to public opinion and to the interests of governing majorities in order to generate compliance. As a result, the power judges can exercise is more like the power of an agenda setter, who can move policy within a set of alternatives acceptable to other players, than the power of an unconstrained dictator. How wide or narrow the bounds of judicial discretion are depends significantly on the political environment, most importantly the support a court enjoys, the preferences of governing majorities, and the transparency surrounding a decision. Naturally, this argument does not imply that court decisions find universal approval or that citizens (or scholars) could not imagine policies they would prefer to those selected by the court. Thus, the results may still trouble those who want a tight connection between current majority preferences and public policy. But the argument does imply that constitutional courts cannot consistently subvert and frustrate the wishes of a clear citizen majority. While judges may not have to worry about the electoral connection directly, they are made *indirectly* accountable to citizens through the implementation problem. The specter of a government of judges does not reflect political reality.

In a larger sense, this study thus suggests that the interactions between judges and governing majorities that are at the heart of constitutionally constrained but democratic government cannot be understood purely in jurisprudential or legal terms. Courts are not apolitical guardians towering above the fray, unmoved by political considerations. To be successful in shaping policy, judges must adjust their decisions to the political environment in which they work. They cannot simply act as jurists. They must be *prudent jurists*.

Bibliography

Adenauer, Konrad. 1966. *Erinnerungen Band 1:1953–1955*. Stuttgart: Deutscher Bücherbund.
Alexander, Herbert (ed.). 1989. *Comparative Political Finance in the 1980s*. Cambridge: Cambridge University Press.
Alexander, Herbert, and Rei Shiratori (eds.). 1994. *Comparative Political Finance among the Democracies*. Boulder: Westview Press.
Alter, Karen. 1998. "Who Are the Masters of the Treaty? European Governments and the European Count of Justice." *International Organization* 52:125–52.
Alter, Karen. 2001. *Establishing the Supremacy of European Law*. Oxford: Oxford University Press.
Arnim, Hans Herbert von. 1993. *Der Staat als Beute: Wie Politiker in eigener Sache Gesetze machen*. München: Knaur.
Arnim, Hans Herbert von. 1996. *Die Partei, der Abgeordnete und das Geld: Parteienfinanzierung in Deutschland*. München: Knaur.
Arnim, Hans Herbert von. 2002. "Die Neue Parteienfinanzierung." *Deutsches Verwaltungsblatt*. 16/2002:1065–78.
Arnold, R. Douglas. 1990. *The Logic of Congressional Action*. New Haven: Yale University Press.
Baring, Arnulf. 1969. *Außenpolitik in Adenauers Kanzlerdemokratie*. München: R. Oldenbourg Verlag.
Bark, Dennis, and David Gress. 1993. *From Shadow to Substance 1945–1963*. Oxford: Blackwell.
Bates, Robert, Avner Greif, Margaret Levi, Jean-Laurent Rosenthal, and Barry Weingast. 1998. *Analytic Narratives*. Princeton: Princeton University Press.
Baum, Lawrence. 1976. "Implementation of Judicial Decisions." *American Politics Quarterly* 4:86–114.
Baum, Lawrence. 1981. "Comparing the Implementation of Legislative and Judicial Policies." In Daniel Mazmanian and Paul Sabatier (eds.). *Effective Policy Implementation*. Lexington: Lexington Books.
Bickel, Alexander. 1962. *The Least Dangerous Branch: The Supreme Court at the Bar of Politics*. New York: Bobbs-Merrill.

Blair, Philip. 1981. *Federalism and Judicial Review in West Germany*. Oxford: Clarendon Press.
Blankenburg, Erhard, Rainer Staudhammer, and Heinz Steiner. 1990. "Political Scandals and Corruption Issues in West Germany." In A. Heidenheimer, M. Johnston, and V. Levine (eds.). *Political Corruption: A Handbook*. New Brunswick: Transaction Publishers.
Boldt, Hans. 1993. *Deutsche Verfassungsgeschichte*. München: Deutscher Taschenbuch Verlag.
Booms, Hans. (ed.). 1989. *Die Kabinettsprotokolle der Bundesregierung: Band 5: 1952*. Boppard am Rhein: Harald Boldt Verlag.
Bösch, Frank. 2001. "Die Enstehung des CDU-Spendensystems und die Konsolidierung der deutschen Parteinlandschaft." *Zeitschrift für Geschichtswissenschaft*. 49:695–711.
Brace, Paul, and Laura Langer. 2001. "The Preemptive Power of State Supreme Courts: Enactment of Abortion and Death Penalty Laws in the American States." Paper presented at the Midwest Political Science Association meeting, Chicago, April 19–22.
Brewer Carias, A. R. 1989. *Judicial Review in Comparative Law*. Cambridge: Cambridge University Press.
Buchstab, Günter. (ed.). 1986. *Die Protokolle des CDU-Bundesvorstandes 1950–1953*. Stuttgart: Klett-Cotta Verlag.
Buchstab, Günter (ed.). 1990. *Die Protokolle des CDU-Bundesvorstandes 1953–1957*. Düsseldorf: Droste Verlag.
Caldeira, Greg. 1986. "Neither the Purse Nor the Sword: Dynamics of Public Confidence in the Supreme Court." *American Political Science Review* 80:1209–26.
Caldeira, Greg. 1987. "Public Opinion and the U.S. Supreme Court: FDR's Court Packing Plan." *American Political Science Review* 81:1139–53.
Caldeira, Greg, and James Gibson. 1992. "The Etiology of Public Support for the Supreme Court." *American Journal of Political Science* 36:635–64.
Caldeira, Greg, and John Wright. 1990. "Amici Curiae before the Supreme Court: Who Participates, When, and How Much?" *The Journal of Politics* 52:782–806.
Canache, Damarys. 1999. *Political Support in a Fragile Democracy*. Ph.D. Thesis, University of Pittsburgh.
Canon, Bradley, and Charles Johnson. 1999. *Judicial Policies: Implementation and Impact*. Washington, DC: Congressional Quarterly Press.
Capelletti, Mauro. 1989. *The Judicial Process in Comparative Perspective*. Oxford: Clarendon Press.
Carrubba, Clifford. 2003. "The Politics of Supranational Legal Integration: National Governments, the European Court of Justice, and the Development of EU Law." Manuscript, Department of Political Science, Emory University.
Carrubba, Clifford, and James Rogers. 2003. "National Judicial Power and the Dormant Commerce Clause." *Journal of Law, Economics, and Organization* 19:543–70.
Clinton, Robert. 1994. "Game-Theory, Legal History, and the Origins of Judicial Review: A Revisionist Analysis of *Marbury v. Madison*." *American Journal of Political Science* 38:285–302.

Dahl, Robert. 1957. "Decision-Making in a Democracy: The Supreme Court as National Policy-Maker." *Journal of Public Law* 6:279–95.
Dahl, Robert. 1989. *Democracy and Its Critics*. New Haven: Yale University Press.
Dehousse, Renaud. 1998. *The European Court of Justice: The Politics of Judicial Integration*. London: Macmillan.
Dübber, Ulrich. 1970. *Geld und Politk: Die Finanzwirtschaft der Parteien*. Freudenstadt: Lutzeyer.
Durr, Robert, Andrew Martin, and Christina Wolbrecht. 2000. "Ideological Divergence and Public Support for the Supreme Court." *American Journal of Political Science* 44:768–76.
Easton, David. 1975. "A Re-Assessment of the Concept of Political Support." *British Journal of Political Science* 5:435–57.
Elster, Jon, Claus Offe, and Ulrich Preuss. 1998. *Institutional Design in Post-Communist Societies*. Cambridge: Cambridge University Press.
Emnid Institut. 1992. "Einstellung zum Paragraphen 218." *Umfrage und Analyse* Nr.7/8:52–62.
Emnid Institut. 1995. "Vertrauen in Institutionen." *Umfrage und Analyse* Nr.1/2:72–8.
Epp, Charles. 1998. *The Rights Revolution: Lawyers, Activists, and Supreme Courts in Comparative Perspective*. Chicago: University of Chicago Press.
Epstein, Lee, and Jack Knight. 1996. "On the Struggle for Judicial Supremacy." *Law and Society Review* 30(1):87–120.
Epstein, Lee, and Jack Knight. 1998. *The Choices Justices Make*. Washington, DC: Congressional Quarterly Press.
Epstein, Lee, Jack Knight, and Olga Shvetsova. 2001. "The Role of Constitutional Courts in the Establishment and Maintenance of Democratic Systems of Government." *Law and Society Review* 35:117–64.
Fenske, Hans. 1994. *Deutsche Parteiengeschichte*. München: Schöningh.
Ferejohn, John. 1995. "Law, Legislation, and Positive Political Theory." In J. Banks and E. Hanushek (eds.). *Modern Political Economy*. Cambridge: Cambridge University Press.
Ferejohn, John, and Charles Shipan. 1990. "Congressional Influence on Bureaucracy." *Journal of Law, Economics and Organization* 6:1–27.
Ferejohn, John, and Barry Weingast. 1992. "A Positive Theory of Statutory Interpretation." *International Review of Law and Economics* 12:263–79.
Fisher, Louis. 1993. "The Legislative Veto: Invalidated, It Survives." *Law and Contemporary Problems* 56:273–92.
Frankfurter, Felix. 1924. "A Note on Advisory Opinions." *Harvard Law Review* 37:1002–9.
Frankfurter, Felix. 1930. "Advisory Opinions." In Edwin Seligman and Alvin Johnson (eds.). *Encyclopedia of the Social Sciences*. New York: Macmillan.
Franklin, Charles, and Liane C. Kosaki. 1995. "Media, Knowledge, and Public Evaluations of the Supreme Court." In Lee J. Epstein (ed.). *Contemplating Courts*. Washington, DC: Congressional Quarterly Press.
Friedman, Barry. 2003. "The Myths of Marbury." Typescript. New York University School of Law.

Bibliography

Garrett, Geoffrey. 1995. "The Politics of Legal Integration in the European Union." *International Organization* 49:171–81.
Garrett, Geoffrey, and Barry Weingast. 1993. "Ideas, Interests, and Institutions: Constructing the EC's Internal Market." In Judith Goldstein and Robert Keohane (eds.). *Ideas and Foreign Policy*. Ithaca: Cornell University Press.
Gibson, James. 1989. "Understandings of Justice: Institutional Legitimacy, Procedural Justice, and Political Tolerance." *Law and Society Review* 23:469–96.
Gibson, James. 1991. "Institutional Legitimacy, Procedural Justice, and Compliance with Supreme Court Decisions: A Question of Causality." *Law and Society Review* 25:631–6.
Gibson, James, Greg Caldeira, and Vanessa Baird. 1998. "On the Legitimacy of National High Courts." *American Political Science Review* 92:343–58.
Gordon, Scott. 1999. *Controlling the State: Constitutionalism from Ancient Athens to Today*. Cambridge: Harvard University Press.
Graber, Mark. 1998. "Establishing Judicial Review? *Schooner Peggy* and the Early Marshall Court." *Political Research Quarterly* 51:221–39.
Grosskopf, Anke, and Jeffrey Mondak. 1998. "Do Attitudes Toward Specific Supreme Court Decisions Matter? The Impact of Webster and *Texas v. Johnson* on Public Confidence in the Supreme Court." *Political Research Quarterly* 51:633–4.
Hamilton, Alexander. 1961. *Federalist 78*. In *The Federalist Papers*. New York: Mentor.
Heidenheimer, Arnold. 1957. "German Party Finance: The CDU." *American Political Science Review* 51:369–85.
Helmke, Gretchen. 2002. "The Logic of Strategic Defection: Court–Executive Relations in Argentina under Dictatorship and Democracy." *American Political Science Review* 96:291–303.
Herbst. Ludolf. 1996. *Option für den Westen: Vom Marshallplan bis zum deutsch-französischen Vertrag*. München: Deutscher Taschenbuch Verlag.
Hesse, Konrad. 1995. *Grundzüge des Verfassungsrechts der Bundesrepublik Deutschland*. Heidelberg: C. F. Müller.
Hirsch, Heidi-Karin. 1981. "Die persönlichen parlamentarischen Mitarbeiter der Bundestagsabgeordneten." *Zeitschrift für Parlamentsfragen* 81(2):203–23.
Holland, Kenneth (ed.). 1991. *Judicial Activism in Comparative Perspective*. New York: St. Martin's Press.
Howard, A. E. Dick. 1993. *Constitution Making in Eastern Europe*. Washington, DC: Woodrow Wilson Center Press.
Huber, John. 1996. *Rationalizing Parliament: Legislative Institutions and Party Politics in France*. Cambridge: Cambridge University Press.
Institut für Staatslehre und Politik (ed.). 1952. *Der Kampf um den Wehrbeitrag, Band 2*. München: Isaar Verlag.
Institut für Staatslehre und Politik (ed.). 1958. *Der Kampf um den Wehrbeitrag Ergänzungsband*. München: Isaar Verlag.
Ketcham, Ralph. 1986. *The Anti-Federalist Papers and the Constitutional Convention Debates*. New York: Mentor.

Bibliography

Key, V. O. 1961. *Public Opinion and American Democracy*. New York: Alfred A. Knopf.
Knight, Jack, and Lee Epstein. 1996. "On the Struggle for Judicial Supremacy." *Law and Society Review* 30:87–120.
Kommers, Donald. 1976. *Judicial Politics in West Germany*. Beverly Hills: Sage Publications.
Kommers, Donald. 1994. "The Federal Constitutional Court in the German Political System." *Comparative Political Studies* 26:470–91.
Kommers, Donald. 1997. *The Constitutional Jurisprudence of the Federal Republic of Germany*. Durham: Duke University Press.
Kreps, David. 1990. *Game Theory and Economic Modeling*. Oxford: Oxford University Press.
Küsters, H. J. (ed.). 1984. *Adenauer: Teegespräche 1950–1954*. Rhöndorf: Siedler Verlag.
Landes, William, and Richard Posner. 1975. "The Independent Judiciary in an Interest Group Perspective." *Journal of Law and Economics* 18:875–901.
Landfried, Christine. 1984. *Bundesverfassungsgericht und Gesetzgeber*. Baden-Baden: Nomos.
Landfried, Christine (ed.). 1988. *Constitutional Review and Legislation*. Baden-Baden: Nomos.
Landfried, Christine. 1992. "Judicial Policy-Making in Germany: The Federal Constitutional Court." *West European Politics* 15:50–67.
Landfried, Christine. 1994. *Parteifinanzen und politische Macht*. Baden-Baden: Nomos.
Lenz, Otto. 1989. *Im Zentrum der Macht: Das Tagebuch von Staatssekretär Lenz 1951–1953*. K. Gotto, H. Kleinmann, and R. Schreiner (eds.). Düsseldorf: Droste Verlag.
Leuchtenburg, William. 1995. *The Supreme Court Reborn: The Constitutional Revolution in the Age of Roosevelt*. Oxford: Oxford University Press.
Loewenberg, Gerhard. 1971. "The Influence of Parliamentary Behavior on Regime Stability." *Comparative Politics* 3:177–200.
Löwke, Udo. 1976. *Die SPD und die Wehrfrage 1949 bis 1955*. Bonn-Bad Godesberg: Verlag Neue Gesellschaft GmbH.
Magalhaes, Pedro Coutinho. 2003. "The Limits to Judicialization: Legislative Politics and Constitutional Review in Iberian Democracies." Ph.D. dissertation, Ohio State University.
Marshall, Thomas. 1989. *Public Opinion and the Supreme Court*. Boston: Unwin Hyman.
Martin, Lanny, and Georg Vanberg. 2004. "Policing the Bargain: Coalition Government and Parliamentary Scrutiny." *American Journal of Political Science* 48:13–27.
Mattli, Walter, and Anne-Marie Slaughter. 1998. "Revisiting the European Court of Justice." *International Organization* 52:177–209.
McCloskey, Herbert, and John Zaller. 1984. *The American Ethos*. Cambridge: Harvard University Press.
McCloskey, Robert. 1994. *The American Supreme Court*. Sanford Levinson (ed.). Chicago: University of Chicago Press.

McGuire, Kevin, and Greg Caldeira. 1993. "Lawyers, Organized Interests, and the Law of Obscenity: Agenda Setting in the Supreme Court." *American Political Science Review* 87:717–26.

McGuire, Kevin, and James Stimson. In press. "The Least Dangerous Branch Revisited: New Evidence on Supreme Court Responsiveness to Public Preferences." *Journal of Politics*.

Mensing, H. P. (ed.). 1987. *Adenauer: Briefe 1951–1953*. Rhöndorf: Siedler Verlag.

Mishler, William, and Reginald Sheehan. 1993. "The Supreme Court as a Countermajoritarian Institution? The Impact of Public Opinion on Supreme Court Decisions." *American Political Science Review* 87:87–101.

Mishler, William, and Reginald Sheehan. 1994. "Response to Norpoth and Segal." *American Political Science Review* 88:716–24.

Mondak, Jeffrey. 1991. "Substantive and Procedural Aspects of Supreme Court Decisions as Determinants of Institutional Approval." *American Politics Quarterly* 19:174–88.

Mondak, Jeffrey. 1992. "Institutional Legitimacy, Policy Legitimacy, and the Supreme Court." *American Politics Quarterly* 20:457–77.

Mondak, Jeffery, and Shannon Ishiyama Smithey. 1997. "The Dynamics of Public Support for the Supreme Court." *Journal of Politics* 59:1114–42.

Murphy, Walter. 1964. *Elements of Judicial Strategy*. Chicago: University of Chicago Press.

Murphy, Walter, and Joseph Tannenhaus. 1990. "Publicity, Public Opinion, and the Court." *Northwestern University Law Review* 84:985–1023.

Nassmacher, Karl-Heinz. 1989. "Structure and Impact of Public Subsidies to Political Parties in Europe: The Examples of Austria, Italy, Sweden, and West Germany." In H. Alexander (ed.). *Comparative Political Finance in the 1980s*. Cambridge: Cambridge University Press.

Noelle-Neumann, Elisabeth, and Renate Köcher. 1997. *Allensbacher Jahrbuch der Demoskopie 1993–1997*. München: KG Saur Muenchen.

Noelle-Neumann, Elisabeth, and Renate Köcher. 2002. *Allensbacher Jahrbuch der Demoskopie 1998–2002*. München: KG Saur Muenchen.

Noelle, Elisabeth, and Erich Peter Neumann. 1974. *Jahrbuch der Öffentlichen Meinung*. Bonn: Verlag für Demoskopie.

Norpoth, Helmut, and Jeffrey Segal. 1994. "Popular Influence on Supreme Court Decisions." *American Political Science Review* 88:711–16.

Note. 1956. "Advisory Opinions on the Constitutionality of Statutes." *Harvard Law Review* 69:1302–13.

Orkeny, Antal, and Kim Lane Scheppele. 1996. "Rules of Law: The Complexity of Legality in Hungary." *International Journal of Sociology* 26:76–94.

Page, Benjamin, Robert Shapiro, and Glenn Dempsey. 1987. "What Moves Public Opinion." *American Political Science Review* 81:23–44.

Perry, H. W. 1991. *Deciding to Decide: Agenda Setting on the U.S. Supreme Court*. Cambridge: Harvard University Press.

Pinto-Duschinsky. 1991. "The Party Foundations and Political Finance in Germany." In L. Seidle (ed.). *Comparative Issues in Party and Election Finance*. Volume 4 of the Research Studies. Royal Commission on Electoral Reform and Party Financing. Toronto: Dunburn Press.

Powell, G. Bingham. 2000. *Elections as Instruments of Democracy.* New Haven: Yale University Press.
Pritchett, C. Herman. 1977. *The American Constitution,* 3rd ed. New York: McGraw-Hill.
Ramseyer, Mark. 1994. "The Puzzling (In)dependence of Courts: A Comparative Approach." *Journal of Legal Studies* 23:721–47.
Riker, William, and Barry Weingast. 1988. "Constitutional Regulation of Legislative Choice: The Political Consequences of Judicial Deference to Legislatures." *Virginia Law Review* 74:373–401.
Rogers, James. 2001. "Information and Judicial Review: A Signaling Game of Legislative–Judicial Interaction." *American Journal of Political Science* 45:84–99.
Rogers, James, and Georg Vanberg. 2002. "Judicial Advisory Opinions and Legislative Outcomes in Comparative Perspective." *American Journal of Political Science* 46:379–97.
Rosenberg, Gerald. 1991. *The Hollow Hope: Can Courts Bring about Social Change?* Chicago: University of Chicago Press.
Rubinstein, Ariel. 1991. "Comments on the Interpretation of Game Theory." *Econometrica* 59:909–24.
Rudzio, Wolfgang. 1994. "Das neue Parteienfinanzierungsmodell und seine Auswirkungen." *Zeitschrift für Parlamentsfragen* 3:390–401.
Schindler, Peter. 1994. *Datenhandbuch zur Geschichte des Deutschen Bundestages, 1983–1991.* Baden-Baden: Nomos.
Schlaich, Klaus. 1994. *Das Bundesverfassungsgericht: Stellung, Verfahren, Entscheidungen.* München: C. H. Beck.
Schleth, Uwe. 1971. "Analyse der Rechenschaftsberichte der Parteien für 1968." *Zeitschrift für Parlamentsfragen* 1:139–53.
Schneider, Hans-Peter. 1989. "The New German System of Party Funding: The Presidential Committee Report of 1983 and Its Realization." In H. Alexander (ed.). *Comparative Political Finance in the 1980s.* Cambridge: Cambridge University Press.
Schwartz, Herman. 2000. *The Struggle for Constitutional Justice in Post-Communist Eastern Europe.* Chicago: University of Chicago Press.
Schwarz, Hans Peter. 1981. *Die Ära Adenauer: Gründerjahre der Republik 1949–1957.* Stuttgart: Deutsche Verlags-Anstalt.
Segal, Jeffrey. 1997. "Separation-of-Powers Games in the Positive Theory of Congress and Courts." *American Political Science Review* 91:28–44.
Segal, Jeffrey, and Harold Spaeth. 1993. *The Supreme Court and the Attitudinal Model.* Cambridge: Cambridge University Press.
Shapiro, Martin. 1981. *Courts: A Comparative and Political Analysis.* Chicago: University of Chicago Press.
Shapiro, Martin, and Alec Stone (eds.). 1994. Special Issue: The New Constitutional Politics of Europe. *Comparative Political Studies* 26.
Shapiro, Martin, and Alec Stone Sweet. 2002. *On Law, Politics, and Judicialization.* Oxford: Oxford University Press.
Shipan, Charles. 2000. "The Legislative Design of Judicial Review: A Formal Analysis." *Journal of Theoretical Politics* 12: 269–304.

Smith, Jean Edward. 1996. *John Marshall: Definer of a Nation*. New York: Henry Holt.

Solzhenitsyn, Aleksandr. 1997. "What Kind of Democracy Is This?" *New York Times*, January 4, 1997:23.

Sontheimer, Kurt. 1991. *Die Adenauer Ära: Grundlegung der Bundesrepublik*. München: Deutscher Taschenbuch Verlag.

Spriggs, James. 1997. "Explaining Federal Bureaucratic Compliance with Supreme Court Opinions." *Political Research Quarterly* 50:567–93.

Spriggs, James, and Paul Wahlbeck. 1997. "Amicus Curiae and the Role of Information at the Supreme Court." *Political Research Quarterly* 50:365–86.

Staton, Jeffrey. 2003. "Public Support and Spin: Judicial Policy Implementation in Mexico City and Merida." Manuscript, New York University.

Stephenson, Matthew. 2003. "When the Devil Turns...: The Political Foundations of Independent Judicial Review." *Journal of Legal Studies* 32:59–90.

Stone Sweet, Alec, and Thomas Brunell. 1998. "Constructing a Supranational Constitution: Dispute Resolution and Governance in the European Community." *American Political Science Review* 92:63–80.

Stone, Alec. 1992. *The Birth of Judicial Politics in France*. Oxford: Oxford University Press.

Stone Sweet, Alec. 1998. "Rules, Dispute Resolution, and Strategic Behavior. Comment on Vanberg." *Journal of Theoretical Politics* 10:327–38.

Stone Sweet, Alec. 2000. *Governing with Judges*. Oxford: Oxford University Press.

Sunstein, Cass. 1991. "Constitutionalism, Prosperity, Democracy." *Constitutional Political Economy* 2:371–94.

Tate, C. Neal, and Torbjoern Vallinder. 1995. *The Global Expansion of Judicial Power*. New York: New York University Press.

Tocqueville, Alexis de. 1835/1988. *Democracy in America*. New York: Harper-Perennial.

Trochev, Alexei. 2002. "Implementing Russian Constitutional Court Decisions." *East European Constitutional Review* 11:95–103.

Tyler, Tom, and Kenneth Rasinski. 1991. "Legitimacy and the Acceptance of Unpopular U.S. Supreme Court Decisions: A Reply to Gibson." *Law and Society Review* 25:621–30.

Vanberg, Georg. 1998a. "Abstract Judicial Review, Legislative Bargaining, and Policy Compromise." *Journal of Theoretical Politics* 10:299–326.

Vanberg, Georg. 1998b. "Reply to Stone Sweet." *Journal of Theoretical Politics* 10:339–46.

Vanberg, Georg. 2000. "Establishing Judicial Independence in West Germany: The Impact of Opinion Leadership and the Separation of Powers." *Comparative Politics* 32:333–53.

Vanberg, Georg. 2001. "Legislative–Judicial Relations: A Game-Theoretic Approach to Constitutional Review." *American Journal of Political Science* 45:346–61.

Volcansek, Mary. 2000. *Constitutional Politics in Italy*. New York: St. Martin's Press.

Volcansek, Mary. 1991. "Judicial Activism in Italy." In K. Holland (ed.). *Judicial Activism in Comparative Perspective.* New York: St. Martin's Press.
Weber Fas, Rudolf. 2002. *Der Verfassungsstaat des Grundgesetzes.* Tübingen: Mohr Siebeck.
Weingast, Barry. 1997. "The Political Foundations of Democracy and the Rule of Law." *American Political Science Review* 91:245–63.
Wengst, Udo. 1984. *Staatsaufbau und Regierungspraxis 1948–1953: Zur Geschichte der Verfassungsorgane der Bundesrepublik Deutschland.* Düsseldorf: Droste.
White, G. Edward. 2000. *The Constitution and the New Deal.* Cambridge: Harvard University Press.
Whittington, Keith. 2003. "Legislative Sanctions and the Strategic Environment of Judicial Review." *I-Con: The International Journal of Constitutional Law* 1:446–74.
Widner, Jennifer. 2001. *Building the Rule of Law: Francis Nyalali and the Road to Judicial Independence in Africa.* New York: W. W. Norton.
Zaller, John. 1992. *The Nature and Origin of Mass Opinion.* Cambridge: Cambridge University Press.

UNPUBLISHED PRIMARY SOURCES

Adenauer's Ministerkorrespondenz (StBkAH)
Nachlaß Laforet (ACDP)
Nachlaß Lenz (ACDP)
Nachlaß v. Brentano (ACDP)

PARLIAMENTARY AND COURT RECORDS

Drucksachen des Deutschen Bundesrates
Drucksachen des Deutschen Bundestages
Entscheidungen des Bundesverfassungsgerichtes
Verhandlungen des Deutschen Bundesrates
Verhandlungen des Deutschen Bundestages
Verhandlungen des Parlamentarischen Rates

U.S. SUPREME COURT CASES

Brown v. Board of Education 347 U.S. 483.
Cohens v. Virginia 19 U.S. 264.
Immigration and Naturalization Service v. Chadha 462 U.S. 919.
Marbury v. Madison 5 U.S. 137.
Worcester v. Georgia 31 U.S. 515.

Index

abortion policy, Germany 126–8
abstract judicial review, *see* constitutional review
Adams, John 34
Adenauer, Konrad 1, 62, 70, 72, 74–6, 175
Alexander, Herbert 144
Alter, Karen 11, 168, 171
Armin, Hans Herbert von 5, 48, 144–5, 151, 152, 154, 155, 158, 160, 161, 162, 164
Arnold, R. Douglas 46
asylum policy, Germany 128–9
attitudinal model 26, 35
Austria
  Constitutional Court 11, 72
  Constitution of 1920 10
autolimitation 31–2

Baird, Vanessa 21, 39, 44, 50
Baring, Arnulf 67, 69, 70
Bark, Dennis 68
"base amount" 4, 162, 163
Bates, Robert 17
Baum, Lawrence 49
Bickel, Alexander 172
Blair, Philip 168, 173
Blankenburg, Erhard 158, 162
Böckenförde, Ernst-Wolfgang 138, 142, 160
Boldt, Hans 150
Booms, Hans 69, 70, 72
Bösch, Frank 148

Brace, Paul 32
Brewer-Carias, A. R. 168
Brown v. Board of Education 48
Brunell, Thomas 168, 171
Buchstab, Günter 74
Bundestag
  funding of factions and staff 153–6
  legislative salaries 48
Bundesverfassungsgericht
  and abortion policy 126–8
  appointment process 81–5
  and asylum policy 128–9
  caseload 87
  chambers 88–9
  decision-making procedures 91
  empirical focus on 17
  and European Defense Community 67
  establishment of 62–6
  First Senate 69, 70, 84, 127, 134
  jurisdiction 87
  organization 80
  (and party finance), *see* party finance
  Second Senate 69, 76, 86, 114, 134, 162
  support for 97–9
  taxation decisions 114, 122–3, 132, 134
Bundesverfassungsgerichtsgesetz, *see* Federal Constitutional Court Act

Index

Caldeira, Greg 21, 39, 44, 50, 51, 102, 103, 170
Canache, Damarys 50
Canon, Bradley 6, 170
Cappelletti, Mauro 1, 10, 11, 52, 79, 90, 169, 176
Carrubba, Clifford 13, 14, 19, 53, 55, 171, 172, 174
Carstens, Karl 158
Chancenausgleich, see "equal chances scheme"
Clinton, Robert Lowry 33–4
Cohens v. Virginia 34
complexity, *see* issue complexity
constitutional complaint 82, 87, 88, 89
constitutional review
    abstract judicial review 82, 87, 88, 89
    American Model 10, 77–9
    and countermajoritarianism 175–7
    concrete judicial review 82, 87, 88, 89, 110
    European model 10–12, 79–80, 82, 87, 89
Crucifix Decision 2–4, 6, 21–2, 48, 87, 99, 121, 126, 128

Dahl, Robert 175
de Toqueville, Alexis 1–2, 10, 175
Dehler, Thomas 70, 72, 142
Dehousse, Renaud 11
Dempsey, Glenn 45
Dieterich, Thomas 138
Dübber, Ulrich 146, 154
Durr, Robert 51

Eastern Europe, Constitutional Courts 11, 173–4
Easton, David 49
Elster, Jon 168
Emnid Institut 98, 128
Epp, Charles 11, 13, 47, 96
Epstein, Lee 8, 13, 33, 81, 169, 174
"equal chances scheme" 159, 160, 163
equilibria (contentious equilibrium) 36, 39, 42, 44, 143, 145, 174

equilibria (judicial self-censoring equilibrium) 32–4, 39, 40, 44, 143, 145, 174
equilibria (legislative self-censoring equilibria) 30–2, 39, 44
equilibria (separation-of-powers equilibrium) 34–5, 39, 42, 44, 174
European Court of Justice (ECJ) 11, 85, 168, 169, 171–2
European Defense Community (EDC) 142
European Defense Community (EDC) Treaty 67
evasion
    impact of costs of compliance on 130–2
    and party finance decisions 4–5, 145, 148, 150, 151, 165–7
Existenzminimum 114
Eylmann, Horst 138

Faller, Hans 138
Federal Constitutional Court Act (FCCA) 62, 80
Federalist 78 6, 9
Fenske, Hans 150
Ferejohn, John 8, 13
Fisher, Louis 5
Flick scandal 158
France (Constitutional Council) 10, 11, 80, 81, 83, 85, 89, 90, 114
Frankfurter, Felix 79
Franklin, Charles 51
Friedman, Barry 49, 67, 174

Garrett, Geoffrey 171
Geiger, Willi 70
Geißler, Heiner 155
General Treaty ("Convention on Relations with the Federal Republic of Germany") 67
Germany
    Constitutional Court, *see* Bundesverfassungsgericht
    Party Finance 4–5, 146
    Revolution of 1848 10

Index

Gibson, James 21, 39, 44, 50, 51, 52, 170
Gordon, Scott 9
Graber, Mark 34, 174
Greif, Avner 17
Gress, David 68
Grosskopf, Anke 50
Guardian Vision 175–7

Hamilton, Alexander 2, 6, 9, 141
Heidenheimer, Arnold 148
Helmke, Gretchen 8, 13
Herbst, Ludolf 67, 68
Herzog, Roman 85
Hesse, Konrad 93, 129, 138
Heuss, Theodor 69, 70, 71
Hirsch, Heidi-Karin 155
Höpker-Aschoff, Hermann 66, 69, 71, 142
Holland, Kenneth 169, 176
Howard, A. E. Dick 168
Huber, John 16
Hungary (Constitutional Court) 80, 83, 85, 89, 173–4

implementation of judicial decisions 6–7, 8, 12
INS v. Chadha 5, 22
interest groups (impact on transparency) 46–7, 103, 107
issue complexity
  coding of 104
  impact on judicial behavior 111–12
  impact on transparency 40, 47
Italy (Constitutional Court) 7, 11, 33, 80, 83, 93

Jackson, Andrew 19
Jäger, Renate 138
Jefferson, Thomas 34
Johnson, Charles 6, 170
Judicial Selection Committee 83

Kelsen, Hans 10–11, 79–80
Ketcham, Ralph 9
Key, V. O. 46
Kirchhof, Paul 85, 138

Klein, Hans Hugo 138, 141
Knight, Jack 8, 13, 33, 81, 169, 174
Köcher, Renate 98
Kohl, Helmut 3
Kommers, Donald 61, 66, 69, 87, 93, 119, 130, 135
Kosaki, Liane C. 51
Kreps, David 16
Kruis, Konrad 138
Kruzifix Decision, *see* Crucifix Decision
Kühling, Jürgen 138
Küsters, H. J. 72

Landes, William 19, 53, 54
Landfried, Christine 12, 32, 85, 155, 156, 157, 158, 160, 161, 162, 164, 176
Langer, Laura 32
legal briefs (impact on judicial behavior) 103, 108–11
legislative veto (United States) 5
Leibholtz, Gerhard 141
Lenz, Otto 69, 70–1, 72, 74–5, 142
Leuchtenburg, William 51
Leutheusser-Schnarrenberger, Sabine 138
Levi, Margaret 17
Limbach, Jutta 85
Loewenberg, Gerhard 50
Löwke, Udo 68

Magalhaes, Pedro Coutinho 10
Marbury v. Madison 9, 34, 77
Marshall, John 19, 77
Marshall, Thomas 51, 172
Martin, Andrew 51
Martin, Lanny 145
Mattli, Walter 168, 171
McCloskey, Robert 45, 172
McGuire, Kevin 103, 172
Mexico (Supreme Court) 49
Meyer, Jürgen 138
Mishler, William 172
Mondak, Jeffrey 50, 51, 64
Murphy, Walter 13, 21

Nassmacher, Karl-Heinz 146
National Labor Relations v. Jones & Laughlin Steel Corporation 51
Neumann, Erich Peter 128
Noelle-Neuman, Elisabeth 98, 128
Norpoth, Helmut 172

Offe, Claus 168
Organstreit 90
Orkeny, Antal 174

Page, Benjamin 45
Parties Act of 1967 148–50, 151
    revision of 1969 152
    revision of 1983 158, 159
    revision of 1988 162
    revision of 1994 164–5
party finance
    introduction of 146
    1958 decision 146
    1966 decision 147–8, 152
    1968 decision 151, 152
    1986 decisions 159–61
    1992 decision 4–5, 162–4
    see also evasion
party foundations 156–7, 161
party taxes 160–1
Penner, Wilfried 138
Perry, H. W. 118
Pinto-Duschinsky, Michael 148, 156, 157, 158
Political Parties Act, *see* Parties Act of 1967
Portugal
    Constitutional Court 11
    Constitution of 1911 10
Posner, Richard 19, 53, 54
Powell, G. Bingham 175
Preuss, Ulrich 168
Pritchett, C. Herman 34
public opinion (impact on judicial behavior) 172–3
public support (for Bundesverfassungsgericht), *see* Bundesverfassungsgericht
    as a double edged sword 121–2
    as a shield 119–21
    as a constraint on judicial behavior 124
    for courts 50–1
    impact on judicial behavior 39, 40–3, 51–3, 112
    role in enforcing judicial decisions 14, 19–22, 28, 119–21
    specific and diffuse 49–51
Putin, Vladimir 7–8

Ramsmeyer, Mark 14, 19, 53, 54, 55
Raskinski, Kenneth 52
rights revolution 47
Riker, William 176
Rogers, James 13, 19, 54, 56, 78, 79, 174
Roosevelt, Franklin D. 51
Rosenberg, Gerald 42, 175, 176
Rosenthal, Jean-Laurent 17
Rubinstein, Ariel 17, 116
Russia (Constitutional Court) 7, 11, 33, 80, 83, 89, 90, 173

Scheppele, Kim Lane 174
Schindler, Peter 149, 155
Schlaich, Klaus 92, 93, 135
Schleth, Uwe 155
Schmalz-Jacobsen, Cornelia 139
Schmid, Carlo 68
Scholz, Rupert 139
Schumacher, Kurt 68
Schwartz, Herman 7, 11, 52, 61, 168, 173, 174, 175, 176
Schwarz, Hans Peter 68
Segal, Jeffrey 26, 35, 172
Senate, First, *see* Bundesverfassungsgericht
Senate, Second, *see* Bundesverfassungsgericht
Shapiro, Martin 52, 168, 169
Shapiro, Robert 45
Sheehan, Reginald 172
Shipan, Charles 8, 13
Shiratori, Rei 144
Shvetsova, Olga 8, 13, 33, 169, 174
Slaughter, Anne-Marie 168, 171
Smith, Jean Edward 19, 34

Index

Smithey, Shannon Ishiyama 51
Sockelbetrag, see "base amount"
Soldier Cases 52–3, 99, 121, 126, 130
Söllner, Alfred 138
Solzhenitsyn, Aleksandr 173
Sontheimer, Kurt 68
South Africa (Constitutional Court) 80
Southwest Case 63–6, 129
Spaeth, Harold 26, 35
Spain (Constitutional Court) 11
Spriggs, James 49, 103
stare decisis 10, 78, 79
Staton, Jeffrey 13, 40, 49, 169
Stephenson, Matthew 53
Stiegler, Ludwig 139
Stimson, James 172
Stoiber, Edmund 3
Stone Sweet, Alec 10, 11, 12, 31, 32, 81, 83, 85, 88, 89, 90, 93, 114, 168, 169, 171, 176
Strauß, Franz Josef 76
Sunstein, Cass 176

Tanenhaus, Joseph 21
Tate, C. Neal 11, 12, 168, 169
taxation, *see* Bundesverfassungsgericht
transparency 45, 95–6
   and issue complexity 47
   impact on judicial behavior 39, 97, 99–100, 111–13, 170–1
   interest group impact on 46–7
   judicial and legislative influence on 47–9, 164
   media impact on 45–6
   role in enforcing judicial decisions 22–3, 28

Trochev, Alexei 7–8
Tucholsky, Kurt 52
Tyler, Tom 52

United States Supreme Court 13, 15, 19, 33–4, 49, 50, 81, 87, 174
   and court-packing plan 51–2
United States v. Nixon 6

Vallinder, Torbjoern 11, 12, 168, 169
Vanberg, Georg 8, 17, 32, 45, 62, 66, 78, 79, 90, 128, 145, 169
Vogt, Ute 139
Volcansek, Mary 7, 33, 169, 172

Wahlbeck, Paul 103
Weber Fas, Rudolf 93
Wehner, Herbert 147
Weingast, Barry 8, 13, 17, 21, 25, 171, 176
Weizsäcker, Richard von 5, 152
Wengst, Udo 69
West Coast Hotel v. Parrish 51
White, G. Edward 175
Whittington, Keith 14, 53
Widner, Jennifer 168
Wohlleb, Leo 64, 65
Wolbrecht, Christina 51
Worcester v. Georgia 19
Wright, John 103
Wüppesahl, Thomas 156

Yeltsin, Boris 33

Zaller, John 45, 46

Other Books in the Series (*continued from p. iii*)

Gary W. Cox and Jonathan N. Katz, *Elbridge Gerry's Salamander: The Electoral Consequences of the Reapportionment Revolution*

Jean Ensminger, *Making a Market: The Institutional Transformation of an African Society*

David Epstein and Sharyn O'Halloran, *Delegating Powers: A Transaction Cost Politics Approach to Policy Making under Separate Powers*

Kathryn Firmin-Sellers, *The Transformation of Property Rights in the Gold Coast: An Empirical Study Applying Rational Choice Theory*

Clark C. Gibson, *Politicians and Poachers: The Political Economy of Wildlife Policy in Africa*

Ron Harris, *Industrializing English Law: Entrepreneurship and Business Organization, 1720–1844*

Anna L. Harvey, *Votes without Leverage: Women in American Electoral Politics, 1920–1970*

Murray Horn, *The Political Economy of Public Administration: Institutional Choice in the Public Sector*

John D. Huber, *Rationalizing Parliament: Legislative Institutions and Party Politics in France*

Jack Knight, *Institutions and Social Conflict*

Michael Laver and Kenneth Shepsle, eds., *Cabinet Ministers and Parliamentary Government*

Michael Laver and Kenneth Shepsle, eds., *Making and Breaking Governments: Cabinets and Legislatures in Parliamentary Democracies*

Margaret Levi, *Consent, Dissent, and Patriotism*

Brian Levy and Pablo T. Spiller, eds., *Regulations, Institutions, and Commitment: Comparative Studies of Telecommunications*

Leif Lewin, *Ideology and Strategy: A Century of Swedish Politics* (English Edition)

Gary Libecap, *Contracting for Property Rights*

John Londregan, *Legislative Institutions and Ideology in Chile*

Arthur Lupia and Mathew D. McCubbins, *The Democratic Dilemma: Can Citizens Learn What They Need to Know?*

C. Mantzavinos, *Individuals, Institutions, and Markets*

Mathew D. McCubbins and Terry Sullivan, eds., *Congress: Structure and Policy*

Gary J. Miller, *Managerial Dilemmas: The Political Economy of Hierarchy*

Douglass C. North, *Institutions, Institutional Change, and Economic Performance*

Elinor Ostrom, *Governing the Commons: The Evolution of Institutions for Collective Action*

J. Mark Ramseyer, *Odd Markets in Japanese History: Law and Economic Growth*

J. Mark Ramseyer and Frances Rosenbluth, *The Politics of Oligarchy: Institutional Choice in Imperial Japan*
Jean-Laurent Rosenthal, *The Fruits of Revolution: Property Rights, Litigation, and French Agriculture, 1700–1860*
Michael L. Ross, *Timber Booms and Institutional Breakdown in Southeast Asia*
Alastair Smith, *Election Timing*
David Stasavage, *Public Debt and the Birth of the Democratic State: France and Great Britain, 1688–1789*
Charles Stewart III, *Budget Reform Politics: The Design of the Appropriations Process in the House of Representatives, 1865–1921*
George Tsebelis and Jeannette Money, *Bicameralism*
Nicolas van de Walle, *African Economies and the Politics of Permanent Crisis, 1979–1999*
John Waterbury, *Exposed to Innumerable Delusions: Public Enterprise and State Power in Egypt, India, Mexico, and Turkey*
David L. Weimer, ed., *The Political Economy of Property Rights: Institutional Change and Credibility in the Reform of Centrally Planned Economies*

For EU product safety concerns, contact us at Calle de José Abascal, 56–1°,
28003 Madrid, Spain or eugpsr@cambridge.org.

www.ingramcontent.com/pod-product-compliance
Ingram Content Group UK Ltd.
Pitfield, Milton Keynes, MK11 3LW, UK
UKHW040158230326
469255UK00012B/165